How Wall Street Created a Nation

How
WALL STREET
Created a Nation

J.P. MORGAN, TEDDY ROOSEVELT,

AND THE PANAMA CANAL

Ovidio Diaz Espino

FOUR WALLS EIGHT WINDOWS
New York /London

© 2001 by Ovidio Diaz Espino

Published in the United States by
Four Walls Eight Windows
39 West 14th Street, room 503
New York, NY 10011
http://www.4W8W.com

UK offices:
Four Walls Eight Windows/Turnaround
Unit 3 Olympia Trading Estate
Coburg Road, Wood Green
London N22 6TZ

Library of Congress Cataloging-in-Publication Data:

Diaz Espino, Ovidio.
    How Wall Street Created a Nation : J.P. Morgan, Teddy Roosevelt, and the Panama Canal / Ovidio Diaz Espino.
      p.   cm.
    Includes bibliographic references and index.
    ISBN 1-56858-196-3

      1. Panama Canal (Panama)–Finance–History. 2. Panama—History—20th century. 3. Wall Street. 4. Roosevelt, Theodore, 1858-1919. 5. Cromwell, William Nelson, 1854-1948. 6. Morgan, J. Pierpont (John Pierpont), 1837-1913. 7. Compagnie universelle du canal interocaanique de Panama.
    I. Title.

HE537 .D5 2001
972.87'503–dc21   2001023187

Printed in the United States of America
10 9 8 7 6 5 4 3 2 1

Interior book design by Terry Bain

To my family

The exact contrary of what is generally believed is often the truth.

Jean de la Bruyere (1645-1696)

The canal was stolen property. . . . The partners in the theft are a group of canal promoters and speculators and lobbyists who came into their money through the rebellion [the U.S. government] encouraged, made safe, and effectuated.

The New York Times, December 29, 1903

Contents

Preface and Acknowledgments

As a child growing up in Panama, I was taught an idealized but false view of our country's history. The official story written in schoolbooks made our liberators to be heroes who won a war of independence that, as it happened, never occurred. This misguided view was shattered during a Christmas party in New York City.

A witty and animated young man named Webster Stone approached me. Noticing my accent, he asked me where I was from and what I did for a living. At that time, I was a lawyer working for J.P. Morgan. He threw his arms up in the air. "Are you aware that J.P. Morgan was the treasurer of Panama during its first decade?" "Did you know that your country was conceived in Room 1162 of the Waldorf Astoria?"

Mr. Stone had written the treatment for a screenplay about the history of the Panama Canal. While snooping around, he had stumbled on some questions that had not been answered for a hundred years. After several coffees in a Tribeca cafe, he convinced me that I had the unique opportunity, as lawyer, J.P. Morgan officer, and Panamanian, to dig up the truth about the untold story of Panama.

For the next year and a half, I camped inside the main reading room of the New York Public Library, perusing records of original congressional hearings, period newspapers, and unpublished papers, finding flagrant inconsistencies with the official story that I had learned as a child. A weekend hobby led to a full-time job. By the end of 1998, I had the outlines of a story hidden for almost a century.

When I went home to Panama for the Christmas vacation, I told my family what I had found, thinking they would share in my excitement, but they reacted with hesitation and even resistance. They warned that they would face retribution from the elite of the country, the wealthy families who were the direct descendants of the people I profiled in the story. Even my father objected for patriotic reasons. He had spent his youth fighting the Americans to make them surrender the Panama Canal to the Panamanians, and this transfer was only a year away. He warned that my book diminished not only the Americans, but our own patriots, and begged me to suppress the truth about the corruption and the Wall Street ties. After all, he claimed, every country needs heroes.

Gathering evidence also became a daunting task. Copies of checks paid by J.P. Morgan to Panamanian patriots, original testimonies taken under oath, and many other papers that proved the conspiracy by Wall Street were mysteriously missing from libraries and private collections. Also, for years, people who had an interest in hiding the truth about the corruption had been buying and taking out of circulation incriminating photographs and revealing documents.

Nevertheless, I decided to publish *How Wall Street Created a Nation* because I wanted to give Panama its own history. The book not only details the beginnings of American imperialism in Latin America, but it tells the story of how a powerful, unchecked financial elite can rule and set the course of U.S. foreign and military policy. The picture that emerges of the period is unsettling; it reminds us of our own days.

I wish to thank a number of people who contributed to the book. Webster Stone, of course, for suggesting the idea. Sylvana Paternostro, James Linville, and my agent Ana Ghosh of Scovil, Chichak & Galen for their creative direction. My publisher John Oakes and my editor JillEllyn Riley of Four Walls Eight Windows provided tremendous editorial advice. In Panama, Jorge Ritter and historian Jorge Conte Porras gave me insights and clues. Most importantly, I wish to thank my father, Ovidio Diaz Vazquez, who inspired me with his nationalism; my mother Marina Espino, and my brother Ovidio Alberto; and my wife, Laura Maria Guardia, who encouraged me to go on when I was ready to quit.

Major Characters
(in order of appearance)

JOSEPH PULITZER

Famed publisher, his newspaper, the *World*, published accusations against Theodore Roosevelt claiming that he had assisted a Wall Street syndicate that fomented the Panamanian revolution and made a sizable fortune speculating on the Panama Canal. Roosevelt counterattacked with a libel suit, and Pulitzer launched a three-year campaign to discover the truth.

WILLIAM NELSON CROMWELL

Lawyer and hired gun, he was the founder of Sullivan & Cromwell, one of Wall Street's preeminent law firms, and adviser to many turn-of-the-century robber barons. In 1896, he was hired by the bankrupt French Panama Canal Company to convince the U.S. government to buy the French company's right to build the Panama Canal. He defeated the Nicaragua canal forces in Congress and masterminded the independence of Panama. Allegedly, he was behind a Wall Street syndicate that speculated on French Panama Canal Company shares.

THEODORE ROOSEVELT

The twenty-sixth president and one of the most vigorous and intellectual men ever to occupy the White House. He believed that an Isthmian Canal under American control would make the United States the most powerful nation in the world. Despite his mistrust of big business, in Panama he colluded with Wall Street tycoons to obtain the rights to build the canal. He personally maneuvered the military movements that led to the independence of Panama.

J.P. MORGAN

Head of J.P. Morgan & Co., America's preeminent banking house. As one of the leading members of Cromwell's syndicate, he allegedly funded the purchase of French Panama Canal Company shares and lent money for the independence of Panama.

PHILIPPE BUNAU-VARILLA

An enigmatic Frenchman, for two decades he launched a personal campaign to build the Panama Canal. He helped convince Congress to adopt the Panama route instead of the Nicaragua route, concocted the plan for the independence of Panama, and then double-crossed the country by rushing to signature a grossly unjust Panama Canal treaty.

SENATOR JOHN TYLER MORGAN

Chairman of the interoceanic canals committee, he devoted his life to building a canal through Nicaragua. Just when his triumph was secured, his lifelong quest was quashed by the Panama lobby. Convinced that heinous crimes were committed, he led two congressional investigations on the activities of the Wall Street syndicate in Panama.

SENATOR MARK "DOLLAR" HANNA

Chairman of the ruling Republican party, he was the most powerful man in Washington before Theodore Roosevelt's ascendancy. His participation during the Senate debates over the Isthmian canal route was decisive for Panama. He had extensive relations with the Wall Street syndicate.

JOHN HAY

The secretary of state during the McKinley and Roosevelt administrations, he negotiated the Panama Canal treaty with Colombia. Heavily influenced by Cromwell when the Colombian Congress rejected the treaty, he conspired to seize Panama from Colombia and then signed the onerous and controversial Hay-Bunau-Varilla treaty.

Manuel Amador Guerrero

The elderly doctor of the Panama Railroad company, in September 1903 he traveled to New York to obtain the support of Cromwell and Roosevelt for the independence of Panama. He led the revolutionary movement of November 1903 using plenty of Wall Street money. He became the first president of Panama.

General Esteban Huertas

Colombian officer, he was in charge of the Colombian forces in Panama. A tiny young man with a mangled left arm, his decision to support the Panamanian revolution and his arrest of the loyal Colombian generals secured the bloodless independence of Panama. He received a small fortune for his participation in the revolution.

Chronology of Events

January 1902   The House of Representatives passes a bill approving the construction of a canal through Nicaragua.

August 1902   The United States Senate reverses the House vote and adopts the Panama route.

August 1903   Colombia rejects the proposed Panama Canal treaty.

November 3, 1903   U.S. warships arrive in Colón and secure the independence of Panama.

November 18, 1903   Secretary of State John Hay and Philippe Bunau-Varilla rush to sign the Panama Canal treaty.

1908   Roosevelt files a libel suit against Joseph Pulitzer for publishing accusations that Roosevelt assisted a Wall Street syndicate.

1914   Panama Canal inaugurated.

1919   Roosevelt dies.

1922   The United States Congress approves a $25 million reparation payment to Colombia for taking Panama.

1964   Riots brake out in Panama demanding a new Panama Canal treaty.

1977   General Omar Torrijos Herrera and President Jimmy Carter sign the second Panama Canal treaty.

1989   U.S. forces invade Panama to oust General Manuel Antonio Noriega.

December 31, 1999   The United States surrenders its control over the Panama Canal after ninety-six years.

Map of the Caribbean Sea (Laura Maria Guardia)

1

Scandal

On October 2, 1908, at 10:30 pm, the managing editor of Joseph Pulitzer's the *World*, Caleb Van Hamm, received an unexpected telephone call. The nervous voice identified himself as Jonas Whitley, a staff member of William Nelson Cromwell's press agency. He told Van Hamm that a libelous and inaccurate story about the Panama Canal involving Cromwell and President Theodore Roosevelt was about to be published by the newspaper the next day, and he wanted to set the record straight. The editor pulled out paper and pen.

Van Hamm knew that any story about William Nelson Cromwell would make sensational news. The senior partner of Sullivan & Cromwell, Wall Street's preeminent law firm, his clients included the huge railroad companies, the nation's most prestigious banks, and the most powerful men in the country, including J.P. Morgan. Known in Wall Street as the "Fox" for his curly white hair and razor-sharp intellect, the lawyer's suspicious involvement in the shady events that had led to the creation of the Republic of Panama and the signature of the Panama Canal treaty had already been reported in the *World*. The story that Whitley was about to narrate, however, would go even further.

Whitley had called because of an error that occurred the day before. Cromwell's senior partner, William J. Curtis, had gone to the offices of New York District Attorney William Travers Jerome to ask him to take action against some Panamanians who were allegedly trying to blackmail Cromwell. Curtis had claimed that they were demanding money for their share of the work in the profit-driven independence of Panama and for keeping silent about Cromwell's role.

Jerome decided not to pursue the matter, but his office leaked the information to the *World*'s city editor, who put a reporter on the story. The reporter could not find the alleged buccaneers, but his snooping roused Cromwell's entire office staff. That night at ten o'clock, Jonas Whitley telephoned Caleb Van Hamm.

Van Hamm knew nothing of the story, but asked Whitley to excuse him for a few minutes to check on it. He called on the city editor and learned that thanks to the afternoon's unfruitful efforts, the article would not be published. Van Hamm returned to the telephone and bluffed to Whitley.

"Dear, dear, Jonas. Sorry to hear that. Tell us all about it."

For the next hour, Whitley narrated the story while Van Hamm took copious notes. Van Hamm asked Whitley to come the *World*'s offices in an hour as supposedly the reporter would have his story ready by then, and Van Hamm promised to give Whitley a chance to have "a look in." Van Hamm immediately called in a stenographer and recounted the story as dictated by Whitley.

When Whitley arrived, Van Hamm handed him a copy of the story which he himself had drafted, claiming that this was the investigation made by the city editor. A distressed Whitley rushed back to Sullivan & Cromwell's offices and immediately sent a cable to Cromwell in Panama.

That night, Cromwell was President Roosevelt's official delegate to the inauguration ceremony of Panama's second president, José Domingo de Obaldiá. He was sitting next to former president Manuel Amador Guerrero and Obaldiá's wife when he received the alarming cable from New York. The lawyer left the lofty ceremonies under the lush palm trees of Panama's Cathedral Park to fire back a response and try to nullify the damaging report.

But the following morning, October 3, the story ran on the front page of the *World*, with a prominent headline next to a picture of

Cromwell and Roosevelt's brother-in-law, an alleged conspirator. The report made Cromwell out to be a virtuous lawyer fighting the vice of Panamanian blackmailers, but the charges received as much publicity as Cromwell's denial. The *World* described how a secret Wall Street syndicate headed by Cromwell had conspired to buy the shares of the defunct French company that had tried, but failed, to build the Panama Canal; the syndicate then convinced Theodore Roosevelt to buy its concessions for $40 million, reaping an enormous profit. When Colombia refused to ratify the treaty with the United States, the syndicate plotted and fomented a revolution in the then province of Panama with the aid of the United States military. The conspiracy included J.P. Morgan, Philippe Bunau-Varilla, the former chief engineer of the French company, Charles P. Taft, brother of secretary of war and Republican party presidential candidate William Taft, and Douglas Robinson, Roosevelt's brother-in-law. The *World* reported:

> Financiers invested their money because of a full knowledge of the intention of the Government to acquire the French property at a price of $40,000,000, and thus because of the alleged information from high Government sources were enabled to reap a rich profit.

The early edition did not carry Cromwell's denial, but the later editions did. He called the story a "lying fabrication without a shadow of truth in it" and stated that "neither me nor any one allied with me ever bought, sold, dealt in or ever made a penny or profit" speculating on the Panama Canal. Taft immediately cabled the *World* denying any connection to a syndicate; Robinson would not comment, but later, he too denied the charges.

Despite the denials, on October 6, the *World* published another inflammatory story. This time it claimed that Cromwell was "practically the Secretary of War as far as the Panama Canal was concerned" and that his "law offices at No. 41 Wall Street were even regarded by many as the real executive offices of the Panama Canal."

At the White House, President Theodore Roosevelt heard the allegations, but refused to comment. Though the *World* published five more stories on the alleged Panama syndicate, the president ignored them. He saw it as a futile attempt by the Democratic Party to discredit the Republicans in the presidential campaign.

But the day before the presidential election, November 2, 1908, the largest newspaper in Indiana, the *Indianapolis News* (tradition- ally a Republican newspaper) picked up on the story from the *World*, and ran an editorial that said, in part:

> The campaign is over, and the people will have to vote tomorrow with- out any official knowledge concerning the Panama Canal deal. It has been charged that the United States bought from American citizens for $40,000,000 property that cost those citizens only $12,000,000. Mr. Taft was Secretary of War at the time the negotiation was closed. There is no doubt that the Government paid $40,000,000 for the property: *But who got the money?*

The smear campaign worked. Although Taft carried Indiana by 10,731 votes over William Jennings Bryan, the Republican candidate, the Democrats lost the governorship, a United States senator, and got only three of fifteen congressional seats.

An enraged Roosevelt blamed the upset on the newspaper articles and swore to exact revenge. He sent a message to the Associated Press asserting that there was no syndicate in Panama and that the "abom- inable falsehood that any American had profited from the sale of the Panama Canal is a slander." He finished by launching a vociferous attack upon Delevan Smith, editor of the *News*, and Joseph Pulitzer of the *World*.

During this time, the old, blind, and rickety Joseph Pulitzer had no inkling of the controversy. He had given up active management of his tabloid newspaper for a life of leisure, and, as usual, was cruis- ing on his gigantic yacht, the *Liberty*, off the coast of the Carolinas. When the story broke, his aides immediately went searching for him and found the *Liberty* temporarily docked outside Charleston. Don Seitz, a senior editor, boarded the ship, bringing with him the news- paper articles and Delavan Smith.

When Pulitzer asked Smith where he got the tip for his story, Smith nervously replied that he had based his editorial on statements "from a prominent New York newspaper." Smith admitted that he had made a mistake when he printed his article having read only the morning edition of October 3, which did not carry Cromwell's denial. After Smith left, Pulitzer asked, "What New York paper does Smith mean?"

"The *World*," answered Don Seitz.

"I knew damned well it must be. If there is any trouble, you fellows are sure to be in it."

Nevertheless, the elderly Pulitzer decided to answer Roosevelt's accusations in the *World* the following day:

The Panama Scandal—
Let Congress Investigate

In view of President Roosevelt's deliberate misstatements of fact in his scandalous personal attack . . . the *World* calls upon the Congress of the United States to make immediately a full and impartial investigation of the entire Panama Canal scandal.

WHO GOT THE MONEY?

The newspaper accused Cromwell of fomenting a revolution in Panama and bribing Panamanian patriots, Colombian troops, and American officials to achieve his aims. It claimed that after the revolution, he and J.P. Morgan personally controlled the disbursement of funds for the benefits of the American speculators. The article concluded:

Who did the United States pay $40,000,000 for a bankrupt property whose control could undoubtedly have been bought in the open market for less than $4,000,000?

Who bought up the obligations of the old Panama Canal Company for a few cents on the dollar?

Whether all the profits went into William Nelson Cromwell's hands, or whatever became of them, the fact that Theodore Roosevelt as President of the United States issues a public statement about such an important matter full of flagrant untruths, reeking with misstatements, challenging line by line the testimony of his associate Cromwell and the official record, makes it imperative that full publicity come at once through the authority and by the action of Congress.

The editorial provoked a sensational scandal; myriad newspapers supported the *World*'s call for a congressional investigation. On December 15, an infuriated President Roosevelt launched the most savage attack of his eight-year reign. He considered the Panama Canal to be his greatest achievement, and he was determined not to have it tainted by a tabloid newspaper editor. In a special message to Congress, he railed against Joseph Pulitzer, holding him personally responsible for the scandal.

> These stories need no investigation whatever . . . they are in fact wholly and in form partly a libel upon the United States Government . . . . The real offender is Mr. Joseph Pulitzer, editor and proprietor of the *World*. . . . It is therefore a high national duty to bring to justice this vilifier of the American people, this man who wantonly and wickedly and without one shadow of justice seeks to blacken the character of reputable private citizens and to convict the Government of his own country in the eyes of the civilized world of wrongdoing of the basest and foulest kind, when he has not one shadow of justification of any sort or description for the charges he has made.

Pulitzer arrived in New York City in a very agitated state of mind. He remained on the *Liberty*, docked at the Chelsea Piers, ready to set sail to the high seas if Roosevelt sent U.S. marshals to arrest him. He summoned Caleb Van Hamm to his yacht and asked, "What proof have you that Douglas Robinson and Charles Taft are involved in this matter?"

"None at all," Van Hamm nervously replied.

"My God! No proof? You print such stories without proof?"

Van Hamm explained that all of the evidence had come from Whitley, Cromwell's own press agent.

"All right. Just remember—Roosevelt is likely to make trouble . . . He will try to make trouble for me. If he does, I will fight him to the finish."

In the meantime, at the White House, Roosevelt assigned detectives to investigate his own vice president, Douglas Fairbanks, because he suspected that Fairbanks was responsible for the *Indianapolis News* report. Indianapolis was Fairbanks's hometown; the *News* enjoyed a monopoly there; the newspaper had traditionally supported Republicans; and editor Delavan Smith was Fairbanks's cousin. Fairbanks had ample reason to launch the smear campaign against Roosevelt, since he had shut Fairbanks out of the running for president and instead endorsed his Secretary of War William Taft. Roosevelt decided that he would sue his own vice president for criminal libel if investigators found any evidence that he had inspired the report. Secret service agents tapped the vice president's telephone and followed him for months, but they found nothing incriminating.

On February 17, 1909, Attorney General Charles Bonaparte (great-grandnephew of Napoleon) indicted Pulitzer, Van Hamm, and Smith, among others, for libeling Roosevelt, Morgan, Elihu Root, Cromwell, Taft, and Robinson. The indictment relied on obscure laws that preceded the American revolution and strapped a tight muzzle on the press.

Pulitzer was at the *Liberty* when he heard the news and figured his days of leisure were over. He became convinced that Roosevelt and Cromwell would walk over courts, judges, and juries to put him in jail. He sent his agents all over the country to find the best prison in which to spend the last years of his life. He sailed to the high seas, but every time his yacht docked for supplies, he anticipated a U.S. marshal would be waiting to take him. Eventually, he decided to take off for Lisbon.

Nevertheless, the ailing newspaperman called his editors to announce that he was going to face the stormy Roosevelt head on. "Roosevelt cannot muzzle the *World*," he proclaimed. If the president is allowed to win this case, he claimed, the constitutional right to a free press would be severely compromised. Newspapers around the country rallied to his support.

Pulitzer sent two reporters, the brilliant Earl Harding and the inquisitive Henry Hall, on a long and arduous mission that would take them to Paris, Panama, Bogota, and Washington in search of the truth for his defense.

At last, the press clamored, the true story of what happened in Panama would be known. The lies and cover-ups regarding the "national chapter of dishonor" would be exposed, Cromwell's mysterious control over the Isthmus would end, and the question that had haunted the world since the canal was begun would finally be answered: What happened in Panama in 1903?

2

Wall Street Faces Congress

CROMWELL PLANNED EVERYTHING he did with an incredible precision. Every letter went three ways, by regular mail, by cable, and by special messenger. He never took risks. "Accidents don't happen," he would acidly tell his lawyers every time they would use floods or strikes as excuses for not carrying out his orders, "they are permitted to happen by fools who take no thought of misadventure!"

A little man, Cromwell was "strikingly pretty, with aquiline features and a mane of white wavy hair which added to his air of authority and made him conspicuous in any company." "In striped trousers and morning coat," one commentator noted, "he looked like a clever drama student dressed for the part of elder statesman." He was controlling, shameless, and utterly persuasive. "No life insurance agent could beat him," a *World* reporter wrote, "he talks fast and when he wishes to, never to the point." With his "wizardry with figures and an intellect like a flash of lighting that swings with the agility of an acrobat," he planned all his movements in advance.

Originally from a modest Brooklyn family, he had risen from poverty in the best American way after his father was killed in the Civil War. At the end of the century, at the age of forty-six, he was already an institution, "a distinguished autocrat in his office, whose juniors lived in awe of him but told stories with certain pride and affection of his eccentricity and structures." He enjoyed his authority, but he was always "the kind of man who likes to be a power behind the throne, not on it: he loved to be regarded as a mystery man." His clients included J.P. Morgan, whom he helped create the United States Steel Corporation, the biggest company in the world, W.K. Vanderbilt (the shipping tycoon), and Edward Harriman, whom he assisted in designing the complex finances and mergers that led to the first transcontinental railroad company. These financial titans sought him not only for his legal skills, but for his sheer brain force and consistency of purpose that allowed him to get what he wanted.

He offered more than a law firm: he had press agents, accountants, and politicians that helped him lobby his cases in Washington. He had intimate relations, "susceptible of being used to advantage," with men possessing influence and power in all circles, including political, financial, and in the press. Clients came to seek the benefit of this influence and power. He was the obvious choice for the French Panama Canal Company to turn to when it needed a miracle.

On January 26, 1896, Maurice Hutin, president of the Compagnie Nouvelle du Canal Interoceanic, paid a visit to the mahogany paneled offices of Sullivan & Cromwell at 41 Wall Street. He came to sign up Cromwell's services in convincing the United States government to acquire the rights to build the Panama Canal from the bankrupt French company. Cromwell enthusiastically received his guest, but admitted that "to obtain favorable consideration for Panama [was] an impossible task." Given the bankruptcy of the French company, he told his client, the American public was "convinced that the plan for a canal at Panama was chimerical and its realization impossible."

For four hundred years, cutting a strait through the mountains and jungles of Panama to join the Pacific with the Atlantic ocean had been the fractured dream of European nations. As early as 1529, Roman Emperor Charles V ordered a search for a Isthmian canal through Panama. Other proposals were pushed by countries as diverse as England, Germany, and Russia, but no attempt was even made until 1879, when Ferdinand de Lesseps, the visionary French promoter who built the Suez Canal, went against all advice and turned his attention to the centuries-old dream of building the Panama Canal.

No one represented the spirit of the nineteenth century more than de Lesseps. He used the new power of the steam, coupled with his capacity to raise private money, to accomplish what many regarded as impossible, building a canal that united the Mediterranean with the Indian Ocean through the strait of Suez. He saw himself as a prophet of biblical proportions, and even stated that what he was doing was nothing less than undoing the work of Noah: As Noah had separated the oceans with one sweep of his hand, he was uniting them. When the Suez Canal was completed, de Lesseps, already in his late sixties and the most famous citizen of France, sought an even greater challenge in Panama.

He chartered the Compagnie Universelle Pour le Canal Interoceanic, its stated purpose to build the Panama Canal, *la grande enterprise*. It was the greatest human undertaking ever attempted. The cost was calculated at 240 million dollars, twice the cost of the Suez Canal. The time for construction was estimated at twelve years, also twice as long as that of Suez.

The excavation was expected to be finished by 1899, but by that time, only a fifth had been completed. De Lesseps had made crucial engineering mistakes, such as demanding a canal at sea level and underestimating the difference between the dry deserts of Suez and the humid, muddy land in Panama. Also, tuberculosis, yellow fever, and malaria had killed or seriously debilitated two out of every three workers. On December 1889, unable to raise more money to continue the work, the French hero had no choice but to declare that *la grande enterprise* was dead.

The Compagnie Universelle's bankruptcy was a failure of unimaginable proportion. Hundreds of thousands of peasants throughout Europe who had invested their life savings in the company saw their money evaporate. Outraged, the public demanded the guillotine for those responsible. Several of the organizers, including the family of de Lesseps and Gustave Eiffel, the builder of the Eiffel tower and the Statue of Liberty, were imprisoned for fraud and misfeasance of the investors' funds. Many bankers involved in the scandal committed suicide, and a score of politicians implicated in the scandal, including future prime minister Georges Clemenceau, either ended up in prison for accepting bribes, or lost their posts.

In 1894, the French liquidator penalized the large shareholders of the Compagnie Universelle by forcing them to subscribe for shares of a new company, the Compagnie Nouvelle. The company acquired the assets of the old company and launched a campaign to raise enough capital to begin the construction of the canal again, but it was mere fantasy. In Panama, all that remained of the original company were a few rusting dredges, and most of the excavation had disappeared under tropical mudslides. Even the word Panama was synonymous with failure and scandal (*Quel Panama!* was a popular French expression that meant "What a mess!"). The only valuable asset was the concession to build the canal granted by Colombia, of which Panama was a province, but even this was set to expire in a few years. Ferdinand de Lesseps had died, and no one else had the ability to engender the optimism that the new enterprise required. France's only real hope of recouping some of its investment was to sell the rights to build the Panama Canal to the United States.

France knew that the United States had wanted to build an Isthmian route since the 1840s to facilitate the massive migration spurred by the California Gold Rush. During the Spanish-American War in Cuba, the fabled voyage of the warship *Oregon* from the coast of San Francisco around Cape Horn demonstrated to Americans the pressing need to expedite passage between the Atlantic and Pacific Oceans to protect its vast territory. However, given the bankruptcy of the French, public sentiment in the United States supported the long cherished plan to build a canal through Nicaragua, using its two lakes, Lake Managua and Lake Nicaragua.

For France, an American built Nicaragua Canal meant the loss of its $250 million investment. The French thus sought to sway American opinion by any means, and for this purpose they sought the professional assistance of William Nelson Cromwell. The New York lawyer had been a director and general counsel of the Panama Railroad Company since 1893. This was a figurehead position, until Maurice Hutin arrived soliciting his lobbying efforts. From that moment, the destiny of *la grande enterprise* and the dream of centuries rested on the shoulders of the man who, according to the *World*, with his "masterful mind, whetted on the grindstone of corporation cunning, conceived and carried out the rape of the Isthmus."

On December 2, 1898, Cromwell went to Washington D.C. to convince President McKinley and Congress to build the Panama Canal, but found himself against an entrenched Nicaragua lobby. Since the failure of the Panama route, important politicians and businessmen with great influence in Washington had gotten Congress to pass an act chartering the Maritime Canal Co., a private company whose purpose was to build the Nicaragua Canal. Articles and photographs describing the plans were constantly published in newspapers. Boards of trade, state legislatures, party conventions all passed resolutions demanding government action in favor of the canal. Newspapers advocated that a Nicaragua Canal would be the canal of the American people. William Randolph Hearst's *New York Herald* expressed the popular opinion when it said,

> the Nicaragua Canal project is a purely national affair, conceived by Americans, sustained by Americans, and if later on constructed, operated by Americans according to American ideas, and for American needs. In one word, it is a national enterprise.

No one was more identified with the Nicaragua lobby than Senator John Tyler Morgan of Louisiana. Chairman of the Senate Committee on Interoceanic Canals, he had introduced a bill in Congress granting government funds to build the Nicaragua Canal, and everything indicated that it would pass.

Cromwell spearheaded his campaign with an official audience with President McKinley. The president was not convinced in the least, and in December 5, three days after Cromwell's visit, he sent his message to Congress in which he supported Morgan's bill and recommended providing government funds to build the Nicaragua Canal. Cromwell decided to confront Senator Morgan face-to-face.

Few dared disagree with the small, white-haired and bat-eyed senator, since he had the tendency to get angry and to attack viciously, especially on matters relating to the Nicaragua Canal. A former colonel of the Confederate Army, Morgan believed that a canal through Nicaragua would bring to the South the prominence it had lost during the Civil War. Nicaragua would be approximately eight hundred miles closer to the Gulf ports of Mobile and Galveston than to New York and Boston. He foresaw the world markets opening to southern lumber, ore, iron, and manufactured goods, and his own popularity at home soaring. Morgan also believed the Nicaraguan route to be superior: it was closer to the United States; it offered the lowest pass anywhere on the cordillera of Central America; it provided as much as one hundred miles of navigable lakes and rivers; and it was a more stable country than Colombia, which had been ravaged by a fifty-year-old civil war. Furthermore, unknown to the public, Morgan had an interest in the Maritime Canal Co. In short, building the Nicaragua Canal had become the centerpiece of Senator Morgan's career. Cromwell sought to hinder his lifelong quest.

In the senator's office, Cromwell demanded an opportunity to espouse the advantages of Panama in the upcoming Senate debates, but Morgan got so angry he threw the lawyer out of his office. Next day, the diminutive senator discharged his anger before his committee with a violent attack on the "Panama lobby of Cromwell."

Morgan's attack angered Cromwell and created a personal challenge for the Fox. He had been one of the biggest donors to the Republican Party during the 1896 presidential campaign, and many prominent congressmen and senators owed him favors. He visited and castigated them for allowing Morgan and the Democrats to be immortalized with a canal bill, especially during an election year. To each of them he gave pamphlets that his press agents, Roger Farnham and Jonas Whitley, had prepared showing "the true condition, the graveness, and the importance of the Panama Canal." When he realized that arguments were not enough, Cromwell promised the politicians enormous contributions for their upcoming campaigns.

Cromwell then turned his attention to securing the support of the man considered the most powerful in Washington, the chairman of the Republican party, Senator Mark Hanna. At age sixty-four, the portly and electrifying Ohio senator looked slightly weak as he limped with a cane, but "his wide eyes and slightly protuberant ears made him a perpetually attentive adolescent." The Republican party was known for its open alignment with big business, and Hanna was its leader in Congress. For his open support of the railroads and oil monopolies, he was nicknamed Mark "Dollar" Hanna. Cromwell knew that Hanna had opposed the construction of any Isthmian canal to protect the interests of the railroad companies that saw the canal as competition, but recently he had declared his support for a Nicaragua Canal as a member of Senator Morgan's committee.

To get an introduction, Cromwell called on one of his clients and Hanna's banker, J.E. Simmons, who arranged an appointment with the senator. At the meeting, Cromwell opened with a $60,000 donation to the Republican party, compliments of his client, the Compagnie Nouvelle. The outrageously large donation surpassed even the Rockefeller Standard Oil Company $50,000 gift to the party that year. The senator probably knew that it was inappropriate to take money from a foreign company, but Cromwell insisted, and Mark "Dollar" Hanna couldn't resist the temptation.

When Senator Morgan found out about Cromwell's machinations, he denounced his tactics openly on the Senate floor and in the press, accusing the lawyer of being a marionette to the railroad companies who were trying to delay the legislation by proposing an alternative route. But Morgan could not defeat the Fox: at the end of February, Congressman Hepburn, a friend of Cromwell, introduced a canal bill in the House of Representatives in order to take the credit away from Morgan and the Democrats. Morgan counteracted in the Senate, presenting the bill under his name, and the result was a stalemate in Congress. To break the deadlock, Cromwell suggested a commission to investigate the most appropriate Isthmian route. To the bewilderment of the public and Nicaragua supporters, Republicans adopted Cromwell's resolution and held that year's budget hostage until their bill was approved. To avoid shutting down the government, Morgan and the Democrats had no choice but to yield, and on March 3, 1899, Congress appropriated $1 million for a commission to study all possible canal routes, including Panama.

On August 9, the nine members of the Isthmian Canal Commission and some of their wives sailed for Paris, not Central America as originally planned. Cromwell convinced them to go to Paris because he knew that there Panama, and not Nicaragua, would be the only subject of discussion. Also, he would have an opportunity to charm the delegates with the wonders of the City of Lights, which was preparing for the historic 1900 World Fair and the inauguration of the breathtaking Eiffel Tower.

Cromwell departed hastily on a transatlantic ship a few days before the delegates to have everything under his control. When the Americans arrived in Paris, the dapper little lawyer was in the Continental Hotel waiting for them, glasses in hand filled with the best vintage champagne. For the next three weeks, he controlled all the activities, delighting the delegates and their wives with sumptuous dinners and pleasures offered by the marvelous cosmopolitan city.

In the offices of the Compagnie Nouvelle, Cromwell organized an impressive presentation with maps and documents in neatly organized, small colorful folders. Playing the role of an engineer, he vociferously argued that the Panama route was feasible despite de Lesseps' failure. The "silver-tongued" lawyer made the best pitch of his life when he proposed that the rusty machinery and the right to build the canal, which expired in less than two years, were worth $40 million dollars. The amount was exorbitant, given that Nicaragua had offered the land for free and that no territory in world history had fetched nearly half that much.

Only one point did not go well. The president of the commission, Admiral Walker, officially asked Maurice Hutin "on what price and by what means could the United States become the purchaser of the Panama Canal?" To the dismay of Cromwell, Hutin hedged and would not give an answer. He still dreamed that the French could build the canal, and he wanted the United States only as a partner. Disappointed, the commission sailed back for America in mid-September, but Cromwell stayed in Paris to promote another agenda.

During the next two weeks, Cromwell pressed the robust and conservative Maurice Hutin to accept a more aggressive plan, which he called the "Americanization of the Panama Canal." Cromwell argued that the Nicaragua route derived immense advantage because "men of high standing in the United States had a direct personal interest in it" through the Maritime Canal Co., which was not the case with Panama. He thus proposed creating an American company owned by important American capitalists (including himself) to buy the assets of the Compagnie Nouvelle and then sell them to the United States government. A suspicious Hutin opposed the plan because he saw it as merely a scheme to buy the Compagnie Nouvelle's assets cheap and then resell them at a much higher price, benefiting the Americans. Cromwell took his case to the largest shareholders of the Compagnie Nouvelle, insisting that without his plan the United States would never buy the "junk heap" that the French had in Panama. Cromwell's arguments convinced the shareholders, and in October, they pushed Hutin to consent.

Cromwell returned to New York and immediately began to interest important capitalists to join his scheme. The first person he visited was the enigmatic J.P. Morgan. A very secretive man, he spent his days tucked away in the exquisite library of his mansion on 34 Street and Madison Avenue, whose ceiling was painted with Italian frescoes and whose mahogany walls were shelved with precious medieval bibles and rare books. The old financier had a deformed nose that shamed him and kept him out of the public eye. Having achieved unimaginable wealth and power, the business of banking bored him in his later years, and his focus was on religion and antiquity art. He spent hours seeking advice from Episcopalian pastors and sought clues to his own reincarnation in Egyptian mysticism.

When Cromwell came to visit, Morgan might have played solitaire inside his library, as was his habit, while Cromwell explained the details of the plan. Although money was no longer a motivation for Morgan, Cromwell presented an opportunity to become part of a scheme that would make history. On December 27, 1899, Cromwell and Francis Lynde Stetson, Morgan's personal attorney, incorporated the Panama Canal Company of America in New Jersey with $5,000 of capital plus a subscription for another $5,000,000. The subscribers included some of the most influential men in America: Morgan; J.E. Simmons; Kuhn, Loeb & Co.; Levi Morton; Charles Flint; Isaac Seligman, and others. This was a fabulous deal for the American investors who only paid $5,000 to incorporate the company, but who could reap millions if their plan succeeded. (Cromwell knew the business very well; some years earlier, he had made a killing speculating on the shares of the United States Steel Company when it was in the formation stages, netting $2,000,000.)

The American press covered the peculiar event. On December 28,

1899, the *New York Times* published the following headline, "French Stockholders Shares Taken by American Financiers. J.P. Morgan Interested in the Project to Americanize the Great Waterway," while the *World* declared that "capitalists having secured control of the French company . . . Americans to build the Panama Canal." However, in France, the liquidator of the Compagnie Nouvelle found out about the Fox's machinations in the United States and got a French tribunal to rule that the company could not sell its assets to the Americans without the consent of the shareholders. The board of directors was forced to resign three days later, and Hutin was again in command.

With the decision of the French court that the company could not sell its assets, Cromwell's plan seemed dead, but only temporarily. Some months later, in May 1901, a rumor spread in Paris that between May 25, 1900 and June 6, 1901, a confidential "Memorandum of Agreement" was signed by sixteen American capitalists and politicians to speculate on the stock of the Panama Canal Company. According to the secret sources, the Americans planned to buy the shares quietly in the Paris bourse and from thousands of shareholders scattered throughout the country. They calculated that they needed only $5,000,000, and yet they could resell the concessions to the United States government for as much as $40,000,000.

When Hutin heard the rumor, he sent Baron Eugene Oppenheim to America to investigate. Oppenheim returned with other news: Cromwell had made a donation to Hanna of $60,000 on behalf of the Compagnie Nouvelle that the company had not approved. On July 1, 1901, Hutin sent an furious letter to Cromwell dismissing him as general counsel and representative in the United States.

The dismissal came back to haunt Hutin and the Compagnie Nouvelle immediately: On November 1, the Walker Commission issued a unanimous preliminary report in favor of Nicaragua. Without Cromwell, the Panama cause was now in dire straits. Ten days later, Philippe Bunau-Varilla docked in New York City aboard the *Champagne*.

For three decades, Philippe Bunau-Varilla had dedicated his life to building the Panama Canal. An enigmatic Frenchman in his mid-forties, a soldier of fortune and an adventurer, he was characterized by the phrase *pomp and circumstance*. Plump and stiff-necked, he wore a large ornamental moustache waxed to fine spikes. His eyes were steady, unflinching, and grave, which gave him "a fixed look of fierce pride." Roosevelt said that he had the eyes of a duelist. "He does not speak in sentences," Frank Pavey, an American lawyer, said of him, "but rather in proclamations." Alice Roosevelt remarked that "he didn't just come into a room, he made an entrance."

Extremely refined to the point of the ridiculous, he tried to pass as a French aristocrat, even though he had no distinguished lineage (his father, a man of modest means, had gone to great lengths to give him a regal sounding name.) Despite his comic appearance, Bunau-Varilla was very astute, audacious, brilliant, and convincing, particularly regarding any matters dealing with the Panama Canal. He alone was a pint-sized battleship, and well suited for the job of taking on American public opinion regarding the Panama Canal.

Nobody knew his real interest in Panama. The source of his money was questionable. During the Compagnie Universelle's construction of the canal, Ferdinand de Lesseps appointed Bunau-Varilla, a recent graduate from the school of engineering of the famed Ecoles des Ponts et Chaussees, head of excavation, even though he was only twenty-six-years old. But after some months, he contracted yellow fever and returned to France. Bunau-Varilla left the Compagnie Universelle to head a private company, funded with American money from the financier Isaac Seligman. The company was contracted to dig the most difficult part of the canal, the Culebra Cut. It was said that the company only dug a ninth of what it promised, but charged an exorbitant fee because Philippe's brother, Maurice Bunau-Varilla, was the accountant in charge of making the payments. Even though the project failed, the modest engineer who had gone to the Ecole on a scholarship emerged quite well-off. He bought a mansion on the Avenue d'Iena, near the Arc de Triomphe, then the most fashionable address in Paris, and filled his house with "servants of servants." Although Bunau-Varilla swore that he never did anything wrong (to the point of almost jumping out of the window of a third-floor building to protest the charge), when the Compagnie Universelle declared bankruptcy, the French tribunals accused him of fraud and penalized him by forcing him to subscribe 400,000 dollars in shares of the Compagnie Nouvelle.

Despite the bankruptcy, he continued to work behind the scenes to begin the construction again. He prepared maps, plans, budgets, and, just as his mentor Ferdinand de Lesseps had done a decade earlier, launched a personal campaign throughout Europe to "Preach the Truth in the Highways" as a "soldier of the 'Idea of the Canal.'" He said that he did it independently as a crusade of faith for "The Glory of France." However, with his brother Maurice, Bunau-Varilla owned 11,000 shares of the Compagnie Nouvelle. If the United States bought the concessions, he would be a very rich man.

At the beginning of December 1900, Bunau-Varilla left Paris for New York. "The bugle note had been heard," he wrote in his memoirs as he hastened for America on an "apparently impossible" trip. "It was nothing more nor less than to change the settled opinion of eighty million people." He claimed that he rushed to answer a "chance invitation" from a certain Lieut. Asher Baker, a friend and influential diplomat, to give a speech in Cincinnati. His arrival, however, was ten days after the Walker Commission had given the preliminary report favoring Nicaragua, exactly the number of days it would take to sail from Paris to New York after receiving a cable from Cromwell.

Once Bunau-Varilla was in the United States, Lieut. Baker organized a dinner in the Commercial Club of Cincinnati attended by the most prominent businessmen in that city. When the American hosts saw the stiff Frenchman with his ornamentally waxed mustache, they probably laughed. However, Bunau-Varilla surprised them. He presented the advantages of the Panama Canal clearly and persuasively, using the maps and diagrams that he brought while jotting some notes on a blackboard behind him.

During the next month, Baker arranged an extensive tour of the main American cities for Bunau-Varilla. The climax of the tour was New York City's Chamber of Commerce. The lunch in the opulent Wall Street chamber gathered the most influential businessmen in America, including J.P. Morgan, John D. Rockefeller, Andrew Carnegie, Levi P. Morton, and J.E. Simmons.

After the tour, Bunau-Varilla decided to conquer Washington. He wrote to Senator Hanna but did not hear from him for weeks. He decided to secure an appointment by hiding in a corner at the lobby of the Waldorf Astoria where Hanna and other politicians were staying. He would then strike up a conversation with a conveniently placed Cincinnati friend and finagle an introduction to the intended prey. In his memoir, Bunau-Varilla recounts the encounter:

> Towards midnight, as I was about to go out for a breath of fresh air before retiring, I met a party of people in evening dress entering the Waldorf Astoria. My surprise was great when I saw at the head of them Colonel Herrick with a lady on his arm, and behind them a short, stout gentleman who limped slightly. His characteristic face, so frequently reproduced in the papers was familiar to me. It was the famous Senator Hanna.

Colonel Herrick, one of his Cincinnati friends, feigned surprise:

> "Come," said he, "that I may introduce you to Senator Hanna. He is here with us, and he wishes to make your acquaintance."
>
> "Ah" said the Senator, "M. Bunau-Varilla, how glad I am to meet you! It is precisely the wish for a long talk with you which made me postpone answering your letter. The fact is, that I am so pursued by business and men, that it is nearly impossible for me to know twenty-four hours in advance where I shall be, and what I shall do. Your letter is in my pocket, I expected to fix an appointment on my return tomorrow. But do not stand on ceremony, come right in when you like. If I am free we will have a talk; if I am not you will be an excuse for me to get rid of some bore."

The good luck of that evening did not stop there. According to Bunau-Varilla, he continued to walk back and forth in the lobby, when he "coincidentally" saw another Cincinnati friend in the company of L. Dawes, the comptroller of the currency. Again he feigned surprise, and after an extensive introduction, Dawes extended an invitation to Bunau-Varilla to visit him in Washington and promised to introduce him to President McKinley. In his memoirs, Bunau-Varilla insisted that this and many other similar encounters were pure coincidence, because the hands of "protecting divinity" were guiding him: "Every time I was in need of a man he appeared, of an event took place." For the introduction, however, the Cincinnati cohorts received good pay.

With these meetings secured, Bunau-Varilla left for Washington, D.C. on April 3. During this fateful trip, he claimed to have single-handedly won Senator Hanna's support. He told the senator,

> It is for you now, for the heads of the nation to speak your word. Will it be for an unpopular Truth or for a popular Error? You have to choose.

According to Bunau-Varilla, the old senator replied,

> Mr. Bunau-Varilla, you have convinced me. I am an old mining operator. If two mines are offered me, I prefer the one which I know to be good and which is said to be bad, to the one I know to be bad and which is said to be good. As a Senator of the United States I must, in the service of the nation, adhere to the same principles.

On April 7, Mr. Dawes called on President McKinley as promised. Bunau-Varilla admittedly "did not inflict a long lecture on him as I knew that the opinion of Senator Hanna would be his own," as was the case with most matters in Washington those days. He simply gave the president the text of his lecture and its gist in a few words. To accomplish his program in Washington, nothing remained but to see Senator John Tyler Morgan. Admittedly, this meeting did not go so well.

> At last, at eight o'clock one evening, I knocked at the door of the veteran of the Nicaragua campaign. My visit produced a deep impression on him. In spite of his apparent courtesy I saw he was trembling with passion.
>
> I had hardly begun my explanations, when he cut me short to sing the praises of Nicaragua.
>
> After half-an-hour of futile effort to get in a word, I was able to say: "But the volcanoes of Nicaragua—"
>
> "Oh, never think," he retorted, "that volcanoes will ever impress the Senate. The volcano argument is dead; with it you will not win a single vote."
>
> "Well, Mr. Senator," I replied, rising, "we shall see."
>
> The eyes of the aged Morgan shone with antagonism.
>
> "Now," said he, "between ourselves you would not put one dollar of your own money in this absurd project—in this rotten project—of Panama."

If ever in my life I was near the point of slapping an American Senator face, it was at this instant. My hand rose instinctively, when I controlled the mad impulse. Between myself and the old man a picture presented itself showing me the consequences of the trap into which the intentional insult was driving me. I lowered my half-raised hand, and extending it solemnly towards the Senator, I said:

"You have just inflicted upon me, sir, a gratuitous and cruel insult. But I am under your roof, and it is impossible for me to show you my resentment without violating, as you do, the laws of hospitality."

I turned my back on him and went out.

The following day, the Washington newspapers published the story of a violent assault committed by a "foreign adventurer, in the pay of Panama, upon the austere and venerable defender of the National Idea of Nicaragua."

After his Washington trip, Bunau-Varilla returned to New York to publish a pamphlet comparing the Panama and Nicaragua routes. It was the first time that someone had compared the routes from a purely technical point of view, and it received a favorable reception. By the time he sailed back to Paris on April 11, 1901, Bunau-Varilla had made a dent on American public opinion about the Panama Canal.

Many questions about his campaign emerged immediately: Who really invited him to America? Who paid his hotel bills? What were his true intentions? Did he act independently for the "Glory of France," or was he an agent of Cromwell's secret syndicate? Why didn't he meet with Cromwell? The presumed independence only lasted a few months, until the Isthmian Canal Commission rendered its final report in favor of Nicaragua.

In spite of the great campaign by Cromwell and Bunau-Varilla, on November 30, 1901, the Walker Commission gave its final report in favor of Nicaragua. Of the nine members in the commission, only the eminent engineer George Morison voted for Panama. One of the main liabilities of the Panama route was Maurice Hutin's extravagant $110,000,000 demand for the assets of the French company, almost three times what Cromwell had proposed.

With the technical report indicating the superiority of the Nicaragua route, all of the obstacles against it were quickly put aside. Morgan announced that he was dropping his name from the bill, deciding that if anyone was to be immortalized, it would be Hepburn and the ruling Republicans. On November 18, Secretary of State John Hay signed a treaty with Lord Julian Pauncefote of England providing for the neutrality of the canal even in times of war. And on December 10, the United States and Nicaragua signed a formal treaty for the construction of the Nicaragua Canal. Congressman Hepburn slated the Nicaragua bill for immediate consideration when Congress returned from its Christmas recess. Everything was set for the adoption of the Nicaragua route. The funeral bells for Panama had begun to toll.

With Cromwell sidelined, the salvation of the French enterprise now depended entirely on Bunau-Varilla. He published a strong condemnation of the actions of Maurice Hutin and the board, which caused a scandal in Paris. A meeting of shareholders became so violent that the police had to be called in. Hutin was forced to resign, and Maurice Bo, president of the bank Crédit Lyonnais, a friend of Bunau-Varilla and of Cromwell, replaced him even though technically he was prohibited from serving because he was one of the "penalized" shareholders. This restriction was conveniently ignored. Two days later, on January 4, the new board of the Compagnie Nouvelle sent a cable with a new sale offer to the United States for Cromwell's original proposal of $40 million dollars. Bunau-Varilla immediately sailed for America to arrive in time for the congressional debates.

As soon as the congressional session began on January 7, 1902, the House adopted the Hepburn Bill by an almost unanimous vote. On January 14, 1902, Senator Morgan introduced the bill in the Senate in a rush of enthusiasm. But in a surprising declaration, Hanna announced that President Roosevelt, who had been sworn in only a few months earlier as a result of McKinley's assassination, had summoned the Walker Commission. The Senate, he said, had to wait until the president approved the report. When Morgan doubted Hanna's assertions, Hanna replied sardonically, "Go and ask the president if you do not believe it!"

Roosevelt's reign over American politics had begun.

At age forty-two, Theodore Roosevelt was the youngest man ever to become president. He was rushed into the chief executive office when McKinley was assassinated by an anarchist in Buffalo on the afternoon of September 6, 1901. Upon hearing the news, Senator Hanna is said to have remarked, "Now look! That damned cowboy is President of the United States."

Roosevelt craved the limelight and, as one observer put it, "set out to be the bride at every wedding, the corpse at every funeral." Born in 1858 in New York City to a distinguished family, he attended Harvard University and then enrolled in Columbia Law School, but dropped out after one year to run for the state legislature, which he won at the age of twenty-three. His energy and constant struggle against machine politics earned him the nickname the Cyclone Assemblyman.

On Valentine's Day 1884, his wife and mother died. Stricken with grief, he left for two years to become a cattle rancher in the Dakota Territory, where he served as deputy sheriff of Billings County. He was later appointed assistant secretary of the navy by President McKinley in 1897. During the Spanish-American War in Cuba, he resigned his post to be the commander of the First Volunteer Cavalry Regiment, popularly known as the Rough Riders. Through press reports, the Rough Riders electrified the nation in a valiant charge up the San Juan Hills.

With his newfound popularity, he won the governorship of New York State in 1898. But soon he ran into trouble with the Republican party bosses, who nominated him, because he wanted to tax the rich and powerful corporations. To get rid of him, they encouraged him to seek the vice presidency of the United States. At first Roosevelt was reluctant to give up the governorship for the boring office of vice president, but he accepted after his friend Henry Cabot Lodge persuaded him that the position might serve as a springboard to the presidency. In the Republican convention of 1900, he was selected to run with McKinley by unanimous vote and later won the general elections. Roosevelt became chief executive upon McKinley's assassination.

Roosevelt and his large family changed the tenor of the office of the presidency, both formally and domestically. His second wife Edith remodeled the White House into what the president described as "a simple and dignified dwelling for the head of a republic," and to the dismay of many in Washington, turned the former "Executive Mansion" into the quite informal "White House." He took time to romp with his children or gather them around for a story. Every night, Roosevelt excused himself for a few minutes to attend the nightly "look in," that is, intense pillow fight.

A proponent of the "strenuous life," he was a vigorous outdoorsman and athlete. His favorite sports included big game hunting, boxing, horseback riding, tennis, hiking over rough terrain, and in the winter, skinny-dipping in the icy waters of the Potomac River. He was also a voracious reader who could finish two books in a day and had an apparently photographic memory. He also published over a dozen books.

Roosevelt spoke forcefully and gesticulated constantly, his fist pounding the air to emphasize a point, his head jerking back and forth virtually with every word. Some listeners were captivated by the stories of his adventures out West, but others found him self-absorbed and incapable of real conversation, since he had a tendency to lecture. In Washington, they said that the only way to make sure he listened was to go see him at 12:40 PM, the exact moment when he was being shaved. He was impetuous by nature and pursued his goals with unfettered intensity. Vicente Concha, the Colombian ambassador, warned his government to be wary of "the President's vehement character," as well as "the persistence and decision with which he pursues the things to which he commits."

Politically, he attacked corruption and fought against monopolies such as Rockefeller's Standard Oil Company and J.P. Morgan & Co.. In Panama, however, he unashamedly colluded with big business to promote an even mightier goal: to make the United States the most powerful nation in the world.

He sought to end the American isolationism that persisted throughout the nineteenth century. He publicly supported the annexation of Cuba, Puerto Rico, Hawaii, and the Philippines. To Henry Cabot Lodge he said, "I do wish our Republicans would go in avowedly to annex Hawaii and build an ocean canal with the money of Uncle Sam." While others saw the commercial advantages of an Isthmian canal, Roosevelt saw it as a means for the United States to dominate the Western hemisphere. He was greatly influenced by the best-selling *Influence of Sea Power on World History*, in which the author, Captain Alfred Thayer Mahan of West Point, argued that maritime power and world conquest went hand in hand. With an Isthmian canal allowing easy access to the Pacific, Roosevelt concluded, the United States could become the strongest nation in the world. He was willing to use his office to further his vision of America as few other presidents had. Joseph Pulitzer complained that Roosevelt took "such powers as no Monarch, or King, or Emperor ever possessed." (Years later, on the occasion of his birthday, Kaiser William II sent him a note saying, "You and I, there are no others.") In Panama, T.R. found the arena in which to promote his vision and his power.

Roosevelt's ascendancy at first seemed to be a blow for the Panama lobby. During his tenure as vice president, neither Cromwell nor Bunau-Varilla had even bothered to lobby him. It was also generally known that his reign meant an end to the era of supremacy of Hanna, who secretly supported Panama. Also, as Bunau-Varilla pointed out, "the new president was the most vivid expression of popular sentiment and was in direct touch with it. This sentiment had always been obstinately turned towards the idea of Nicaragua." Everything indicated that upon the rendering of the Walker Commission report, Roosevelt would support the construction of the Nicaragua canal the same way McKinley, the Senate, and the House already had.

But Teddy Roosevelt surprised everyone. Unlike McKinley, he wasn't going to let a committee, Congress, or anyone else decide where he was going to build his "ditch." On the week of January 14, Roosevelt called to his office every member of the Walker Commission individually, asking them to reconsider their decision in light of the new offer made by the Compagnie Nouvelle. One member, Professor Haupt, held out. Admiral Walker called him into the corridor outside the commission's offices and told him that President Roosevelt demanded a unanimous report because he feared that any dissent would be used to defeat all canal legislation. Under pressure from T.R., on January 18, the Isthmian Canal Commission annulled its preceding vote. In view of the new offer made by the Compagnie Nouvelle on January 4, it recommended the adoption of the Panama Canal.

No one knows for certain why Roosevelt chose Panama. This was the first major decision of his administration, and he was risking delaying passage of any canal bill and causing more years of congressional quarreling. George Morison, an eminent engineer and member of the Walker Committee, might have persuaded him that Panama was a superior route purely on technical grounds. Hanna is also said to have had an influence on the president.

T.R. got his friend, Senator Bill Spooner, to introduce a bill proposing the Panama Canal. He sent the bill to the Senate floor, where an intense debate was expected.

The press was stupefied and called on the Senate to disregard the recommendation of the Walker Commission. The *New York Herald* published an editorial saying that the recommendation "could not counterbalance the weight of the national sentiment in favor of Nicaragua." In the Senate, Senator John Tyler Morgan pledged a vitriolic attack against the defenders of Panama.

To get ready for the congressional debates, Hanna and J.E. Simmons asked Bunau-Varilla to ask the board of the Compagnie Nouvelle to reinstate Cromwell as general counsel and representative in the United States. He had been working secretly on Hanna to encourage delaying legislation and was behind the January 27 bill by West Virginia Senator Scott to appropriate $15,000 to investigate yet a third Isthmian route, through Darien, the widest part of Panama on the neck of the South American continent. The plan advocated was ludicrous, providing for a five-mile underground tunnel through which the ships would pass. Cromwell was trying to send the U.S. government off on a wild goose chase to delay legislation.

Bunau-Varilla wrote to Paris requesting the reinstatement, and a few days later, Cromwell was back again in his job. (In the letter reinstating him, President Bo warns not to make any "donations" or "promises" without the company's prior consent.) On January 25, Cromwell and Bunau-Varilla allegedly met for the first time at Senator Spooner's house to prepare Hanna's minority report.

Despite the Walker Commission's report, Morgan got the Committee on Interoceanic Canals, which he chaired, to recommend the Nicaragua Canal. Panama would be the alternate route, its advantages espoused only in a minority report. Knowing that such reports would typically be filled with dull engineering data that no one would read, Bunau-Varilla conceived a simple pamphlet with bars and rounds comparing the two routes from a technical point of view and clearly advocating the technical superiority of Panama.

In the meantime, Cromwell sent his partner William Curtis to France to get the consent of the shareholders of the Compagnie Nouvelle for the sale to the U.S. government. Curtis did more than to request signatures. Press reports began to arrive in New York alleging that American lawyers had been seen canvassing thousands of peasants scattered throughout France and offering to buy their shares of the company. The *World* published an exposé alleging that Cromwell and Bunau-Varilla were agents for J. P. Morgan's "gigantic Wall Street syndicate to gain control of the French concession and sell it to the U.S."

Bunau-Varilla's finances were also in question. For months, he had kept a hotel room in New York's posh Waldorf Astoria and in Washington's New Willard Hotel; he often spent great sums of money entertaining his friends, including Mrs. Douglas Robinson, Theodore Roosevelt's sister, and Mrs. H. W. Taft, the wife of the secretary of war. If he was on no one's payroll, as he claimed, but acted independently, where did he get the money and what was his motivation?

All the documents and speeches that Cromwell and Bunau-Varilla had prepared in favor of Panama could not match the effect of one incredible occurrence. On May 6, Mount Pelée in the South Pacific exploded and buried the island city of Saint-Pierre, leaving only one survivor. The disaster sent shudders throughout the world. Every nation, including the United States, sent relief shipments. Bunau-Varilla immediately seized upon the disaster for his advantage. He had been preaching the dangers of volcanoes in Nicaragua as early as 1892, and this supposed danger had been a recurrent theme in his speeches in 1901. He sent every senator a well-crafted pamphlet:

> Look at the coat of arms of the Republic of Nicaragua; look at the Nicaraguan postage stamps. Youthful nations like to put on their coats of arms what best symbolizes their moral domain or characterizes their native soil. What have the Nicaraguans chosen to characterize their country on their coat of arms, on their postage stamps? Volcanoes!

A few weeks later, "Protecting Divinity" intervened with yet another well-timed occurrence. On May 14, a cablegram from New Orleans announced that Momotombo had violently erupted on the shores of Lake Managua, and that it had destroyed the wharves of the railroad's Pacific terminus.

At the urging of Senator Morgan, Luis Correa, the Nicaraguan minister in Washington, cabled the president of Nicaragua asking for confirmation of the volcanic eruption. President José Santos Zelaya wired back, "NEWS PUBLISHED ABOUT RECENT ERUPTIONS OF VOLCANOES IN NICARAGUA ENTIRELY FALSE." Correa sent the cablegram to Senator Morgan with a letter assuring him that "Nicaragua has not had volcanic eruptions since 1835, and at that time Coseguina discharged smoke and ashes, but no lava." It was a blatant lie, but it was official. Morgan used it to open his speech before the Senate on June 4, 1902.

Morgan read Luis Correa's letter and a report from the American minister in Nicaragua, which reiterated that there had been no disturbances. Morgan then accused the Panama lobby of inventing the volcanic eruption and proclaimed that no active volcanoes existed in the whole of Nicaragua. He attacked the political instability in Colombia and Panama, their "mixed and turbulent people." Because of the civil war there, it would be merely a matter of time, he announced prophetically, before the United States would have to take Panama by force. "It would poison the minds of people against us in every Spanish-American republic in the Western Hemisphere, and set their teeth on edge against us." The senator continued extolling the virtues of Nicaragua, "where all the people are anxiously awaiting the coming of the United States to their assistance, with eager hopes and warm welcome, to their fertile, healthy, and beautiful land." He finished with an appeal to his Old South, "I hope to see the water of the Gulf of Mexico and of the Caribbean Sea as busy with commerce as the bay of San Francisco."

The following day, a weary Senator Hanna "limped down the aisles of the Senate," and decided, though unprepared, to address his colleagues. Most people did not know he supported Panama. The gallery was scantly occupied, but when word got around that Hanna supported the Spooner Bill, reporters and diplomats rushed to the Capitol. Rules of order were broken in the gallery as hundreds crowded in.

Hanna delivered the best speech of his eminent career. This was the ailing senator's last chance to dominate American politics. His influence was now overshadowed by the ascendancy of the most powerful president in U.S. history, but despite his dwindling power, he had a chance to prove that that he could still control Congress, even in the face of an unpopular, almost losing cause.

Unlike Senator Morgan, Hanna spoke softly, without emotion, recounting the virtues of Panama in a businesslike and factual manner, occasionally taking material from an aide and using the large visuals provided by Bunau-Varilla and Cromwell. The Russian envoy murmured, "Mais il est formidable."

He began with an exposition on the volcanic dangers of Nicaragua. Bunau-Varilla had produced a large map of volcanoes in Central America, with still active volcanoes marked red, and the extinct volcanoes marked black. Nicaragua had eight active sites, Panama zero. Pelée, on Martinique, Hanna told the audience, was once marked black. He then presented the results of a survey of ship captains that Cromwell had conducted favoring Panama, and he defended de Lesseps' vision. At about this point, he lost his balance, and his face became damp and pale. A spectator exclaimed, "Oh, do make him sit down!" He stopped, only to resume the next day.

Many thought Hanna feigned exhaustion to give Bunau-Varilla time to finish printing his Nicaragua-Panama pamphlet. The following morning, he began to speak as his secretary passed the pamphlet to each person in the chamber. He summarized its content in an almost mechanical fashion. One: a Panama Canal would be shorter; two: it would have less curvature; three: the time of transit would be less than half that of Nicaragua; four: it would have fewer locks, etc. When Senator Mitchell of Oregon, a Nicaragua supporter, tried to interrupt to question the sources of his report, Hanna replied, "I do not want to be interrupted, for I am very tired."

Hanna did not want to admit that Cromwell and Bunau-Varilla provided him with all the data, charts, and maps he relied on during his speeches. The two lobbyists sat together in the gallery, occasionally advising the senator through senate page boys who delivered the messages. The opposition became quite annoyed, and at one point, Senator Morgan openly accused Cromwell of writing Hanna's minority report; the accusation went unchallenged. At a later date, he said, "I warn that distinguished citizen wherever he may be to beware of Mr. Cromwell." In yet another speech, he referred to Cromwell, dramatically looking up at him, "I suppose he is in the gallery listening to me as he always is." During one of Senator Mitchell's speeches, Morgan fixed his unflinching gaze on Bunau-Varilla. The Frenchman recalled:

> He hoped to see the indignation provoked in me by the speech bring forth a shrug of the shoulders or a disdainful smile. I read in his eyes that he wished it intensely. He wanted to seize the least possible pretext to provoke a monumental scandal, and denounce the insolent foreigner who was showing contempt for Senatorial dignity. Beholding his anger increase I preferred not to run risks. I left the Chamber.

One of the most serious accusations against the Panama lobby was that the volcano scare in Nicaragua had been a fabrication, and the Nicaraguan Embassy maintained that the eruption never took place. The *Washington Star* published a cartoon in which Senator Hanna was depicted painting volcanoes on the map of Central America "with an air of keen satisfaction." With him was a man in the attire of an art student, the fancy costume emblematic of a French stereotype, symbolizing Bunau-Varilla. To refute the accusations, Bunau-Varilla searched in Washington for an official document from the Nicaraguan government acknowledging the abundance of active volcanoes. Suddenly, he realized that he had the proof in his possession all along.

> I hastened to call on all the postage-stamp dealers of Washington. I was lucky enough to find there ninety stamps, that is, one for every Senator, showing a beautiful volcano belching forth in magnificent eruption.

The stamp showed a volcano spewing a cloud of smoke; coincidentally, it was Momotombo. The foreground showed the very wharf that had been destroyed by the earthquake according to reports published one month earlier. He pasted his precious postage stamps on sheets of paper. On the top of each was written, "Postage Stamps of the Republic of Nicaragua, An official witness of the volcanic activity of Nicaragua."

The stamps arrived on the senators' desks on June 16, just three days before the vote. They had the desired effect: Senator Gallinger asked the Senate if it were reasonable to undertake this colossal work in a country whose emblem on its postage stamps was a volcano in eruption. Many senators who had been ambivalent were won over to the side of Panama.

During its last days, the debate became especially heated. Senators Platt and Quay worked tirelessly to persuade Roosevelt to withdraw his support of the Spooner Bill. The guests bored the president so much that during their next visit, T.R. arranged for Colonel Montgomery, a friend and staff member, to stand beside him and act attentive. Sitting at his desk, the president scribbled and did not even pretend to listen as the two senators launched into a diatribe in favor of Nicaragua. Frustrated by his inattention, they left. As soon as they were out the door, the president griped, "Montgomery, does the spectacle of human imbecility ever alarm you?"

On June 19, the debate ended. The gallery filled up; the press awaited the most important decision by Congress in years. Everyone knew it would be extremely close, and Morgan claimed that he had the votes to win. The decision came in the afternoon: The vote was forty-two to thirty-four in favor of Panama.

The Spooner Bill gave preference to Panama, but only on the condition that a satisfactory treaty could be negotiated with Colombia. Otherwise, the president had to construct the Nicaragua Canal. During the congressional debates, Colombia had already issued troubling statements about its willingness to grant its consent. Senator Hanna encouraged President Roosevelt to rely heavily on Cromwell during the sensitive negotiations. He told T.R., "You want to be very careful, Theodore; this is very ticklish business. You had better be guided by Cromwell; he knows all about the subject and all about those people down there."

T.R. replied, "The trouble with Cromwell is he overestimates his relation to the cosmos."

"Cosmos?" the seasoned senator replied. "I don't know him—I don't know any of those South Americans, but Cromwell knows them all. You stick close to Cromwell."

3

Colombia's Gamble

Ambassador José Vicente Concha of Colombia sat in his hotel suite in New York City and stubbornly refused to start the negotiations. During the congressional debates, he insisted on talking only to Secretary of State John Hay, and not to Cromwell or any representative of the Compagnie Nouvelle. Cromwell told him that Hay had no authority to deal with any Colombian legation until the Spooner Bill was adopted, and that Concha would have to deal only with him, whether he liked it or not. Concha refused and sat in his hotel room like an angered child giving the silent treatment and leaving Uncle Sam and the Compagnie Nouvelle to fret and wait.

Concha was a peculiar choice for the Colombian minister responsible for negotiating the treaty. Formerly the minister of war, he had never traveled outside Colombia prior to his Washington trip, he spoke no English, and he was frequently ill (which often interrupted negotiations). In a telegram to the State Department, the Colombian foreign affairs minister admitted that Concha was prone to "nervous excitement." Above all, he was proud, stubborn, staunchly nationalistic and suspicious of Americans.

To get Concha to cooperate, Cromwell warned him that if the Nicaragua route was adopted as a result of Colombia's stonewalling, a rebellion in the province of Panama would ensue. To buttress his argument, he brought with him the governor of the Department of

Panama, Mutis Duran, who spoke about the sentiment in Panama against the Bogota government (Duran was on Cromwell's payroll). Concha had never been to Panama, but the threat of a potential rebellion scared him. He thus authorized Cromwell to prepare a draft treaty between the United States and Colombia. In early April, Cromwell personally delivered his draft on behalf of the Colombian government to Secretary of State Hay.

Hay was already badly predisposed to negotiations with Colombia. Stocky, with a stiff posture and a gigantic moustache that curled back toward his ears, he had the distinguished but rigid demeanor of a military officer. In Washington he was regarded as something of a monument because he had served as Abraham Lincoln's private secretary when he was merely twenty years old (Hay-Adams, a posh section of Washington D.C., is named in part after him). His experience in international relations was unrivaled. He had served as British ambassador before he reluctantly accepted the post of secretary of state for McKinley and later for Roosevelt. A hawk, he had approved the annexation of the Philippines, had dispatched a dangerous relief expedition to rescue Americans in China during the Boxer Rebellion, and had supported the Spanish-American War, which he described as a "splendid little war." In Panama, however, he found a challenge that matched his abilities.

Hay shared Roosevelt's view that South American diplomats were "dago ambassadors from powerless, insignificant countries." He complained that negotiating with Colombia was "like holding a squirrel in your lap" because Colombia changed its diplomats in Washington frequently. Colombia had not had a permanent legation in Washington for years because of a vacuum in power caused by its civil war. The war pitted the Liberal party against the Conservative party. The former advocated a type of government similar to that of the United States, with autonomous states and separation of church and state. The Conservatives wanted a strong central government ruled from Bogota, adherence to the church, and law and order. The struggle for power between provincial Liberals and urban Conservatives had sunk a once prosperous and educated country into misery in the years after Simón Bolívar wrestled the country from Spain in the early nineteenth century. Bolívar, the liberator of much of South America, advocated the creation of one single Latin American country modeled after the United States. But after the liberator died in 1830, the dream of a modern nation based on the principles of the French and American revolutions vanished. Instead of a South American Paris or Washington D.C., Bogotá became an isolated hotbed of revolutions and coup d'etats.

To finance the civil war, the government was heavily indebted to foreign lenders. Its only salvation was a canal in Panama, Colombia's golden jewel. High hopes were placed on the payment to be received from the Americans and on the commerce and prosperity that a canal would bring. However, when the negotiations began, the Colombian government was hardly prepared to deal with Washington and the forceful Wall Street lobby.

Colombia's president at the time, José Manuel Marroquín, a conservative, was viewed as a weakling. He was a bearded eighty-year-old professor and man of letters "whose shyness kept him in the background for most of his career." In 1900, the feeble scholar, then vice president, surprised everyone and overthrew his own president in a coup d'etat, but he never fully consolidated his power. Rebel Liberal party troops conquered much of the countryside, including Panama. By 1901, they were almost at the gates of Bogota, and everything was in confusion and disarray. Entire provinces and government ministries acted independently of the Marroquín government.

Despite the confusion, Marroquín insisted on personally giving directions to his diplomats abroad. Negotiators sent to the United States had a difficult task; they often got contradictory instructions, and given the isolation of Bogotá, had to wait months to get an answer to even the simplest question.

Built on the plateau of the Andes at an altitude of 8,700 feet, Bogota was one of the most inaccessible cities in the world. To reach the capital, travelers had to sail for nine days on the Magdalena River from Barranquilla to Honda, a tiny village, and then travel by mule for three more days. "Given its isolation, the echoes of the outer world that arrived thither were all weakened by distance," Bunau-Varilla wrote. "All foreign questions appear at Bogota to be purely theoretical, abstract and remote. They engender semi-philosophical discussions in which the spirit of controversy is sharpened without any regard for tangible realities and their material consequences." With this lack of concern for practical consequences, Colombians approached the negotiations of the canal treaty.

Concha received instructions from President Marroquín to demand a $20,000,000 down payment, a $600,000 annuity, and a hundred-year lease. Secretary Hay counteroffered with a $7,000,000 down payment, a $10,000 annuity, and a perpetual lease. Cromwell went back to Concha with Hay's proposal, but Concha first rejected it and then said that he could not approve it unless he consulted Bogota, which would take weeks. To avoid delays, Bunau-Varilla sent a message to José Gabriel Duque, the editor of the *Panama Star & Herald*, Panama's largest newspaper, saying that Colombia was sabotaging the negotiations with excessive demands. The Colombian authorities quashed publication of the cable, but Duque managed to get copies to influential Panamanians who favored a canal treaty with the United States. When Bunau-Varilla told Cromwell what he had done, the lawyer was astounded. He asked what the Frenchman hoped to achieve. Bunau-Varilla explained that he knew the cablegram would not be published, "The Governor will forbid its being printed, but he will immediately wire it on to Bogota, and this will entail the dispatch of fresh instructions to Concha. Moreover, I am going to communicate it myself to Concha and it will perhaps suffice to open his eyes."

Concha was furious, but the ploy worked. He accepted a compromise proposed by Cromwell: a $7,000,000 down payment, a lease renewable for hundred-year periods, and an annuity to be determined later by a panel of arbitrators. On April 18, Cromwell delivered the signed Hay-Concha treaty to Secretary of State Hay.

A week later, Concha received a message from President Marroquín with instructions not to sign the treaty. Secretary Hay had been informed by the United States charge d'affaires in Colombia, Arthur Beaupré, that Marroquín opposed the treaty as drafted, but decided not to tell Concha in order to commit him and his government. When Concha found out about Hay's connivings, he was furious and announced his resignation, but President Marroquín would not allow it.

When Congress adopted the Spooner Act in June 1902, it required a revision of the Hay-Concha treaty. Under the terms of the Spooner Act, the United States demanded not a lease, but an absolute and perpetual cession of the land. Hay asked Cromwell to prepare an amendment to the treaty and submit it to Concha on July 9, 1902.

Concha immediately objected. He sent a telegram to President Marroquín urging his government to reject the proposed amendment, which he considered to be an affront to Colombian sovereignty. In the same telegram, the paranoid ambassador told his government to use code words to communicate with him because he feared that agents of the State Department were intercepting his cables.

He expected President Marroquín to reject the amendment, but on August 9, the president cabled back telling him to accept the proposal. "In order to render the amendments to memorandum presentable to our Congress, demand ten million cash and annuity of six hundred thousand after 14 years,," the cable said.

Concha was stunned and angered by Marroquín's response. A staunch nationalist, Concha could not comprehend how Colombia could so easily cede its sovereignty for money. Marroquín accepted the offer because he was desperate for cash to finance the civil war, and more importantly, he had concocted a secret scheme to later defraud the United States that he did not communicate to Concha.

The scheme consisted in getting the United States government to help Bogota reclaim the Department of Panama. The deal was struck by Marroquín's son and the American charge d'affairs in Bogota. Under the terms of the deal, Americans would send troops to invade Panama to quash the Liberal party stronghold there, and in exchange Marroquín would ratify the proposed treaty.

But Marroquín's plot did not end there. He was also planning to double-cross the United States. After the Americans would help him win back Panama, he intended to summon a congress that would reject the canal treaty as proposed. Colombia had not had a congress since 1898, and Marroquín intended to personally select delegates that would oppose the treaty, even though he had powers to ratify it by executive decree. Once it was rejected, he would negotiate better terms with the United States.

On September 16, the U.S.S. *Cincinnati* landed in Colón with more than two hundred American marines as planned. They seized the railroad trains and for the next three months, held Panama City and Colón under siege, disarming the Liberal party's rebel troops under the excuse that they were protecting the Panama railroad and the right of passage through the Isthmus.

This was the seventh American invasion of Panama since 1846, when U.S. Ambassador to Colombia John Bidlack and Colombian Minister Pedro Herrán signed the Bidlack-Herrán treaty. The 1846 treaty, as it became known, gave Americans the "right of passage" through the Isthmus and permitted the construction of the first intercontinental railroad in Panama in order to accommodate the massive migration as a result of the California Gold Rush. Work on the railroad began in 1850 and was completed in 1857. For a fee of twenty-five dollars in gold, the Panama Railroad and Steamship Company would take the traveler on a scenic route across the Isthmus, shortening the brutal trip from New York to San Francisco to just over two weeks.

In exchange for the "right of passage," the United States agreed with Colombia to guarantee "that the free transit from one to the other sea may not be interrupted," and more importantly, to protect with military force "the rights of sovereignty and property which Nueva Granada [Colombia] has and possesses over said territory." The original intent of the treaty was to protect Panama against England and European countries that may wish to invade the Isthmus to gain a stronghold there, but over time the Bogota government began to request United States help in quashing local uprisings threatening its own control over Panama.

Although the U.S. troops acted impartially during the invasion, allowing neither Conservative nor Liberal troops access to the railroad, the siege gave Marroquín sufficient time to bring reinforcements from Colombia, and the Panamanian Liberal revolt was summarily quashed. (A U.S. officer was quoted in the local press claiming that if the civil war did not stop, the United States would annex Panama.)

All this time, Concha was unaware of Marroquín's request for American troops and of his intention to later reject the unfavorable treaty. Concha thus became so outraged by the U.S. invasion of Colombian territory that he lost the capacity to negotiate with Americans at all. He asked his president for permission to launch a formal protest to the State Department, which, of course, Marroquín denied. Concha responded with a bitter note, railing against the United States:

> This uncle of ours can settle it all with a single crunch of his jaws. The desire to make themselves appear as the nation most respectful of the rights of others, forces these gentlemen to toy a little with their prey before devouring it. . . . My presence here is not only useless — it is improper.

On October 3 and again on November 7, Concha tried to resign, but Marroquín replied that his resignation was "unpatriotic and inadmissible." To protest, Concha decided to sit idly. On October 30, Hay cabled Bogota about the minister's refusal to cooperate and threatened to start negotiations with Nicaragua.

Concha's correspondence reveals that his intense anger led him to a voluntary, painful seclusion. He had a falling-out with Hay, Cromwell, and the rest of the diplomatic corps. In defiance of his government's instructions, he did not continue negotiations or even consider signing a treaty. On November 25, Concha left for New York. A few days later, Cromwell delightedly reported to Hay that Concha had been taken to Bogota in a straitjacket.

When Concha left the United States, he turned the matters over to fifty-year-old Dr. Tomás Herrán, the only remaining member of the Colombian legation in Washington. A refined, intelligent, and somewhat somber-looking man, Herrán had excellent credentials. He came from a family of Colombian diplomats; his grandfather had signed the Bidlack-Herrán treaty; he was a graduate of Georgetown University; and he was fluent in English. While Herrán waited for his appointment, he noted a worrisome proclamation by the Roosevelt administration: that the Isthmus of Panama constituted "international eminent domain," whereby if Colombia got in the way of a canal, the United States had the right to build it anyway. Herrán had reason to be anxious. In an address to Congress in December, Roosevelt warned that no independent American nation "need have the slightest fear of aggression from the United States," but assured that the canal "would be built."

Mindful of Roosevelt's character and threats, Marroquín instructed Herrán to try to get the best pecuniary advantages possible, namely $10 million and a $600,000 annuity, but to sign the treaty if the United States gave Bogota an ultimatum. In mid-December, Cromwell and Herrán started negotiations. Secretary Hay granted Cromwell authority to negotiate the treaty on behalf of the United States, despite the fact that the lawyer represented the French interests and possibly, if the rumors were true, the American speculators.

Herrán worked without respite and without a staff throughout the lengthy negotiations. A mountain of Herrán's handwritten correspondence made its way to the desks of lobbyists, congressmen, and the State Department. During the Christmas holidays in 1902, he declined an invitation to Cromwell's house at Laurel in the Pines in Lakewood, New Jersey, because of his overwhelming workload. Though he managed on New Year's Day 1903 to breakfast with Hay and then attend the president's always colorful reception for the diplomatic corps, he made an early exit, suffering "under physical pain and mental depression." He was also nervously awaiting the U.S. ultimatum that President Marroquín had warned him to expect.

Given the seeming inability to sign a treaty with Colombia as mandated by the Spooner Bill, Senator Morgan introduced a new bill pushing for the Nicaragua route when Congress reconvened after the Christmas recess. Angered and alarmed by increasing support for Nicaragua in Congress, Cromwell spent the whole day of January 20 in the White House talking to Roosevelt; he then dropped anchor at the State Department the next day. On the afternoon of January 22, Herrán received the expected final offer from the United States government: $10 million and a $250,000 annuity. He accepted.

The Hay-Herrán treaty was signed at Hay's Lafayatte Square house on the evening of January 23, 1903. Cromwell was the sole witness, and Hay gifted to him the pen used in recognition of his work. Two days later, Herrán received his instructions from Marroquín, "Do not sign canal treaty. You will receive instructions in letter today."

A despondent Herrán wrote his government, "I feel as if I am wak-

ing from a horrible nightmare. Gladly shall I gather up all the documents relating to that dreadful canal and put them out of sight."

President Roosevelt sent the Hay-Herrán treaty to the U.S. Senate the
same day it was signed. Opposition to the treaty was strong, and Senator Morgan led the fight, offering up over sixty amendments.
Cromwell lobbied hard, but Morgan filibustered successfully for a
month and a half. When Congress recessed on March 4, the treaty
had not been approved.

With treaty ratification looking dubious, Roosevelt called a special session of Congress. On March, it opened with Senator Morgan's
acidic attack on the treaty, the Compagnie Nouvelle, and especially
Cromwell. Fearing that significant modifications would require
restarting the negotiations, Cromwell forged a letter from Herrán saying that no amendment would be acceptable to Colombia. This time,
Roosevelt himself pushed for ratification. Morgan filibustered again
but he broke down, physically exhausted, on March 16. The next day,
the Senate ratified the treaty without amendments.

President Marroquín called for the landmark session of the Colombian Congress to open on June 20, 1903. The Roosevelt administration could not understand why the treaty had to be submitted to a
congress, since Marroquín had the power to ratify it by executive
decree. Washington was unaware of his plotted duplicity.

Lobbyists from all over the world descended on Bogota. Prominent Panamanian citizens sent a resolution urging ratification; from
Paris, Bunau-Varilla sent letters to Marroquín and the president of
the Congress, Nel Espina; from Washington, Dr. Herrán wrote influential friends recommending ratification. In Bogota, José Vicente
Concha mobilized forces against it.

At the end of March, troubling dispatches began to arrive from
Bogota. The German ambassador to Colombia told his American
counterpart, Arthur Beaupré, to rest assured that the treaty would be
rejected (Germany, too, sought the French concessions; they saw the
canal as an opportunity to gain the colonial hegemony they had so
far failed to achieve). Cromwell's agent in Bogota also reported neg-

ative expectations. A Nicaraguan negotiator was already on his way to Washington.

In mid-April, Cromwell received an alarming dispatch from the Bogota government demanding from the Compagne Nouvelle a substantial portion of the $40,000,000 it would receive from the United States. The Colombian officials reasoned that since the French concessions lasted only until October 1904, just over two years away, Colombia had as much right to the machinery, land, and railroad as the French company.

A furious Cromwell immediately scheduled conferences with Hanna, Spooner, Hay, and Roosevelt, and "began a campaign to discredit Colombia's request." He asserted that the Colombian action was an attempt to blackmail and extract more money from the U.S. government, most likely to pad the private vaults of Marroquín and his cronies. Some U.S. senators feared getting involved in a dispute between Colombia and the French company that did not concern the United States. Nevertheless, on April 28, Cromwell got Secretary Hay to wire a message to Bogota that he himself had drafted, stating unequivocally that the United States opposed Colombia's attempt to seek an indemnity from the Compagnie Nouvelle, "The United States considers this suggestion wholly inadmissible."

Colombia react d by dropping the request, but with a warning that as a result the treaty would most likely be rejected. Urgent meetings between Cromwell, Roosevelt, and Hay followed. On June 9, Hay sent a telegram to Beaupré issuing an ultimatum: "If Colombia should now reject the treaty, action might be taken by next winter which every friend of Colombia would regret."

Hay ordered Beaupré to deliver the message to the Colombian foreign minister personally. The American ambassador would later be criticized for his condescending attitude, rough words, and disregard for the dignity of Colombia. He had had a distinguished diplomatic career, having served in Guatemala, Honduras, and Colombia, and was known for his "urbane, dignified manners and courtly demeanor," which is at odds with the perception Colombians had of him. In fact, he had been working to resolve the situation in a way that would benefit both countries, but had no choice but to be dictatorial given his instructions from Washington.

Instead of cowering at the threat, Colombia reacted by condemning the "aggressiveness" of the United States. On June 13, Cromwell was seen entering the White House at about 8:30 AM, and he did not leave until evening. On the following day, June 14, the *World* printed a prophetic report:

> President Roosevelt is determined to have the Panama Canal. . . . The State of Panama will secede if the Colombian Congress fails to ratify the treaty. . . . The citizens of Panama propose, after seceding, to make a treaty with the United States, giving this government the equivalent of absolute sovereignty over the Canal Zone. In return the President of the United States would promptly recognize the new government.

The remarkably accurate description of what would follow had been given to the *World* by Roger Farnham, Cromwell's press agent. It even set the date of the revolution, November 3.

Secession now seemed to be on everyone's mind. On June 13, Bunau-Varilla cabled President Marroquín from France warning that if the treaty were not ratified, Panama would secede with U.S. protection. On July 8, the Republic of Chile expressed its fears that the United States would annex Panama in violation of the Monroe Doctrine. Concha sent a letter reminding his government of Roosevelt's "violent and abrupt nature." A friend of Secretary Hay remarked, "the fathers at Bogota are eating sour grapes and the teeth of the children in Panama are getting a fine edge to 'em."

On June 29, the Colombian Congress met for the first time since 1898. Feigning support for the treaty, Marroquín sent a weak, disinterested message placing the decision in the hands of Congress. Representatives of the American transcontinental railway pushed for rejection and allegedly resorted to bribery, as did representatives of Germany.

The session opened with the usual lofty philosophical rhetoric, much of it against Marroquín's government. Opposition to the treaty was evident from the outset. One senator grumbled, "The insult which Herrán has cast upon Colombia will never be wiped out. The gallows would be small punishment." The president of the senate pledged, "If it cannot be a Colombian canal, it will not be built!" Bunau-Varilla compared the group debating at Bogota to astronomers discussing "the nature of the Canals of Mars," and theologians from the Middle Ages debating "the question of the Real Presence." The situation did not improve when Hay's forceful message of June 9 was read aloud in a secret session.

The treaty's only proponent in Congress was Panama's Senator José Domingo de Obaldía. On August 12, late in the afternoon, he left the chamber feeling ill. That night, his colleagues in Congress took advantage of his absence and defeated the treaty by unanimous vote.

Colombia's decision was well considered and reasonable. Marroquín had decided that if the Compagnie Nouvelle refused to share its payment with Colombia, Colombia's best course of action would be to delay negotiations for a year. At that time, Colombia would take control of the $200 million French investment, only two-fifths completed, and sell the concessions to the United States for $25 million. The country needed money badly, but the government decided to hold out for more.

Marroquín's error was to underestimate the influence that Cromwell exerted over Hay and Roosevelt. As late as July 9, Beaupré confidentially cabled Secretary Hay reporting that he had assurances from the Colombian Congress that it would ratify the treaty if the Compagnie Nouvelle paid $15,000,000 to Colombia for its consent. At Cromwell's urging, however, Hay again decided that the suggestion was "inadmissible" to his government, even though it did not concern the United States. Henry Hall of the *World* later wrote,

> To whom, in fact, was this suggestion wholly inadmissible—the United States or Mr. Cromwell and his speculative friends, whose profits would thereby be claimed in part or in entirety by Colombia? Was it disadvantageous to the United States for Colombia to dictate terms, just or unjust, to the bankrupt concessionaire that had failed repeatedly to execute its contract?

No one knows with certainty why Hay chose to aid the French shareholders and the American speculators as he did. The secretary of state had no connections with Wall Street, had spent his life working as a civil servant, and was allegedly free from the influence of the monopolies that ruled his Republican party. Most likely, he was relying on the Fox so much during the negotiations that he unwillingly fell under his spell, but this remains one of the open questions about the story of the Panama canal.

If Cromwell had not exerted such influence over Secretary Hay and President Roosevelt, the United States would have gotten the rights to build the canal for as little as half the price quoted by the French. As Congressman Rainey said in 1913, "we could have made better terms with Colombia if we had let the contract expire," because of the inflated price at which the French shares were being sold. But "better terms" meant less for Cromwell and his "speculative friends," who convinced President Roosevelt that "unless I had acted as I did, there would be no canal."

A few days before the final vote of the Colombian Congress, the *New York Herald* outlined the choices available to President Roosevelt: first, to fight Colombia; second, to move in accordance with the Spooner Act and construct the canal in Nicaragua; and third, to continue to negotiate with Colombia until something happened. The *Herald* then alleged that "persons interested in getting the $40,000,000 for the Panama Canal are of course eager that this government shall go ahead and seize the property, even though it leads to war."

On August 13, Senator Shelby Cullom returned from the president's Sagamore Hill summer home and told the press, "We might make another treaty not with Colombia, but with Panama."

4

Panamanian Cohorts

Dr. Manuel Amador Guerrero appeared at first glance to be an unlikely candidate to lead a revolution. Slight, with receding white hair, a walrus moustache, a worried look, and stiff posture, the seventy year old would have been happy to spend his days resting in the hammock of his seafront home in Panama City, if José Agustín Arango had not recruited him to join a secessionist movement. Tall and robust, with a gigantic white beard, a stern face and a confident, dignified demeanor, Arango was the lawyer for the Panama Railroad & Steamship Co., where Amador worked as a doctor. The two of them were chosen to lead a revolution by the representative of the Panama Railroad & Steamship Co. in the United States, their boss, William Nelson Cromwell.

When it became obvious that the Colombians were going to reject the treaty, Cromwell rushed to find "some other satisfactory way." Panamanians, too, were naturally concerned. Early in 1903, prominent citizens cautioned their representative in Bogota that if the treaty were not ratified, the consequences would be severe, since an Isthmian canal was the impoverished country's only salvation.

For centuries, Panama had been a prosperous crossroads between two oceans, but after the French canal failed, it deteriorated. The city was built inside a seawall that once protected its gold altars from buccaneers. Houses with thick limestone walls, colorful interior patios, and large front balconies lined narrow cobblestone streets. At the heart of the city was Cathedral Park, its lush gardens marking the steps to the stone cathedral built in 1675. The courtly Hotel Central stood on one corner, while across the park, the Grand Hotel, a majestic building with arched windows, once served as headquarters of the Compagnie Universelle. A Frenchman who stayed after the Compagnie failed opened a cafe in the first floor that gathered the *rabi-blancos*, the more reclusive and aristocratic Panamanian families that descended from Spanish conquistadores. They were joined by the nouveau riche of Panama, many of them Americans who worked for the Panama Railroad Company, the biggest employer in the Isthmus, or who owned local banks, insurance companies, and freight agencies to satisfy the needs of travelers passing through the Isthmus.

But Panama at the turn of the century was past its prime. The city had deteriorated significantly after the French enterprise failed in 1889. Its streets were dirty and dangerous, its church towers were crumbling, and fires constantly ravaged the pestilent wooden shacks that housed migrant workers from the West Indies and China who came to Panama to build the French canal. Tracy Robinson, an American citizen, wrote:

> The once proud city had fallen in a state of apathy. It had no foreign commerce, and very little domestic trade. A few members of some of the leading families of Spanish ancestry were sent abroad to be educated; but for the most part, poverty or indifference or both kept the inhabitants captive within their picturesque old walls. Dullness held them in a summer snare of contented ignorance. Men were sent up the crumbling towers of the old churches, with stones in their hands, to pound religiously upon the broken bells still suspended there.

A new American canal seemed to be the country's only salvation, but following Bogota's rejection of the treaty, it would take a revolution to make it a reality.

For more than seventy years, Panamanians had tried unsuccessfully to secede from the Colombian government. After obtaining its independence from Spain in 1821, Panama annexed itself to Colombia, then Nueva Granada, in pursuance of Simón Bolívar's dream of a unified South American nation. After Bolívar's dream failed,

Panama sought to regain its independence, but a much stronger Colombian government prevented it. Theodore Roosevelt claimed that in the fifty-seven years before 1903, Panamanians rebelled fifty-three times trying to wrest themselves from the troubled, selfish, and repressive Colombian government. The attempted independence movements were usually not quashed by Colombian forces; rather, the Bogota government would ask the United States to send troops to the Isthmus to put down the rebellion and reclaim its sovereignty under the terms of the 1846 treaty. The United States invasions, thus, became Colombia's main weapon to prevent Panama from seceding.

When Arango set out to foment a revolution in the summer of 1903, Panamanians understandably didn't trust Washington's intentions. Only a few months earlier, they had seen American marines dismantle the Liberal rebel forces that could have liberated Panama. Promises recently uttered by Washington to free the Isthmus, therefore, were interpreted as warnings intended to bully Bogota into ratifying the canal treaty. Most likely, no one would have made a move if the two Panama Railroad Company employees didn't believe that they could overcome fifty years of history by placing their trust in William Nelson Cromwell.

Cromwell was the director, general counsel, and representative in the United States of the Panama Railroad Company. The company was owned by the bankrupt Compagnie Universelle, which used it to mobilize its workers during the excavation phase. After the French failed, the railroad continued to operate under the direction of Americans. Many prominent Panamanians worked for it. Its headquarters were in New York, where Cromwell called all the shots.

In early July, José Agustín Arango asked Captain James Beers, freight agent and port captain for the Pacific terminal of the Panama Railroad, to travel to New York to see if he could procure Cromwell's support for a revolution. A retired sea captain, Beers was a careful, calculating man, a familiar figure in Panama City, and a reputed Cromwell friend and confident. It is possible that Beers suggested to Arango the possibility of approaching Cromwell; his suggestion, in turn, may have emanated from Cromwell himself.

In mid-July, Captain Beers left for New York to meet Cromwell. To hide the lawyer's identity, Arango nicknamed him "the responsible person." In the meantime, Arango was called upon in Panama City to rally local support for a rebellion. On July 28, Tomás Arias, a young and wealthy landowner, gave a luncheon for twenty guests at his cattle ranch outside Panama City. Glasses were hoisted and speeches were ardently given in favor of a free Panama. Guests included Ricardo Arias, Federico Boyd, Nicanor de Obarrio, Carlos Arosemena, Manuel Espinosa, and Manuel Amador Guerrero, among others. Several Americans also were present: Arthur Grudger, American consul general in Panama and one of the prolific speakers; Herbert Prescott, assistant superintendent of the Panama Railroad Company; his brother Dick Prescott, married to Maria de Amador's niece; H.L. Jeffries, an American adventurer; and José Gabriel Duque, a Cuban-American proprietor of the *Panama Star & Herald*. Despite their enthusiasm, everyone knew that the success of their revolution was contingent upon obtaining U.S. support, for which they needed Cromwell.

In New York, Beers's meetings with Cromwell went very well. The lawyer told him that the Panamanians could trust him "to go the distance," but warned that they needed to keep secret the railroad's involvement; if discovered, its concession from Colombia could be forfeited. For communication, Cromwell gave Beers a cable code with special instructions written on the back of a book. He also set the date for the revolution: November 3. Cromwell's press agent, Roger Farnham, had chosen the date because United States midterm elections fell on November 4. The country and the press would be busy with the election results and would not give much attention to news of a revolution emanating from Central America.

Beers called upon Amador and Arango as soon as he returned on August 4, 1903. Cromwell, he told them, would "go to the limit" with them, but they had to keep secret the railroad's conspiracy. Full of hope, Arango and Amador immediately planned the independence of Panama.

Arango hosted a luncheon at his cattle ranch the following Sunday. To avoid leaking the news to the Colombian authorities, he invited only a half-dozen conspirators, including only two Americans, Herbert Prescott and James Beers. Beers reported that they could count on Cromwell to obtain assistance, "which he has promised." Everyone understood that this meant U.S. government military support. The Panamanians decided to send Amador and Arias to New York to meet Cromwell and secure the U.S. government support that he promised.

From that day on, the conspirators met frequently in hideaways throughout the city, including Arango's and Amador's offices at the wooden, barnlike Panama Railroad Pacific depot. Given their access to "the responsible person," the two railroad employees were designated the leaders of the revolution. Many conspirators considered the much younger Arango *El Maestro*, the head of the revolution, as he had been the first to foment discontent. Talkative, good-humored, an intellectual who did nothing after dinner except read, he was probably better fitted to play the role of ruler of a country than Amador. However, Dr. Amador's common sense and cunning schemes kept propelling him to the forefront. Even Amador and Arango had trouble determining which was the leader. One evening, as the two were leaving the railroad building, Amador told Arango that he should be the first president of Panama. To return the compliment, Arango put his arm around the much older Amador, insisting, "No, I think you should do it." Amador immediately replied, "Okay, I'll do it."

Born near Cartagena in 1833, Amador came to Panama in the late 1840s to work as a doctor, and his practice flourished in the disease-stricken country. A member of the Conservative party, he was appointed governor of Panama in 1867, but a revolution prevented him from taking office. The rebel Liberal party forces captured him and sent him into exile for a year. When he returned, he gave up his political ambitions and became superintendent of the Santo Tomás Hospital. His most important role, however, was as chief physician of the Panama Railroad Company. Because of the importance of the railroad in Panama, the position conferred an elevated status upon him. When Ferdinand de Lesseps visited the Isthmus, Amador was one of the Panamanians who welcomed him; when Cromwell needed leaders for the revolution, Amador was an obvious choice.

The conspirators brainstormed over how to co-opt Colombian civil and military officers to join the revolt. Amador suggested bribing the discontented Colombian troops that had not been paid for months. For this purpose, he proposed approaching General Esteban Huertas, a Colombian officer married to a Panamanian, who seemed sympathetic to the cause of Panama. They also needed to enlist the support of the civilian government. As they schemed, a dispatch arrived from Bogota reporting that the patrician Senator Don José Domingo de Obaldiá had been named governor of Panama.

Robust, bald, highly respected, and dignified, Obaldiá was the only senator in the Colombian Congress who had voted in favor of the canal treaty. He had served as a senator of Panama in Bogota for decades. Several Colombian congressmen protested his appointment, as typically the governor of Panama came from the Colombian interior and had little patience for dissent in the rebellious Isthmus. (For example, in July 1903, a Colombian general in Panama City got drunk and destroyed the printing press of a Liberal newspaper and imprisoned its owners; the governor did nothing.) In contrast, Obaldiá told President Marroquín that if the Panamanians revolted, he would side with his native Panama. Many claimed that Americans bribed Marroquín to accept Obaldiá's appointment; most likely, Marroquín appointed him in exchange for help in securing the election of his handpicked successor, General Rafael Reyes.

On September 16, Obaldiá arrived in Panama City to a hero's welcome. The conspirators held a candlelight dinner in his honor on the posh interior patio of the Hotel Central. Amador offered him a room in his large home until the governor found his own house. (The invitation might have been a pretext to get Obaldiá involved in the revolution.)

A few days later, Amador left for New York City as planned. Tomás Arias was supposed to go with him, but at the last minute Arias backed out. So as not to arouse the Colombian government's suspicions, Amador instructed his son Raoul, a United States Army doctor stationed in Fort Revere, Massachusetts, to send a cable: "Father, I am sick, come."

Amador brought with him a code for communicating with the conspirators through cable messages so as not to be detected by the Colombian government. The code consisted of roman numerals and spelled-out numbers, each of which had an assigned meaning. Roman numerals were used by Amador while he was in New York to communicate with the conspirators in Panama, while the spelled-out numbers were used by the conspirators to communicate with Amador. A conspirator would send a cable simply stating one or a combination of roman or written-out numbers, and the recipient would interpret its meaning based on the code. Below is the text of the actual code that was used. It illustrates the goals and the fears of the Panamanians. To transmit Amador's messages from New York to Panama, they used the following:

From Here to There

I.   Have not been satisfied with Hay in my first conference.

II.   Have had my first conference with Hay, and I found him determined to support the movement effective.

III.   Have not been to talk to Hay personally, only through a third person; I believe that everything will turn out in line with our desire.

IV.   Hay is determined to aid us in every way and has asked me for exact details of what we need to insure success.

V.   My agent is going with me, fully authorized to settle everything there.

VI.   Cromwell has behaved very well and has facilitated my interviews with important men who are disposed to cooperate.

VII.   You can hurry up matters, as everything here goes well.

VIII.   I am satisfied with the result and can assure success.

IX.   Minister Herrán has suspected something and is watching.

X.   Have not been able to obtain assurances of support in the form in which I demanded it.

XI.   Delay of Cromwell in introducing me to Hay makes me suspect that all he has said has been imagination and that he knows nothing.

XII.   It appears that Hay will not decide anything definitely until he has received advice from the commissioner who is there [Panama].

XIII.   I understand that Hay does not wish to pledge himself to anything until he hears the result of the operation there.

XIV.   The people from whom I expected support have attached little importance to my mission.

XV.   Those who are decided can do nothing practical for lack of necessary means.

XVI.   I have convinced myself that Hay is in favor of the rival route and for that reason will do nothing in support of our plan.

XVII.   News that have arrived from there on facilitating the construction of the canal has caused opinion here to shift in regard to our plan.

XVIII.   The pretensions manifested in the new draft of an agreement [treaty] render all negotiations between the two Governments impossible, and for this reason I have again resumed conferences.

XIX.   The new commissioner is expected here to negotiate. On this depends my future movements.

XX.   I consider that I can do nothing practical here now, and for this reason I have decided to take passage for home.

XXI.   Await my letter, which I write to-day.

XXII.   Here it is thought best to adopt a different plan in order to obtain a favorable result for the construction of the work.

XXIII.   Cromwell is determined to go the limit, but the means at his disposal are not sufficient to insure success.

XXIV.   Hay, Cromwell, and myself are studying a general plan of procedure.

XXV.   The commissioner there is an agent of Cromwell's, of which fact Hay is ignorant.

XXVI.   I wish to know if anything has been advanced there and can I fix date here to proceed?

XXVII.   Delay in getting a satisfactory reply obliges me to maintain silence.

XXVIII. B. [Bunau-Varilla] communicates here [New York] that the contract can be satisfactorily arranged.

XXIX.   I have considered it prudent to leave the capital [Washington] and continue negotiations from here [New York] by correspondence.

XXX.   I await letters from there [Panama] in reply to mine, in order to bring matters to a close,

For messages from the Panamanian conspirators to Amador in New York, they relied on the following code:

From There to Here

Forty.	The situation here is the same as when you left in every respect.
Fifty.	The object of your trip is suspected here, and in consequence you must be circumspect.
Sixty.	New military commander expected here shortly.
Seventy.	Letters received. All is well. You can proceed.
Eighty.	We write at length on variation of plan, as the one outlined has certain.
Ninety.	We accept indications contained in cable.
One hundred.	Cable received. Go ahead.
Two hundred.	Forces coming from Bolívar will arrive shortly.
Three hundred.	Forces coming from Cauca will arrive here soon
Four hundred.	From Bogota they ask what has been done on the matter.
Five hundred.	The matter is being much talked about. In consequence much precaution is necessary in acting.
Six hundred.	Newspapers of here [Panama] give account of object of your journey.
Seven hundred.	Strong opinion shown in favor of the plan, but this may hamper its realization.
Eight hundred.	Here nothing has been done, awaiting what you have to communicate.
Nine hundred.	Without our being able to tell how, the government has discovered the secret and is on the watch.
One thousand.	We must have the resources asked for to proceed with probabilities of success.

The code reveals that the Panamanians were relying on Cromwell to give them a "general plan of procedure," that success depended upon the attitude of Washington and the financial assistance procured in New York, and that Amador needed to ensure that Secretary Hay and President Roosevelt supported the plan. If the United States did not fully back it, the revolt would be futile, as the much stronger Colombian forces would quickly quash the insurgency; in fact, judging by the prior fifty years, United States forces would land in the Isthmus to help the Colombians.

Amador sailed for New York on August 26, 1903 on the *Seguranca*, a Panama Railroad & Steamship Company steamer. The revolutionaries did not provide him with sufficient money to cover even the expenses of the trip. Fortunately, he was an excellent poker player and won enough money from his fellow passengers during the voyage to tide him over a few days.

José Gabriel Duque, the American proprietor of the *Panama Star & Herald* and the Panama lottery, head of the fire brigade, and reputedly the wealthiest man on the Isthmus, traveled on board the same ship. He was supposedly going to New York on customary business. Later, Duque boasted that he was the first person who got the "goat" of the poker party, thus making him the first contributor to the expenses of the revolution. Amador claimed that he did not inform Duque of his mission; Duque, however, could have made a good guess about the old doctor's intentions.

On September 1, 1903, the day the *Seguranca* arrived in New York City, the *Washington Post* ran a front-page article reporting that Costa Rican sources claimed Panamanian rebels had been collecting thousands of rifles for a revolution and that the Colombian troops stationed in Panama sympathized with it. The source for the information was José Gabriel Duque's son, H.G. Duque; it was a lie intended to scare the Colombians into ratifying the treaty.

Upon his arrival in New York, Amador checked into the Hotel Endicott at Columbus Avenue and 81 Street. The same day he went to see Joshua Lindo, head of the New York branch of Piza, Nephews & Co., a local Panamanian bank. Amador told Lindo of his plans and asked for a loan on his personal credit to pay his hotel bills.

Amador had hoped to see Cromwell immediately, but Cromwell delayed the meeting. Instead, the lawyer sent for José Gabriel Duque. Duque was escorted by Roger Farnham to the offices of Sullivan & Cromwell at 41 Wall Street. At the meeting, Cromwell told Duque that "there was no prospect for favorable action by the Colombian Congress on the pending treaty, and that the Panama department should make a revolution and declare its independence." Duque argued that a revolution was out of the question for lack of funds and arms. Cromwell encouraged Duque to lend $100,000 on Cromwell's security, to be repaid after the independence. He pledged to "make" Duque Panama's first president if he would lead the revolution (Cromwell did not seem to mind that both he and Duque were American citizens). Duque hesitated, mentioning Amador's arrival in New York, but Cromwell insisted that Duque should be the one to lead the insurgency. (Cromwell probably feared that if Amador or Arango were at the helm, Colombia would accuse the Panama Railroad Company of planning the revolution.) Without waiting for Duque's response, Cromwell called Secretary Hay and arranged a meeting between the two men.

On the night of September 2, a reluctant Duque and a former American minister to Bogota took a night train to Washington. Farnham strongly urged them not to check into a hotel, as it would leave evidence of their visit. Duque met the secretary of state between 10 AM and 1 PM in his house at Lafayette Square. It is uncertain what was said at that meeting. Hay later claimed that he told Duque that the United States "would not connive at a revolution," and that when Duque asked him what would happen if Colombia rejected the treaty, he answered, "We will cross that bridge when we get to it." But according to Duque, Hay promised that if the revolution were confined to Colón and Panama City, the United States would send troops to keep the Colombians from landing. More to the point, he assured Duque that the "United States will build the Panama Canal and we do not intend to permit Colombia's standing in the way." Hay asked Duque if he would stay a few days to meet President Roosevelt, but a nervous Duque declined, saying he was sailing for Panama shortly.

Instead of returning to New York as intended, when he left Hay's house, Duque marched straight into the offices of his friend Colombian Ambassador Tomás Herrán. Duque told him about Amador's arrival in New York and his meeting with Hay; he also told Herrán about the revolutionary movement in Panama. No one knows why Duque did this. A proud, stubborn man, he might have been upset that the Panamanians had not chosen him their leader. Most likely, he was trying to scare the Colombian government so they would feel pressure to ratify the treaty.

Duque's news did not surprise Herrán. The Colombian minister had already heard about Amador's arrival and had even placed a detective on him. He sent his government an urgent wire: "Revolutionary agent of Panama here. If treaty not approved by September 22, it is probable that there will be a revolution with American support." He got no reply, so he decided to take up the matter with Cromwell.

Meanwhile, in New York, Amador reported to the offices of his employer, the Panama Railroad & Steamship Company. Its vice president and chief administrator, E.A. Drake, took him to see Cromwell on the afternoon of September 1. The first interview was cordial, and Cromwell made "a thousand offers in assisting us," Amador later wrote in his memoirs. But since Cromwell had placed his hopes on Duque, he told Amador that "nothing could be done except when the Herrán-Hay treaty has been absolutely rejected, for in the end we believe that it will be approved in spite of the great opposition of the houses of Congress." (He had told Duque exactly the opposite only a day earlier.) "Vain were my efforts to convince Mr. Cromwell that no hope whatever should be entertained," recalled Amador, "and we continued the appointment to go on discussing the matter on the following day."

But on the following day, Cromwell received an unexpected letter from Minister Herrán, prompted by Duque's visit. The letter warned that the Colombian government would hold the Panama Railroad Company and the Compagnie Nouvelle responsible for any revolutionary activity in Panama, and that the result would be the forfeiture of their concessions.

When Amador arrived to see Cromwell, the receptionist told the doctor that Cromwell had had an unexpected meeting and could not see him that day. The next day Amador returned and got the same excuse. A distressed Amador returned numerous times over the next few days, even though employees of Sullivan & Cromwell insisted that Cromwell was absent. Unable to comprehend Cromwell's sudden change in attitude, Amador sat on one of the leather chairs in the elegant lobby and refused to move until he saw Cromwell. After a few hours, Cromwell stormed out of his office, and in front of receptionists and other lawyers, screamed at Amador that he would have nothing to do with him, and literally pushed the old doctor out of the office and into the hallway. The next day Amador sent his compatri-

ots a cable with a single word that had never been part of the prescribed code's vocabulary: "Disappointed."

Amador then called upon the secretary of state, but with similar
luck. Willis Johnson, the administration's historian at the time, said
that Amador kept calling at the State Department until he was told
"kindly, but firmly and plainly, that, as he was confessed and notori-
ously the would-be organizer of a revolution against a power with
which the United States was at peace, any further visits at that office
would be improper."

Demoralized and disheartened, Amador began to prepare his
return to Panama. Joshua Lindo begged him to stay in New York a
few more days, in the hopes that Cromwell's attitude would change.
Quite the contrary. On September 10, Cromwell cabled his agents
in Panama, Colonel J.R. Shaler, the superintendent of the Panama
Railroad Company, Herbert Prescott, the assistant superintendent,
and Captain Beers, prohibiting them from becoming involved in any
way with the revolutionary activities. However, he prefaced his letter
by saying, "while there may be no real foundation for newspaper statements of possible revolution in Panama," which contradicted the very
revolutionary activities that he himself had been promoting. Beers
and Shaler concluded that Cromwell had sent the cable solely to protect the company in the event that the revolution failed. They decided
to continue their activities, while at the same time sending Herbert
G. Prescott to New York to clarify the situation.

Next to Colonel Shaler, Prescott was the second in command of
the Panama Railroad Company in Panama. Unlike Shaler, he was
not a soldier but a capable railroad engineer who had lived in Panama
for a long time, had family ties there, and who spoke Spanish fluently.
Enthusiastic and adroit, the Panamanians saw Prescott as one of their
own. On September 18, Herbert Prescott and U.S. General Consul
Grudger, who was on his way to a family vacation in North Carolina,
docked at the Chelsea Piers. They went to see Cromwell that same
afternoon. Consul Grudger spent hours talking with Cromwell
behind closed doors (they later claimed that they never discussed
Panama). The meeting ran so late that Cromwell had no time to talk
to Prescott and told him to come back the next day.

When Prescott arrived the following morning, however, Cromwell would not see him. Roger Farnham ushered him into the offices of Edward Hill, another senior partner of Sullivan & Cromwell. Hill told Prescott that the Panamanians "must be fools if they expected the United States to give them any guarantees before the revolution took place; that they must make the movement themselves." However, he assured Prescott that "once they had established their independence the United States would never permit Colombian troops to land to attack them, as there was precedent for such an action." Farnham went in and out of Hill's office during the interview; at one point, to encourage a disappointed Prescott, he boasted that if the Panamanians started a revolution, he would personally go to the Isthmus to fight. Prescott replied that Panamanians would not revolt unless they got explicit support from the United States.

During the meeting, Prescott asked to see Cromwell several times, but Cromwell did not show up. Prescott was told that Cromwell was scheduled to leave for Paris on other business and could no longer be counted on to help the Panamanians. Prescott left the office without ever talking to Cromwell.

In historical recollections, everyone agreed that Cromwell took off for Paris and did not have anything to do with the events that took place afterwards. In his manuscript, Amador said, "I took leave of him and had no further news of him except several weeks after the 3 of November." Even Cromwell, who took copious notes of all the events, later wrote that he did "not judge it necessary to enter into the details of the events of this period."

However, it is highly unlikely that he remained out of touch. As Henry Hall of the *World* later remarked, it is hard to believe that he "left the fat he had fried so assiduously for seven long, lean years to fall, if it might, in the fire, without so much as knowing what hand might be near to save it or what hostile breath might smother or fan to uncontrolled fury the seditious sparks he had nursed into a revolutionary flame."

Why then did Cromwell disappear from sight? By disassociating himself from the revolution, Cromwell was protecting the Panama Railroad Company's concessions that had been granted by Colombia from forfeiture in case the revolution failed. The other conspirators, including Amador, went along with the ruse, as they also had an interest in protecting their jobs. Disappearing temporarily from the stage was just a sensible move. Before he left the scene, however, Cromwell mapped out the strategy for the liberation of Panama and left its execution in the hands of his French counterpart, Philippe Bunau-Varilla.

5

Teddy's Conspiracy

On September 22, Bunau-Varilla arrived unexpectedly in New York City. He claimed that he had come to see his son Etienne, who was recovering from hay fever at the house of his friend and mentor, the eminent American ambassador to Paris, John Bigelow. His arrival, however, was exactly two weeks from the date when Cromwell received Dr. Herrán's letter and the exact time required to sail from Paris to New York.

Bunau-Varilla later claimed that he was not aware of any revolutionary activities in Panama until he made a casual telephone call to his friend Joshua Lindo.

"Is the rumor true that the people in Panama are going to make a revolution?" Bunau-Varilla inquired innocently.

Lindo allegedly shrugged his shoulders and responded in a disheartened tone, *"Faltan recursos!"* ("We have no financial means.")

Bunau-Varilla couldn't believe Panamanians would do nothing, to which Lindo responded, "Without money a revolution cannot be brought about any more than a war. But if you care to know what the situation really is I will ask Amador to come and see you."

"What!" Bunau Varilla exclaimed. "Amador is here?"

On September 23, at 10:30 AM, Amador went to suite 1162 of the Waldorf Astoria Hotel to confer with Bunau-Varilla. They knew each other from Panama, when Dr. Amador used to report to Chief Engineer Bunau-Varilla. According to Bunau-Varilla's own version of the meeting, Amador filled him in on the revolution, Captain Beers's mission, Secretary Hay's unwillingness to meet him, and the "sudden reversal of the person who was to take me to Washington." Amador was almost overcome with tears because he feared that the Colombian authorities in Panama, who still did not know about the conspiracy, would find out and execute him, his family and friends.

Bunau-Varilla interrupted him. "Dr. Amador, you are telling me a very sad story, but why did you withhold the name of the man who thus promised you the gold of the American Treasury—the Army and the Navy of the United States? This childish proposition bears the stamp of the man who formulated it. There is but one person in the United States capable of expressing himself thus."

Confronted point-blank with Cromwell's role, Amador admitted everything and Bunau-Varilla replied, "He has a habit of speaking of the highest persons of the State in the way you just described to me. What, you believed in such empty talk? It is an unpardonable folly. With your imprudence you have indeed brought yourselves to a pretty pass."

Bunau-Varilla ordered Amador to "appeal to reason and not to passion" and to tell him what he wanted. Bunau-Varilla boasted that he alone would deliver what Cromwell could not. Amador gave him the details of the plan: Colombia kept only a small garrison of troops in Panama; the troops had not been paid their salary for three months, leading to great discontent; and General Huertas could be trusted to bribe the troops and to aid the revolution. Bogota, however, could send reinforcements, so Panama wanted from the United States government "all the money we need to buy arms and ships and to pay the troops."

"How big a sum do you consider necessary?" Bunau-Varilla asked. "We need $6,000,000."

Bunau-Varilla thought the amount excessive, but told Amador he would look into it. As a precaution, they agreed that henceforth Amador would go by the name of Jones and Bunau-Varilla would go by Smith. Amador went back to the Hotel Endicott and sent to Panama a one word cable: "Hope."

A few days later, Amador saw Herbert Prescott off to Panama at the

Chelsea Piers. Using Prescott as a messenger, Amador reported to his cohorts that Duque had upset everything; that Cromwell seemed unwilling; that he himself had been to Washington but had accomplished nothing concrete; but that he had just met the man who could get everything done. This man, Bunau-Varilla, had promised to take him to Washington to obtain the anticipated American assistance. Even though Bunau-Varilla had offered no assurance that he could deliver what he promised, Amador presumptuously predicted that everything would be arranged in a few days and that he would sail on the next week's ship to Panama.

Meanwhile, Bunau-Varilla traveled by train to Washington and booked a room in the luxurious New Willard Hotel. According to his own version of events, he "made appointments, telephone calls, wrote notes, cables and sat in waiting rooms" to get an introduction to Hay or Roosevelt but had no luck. He sent an articulate letter to the eminent professor of international law J.B. Moore, a friend of President Roosevelt, claiming that under the 1846 treaty with Colombia, the United States was entitled to take the Isthmus by force if Colombia prevented the construction of the canal. The argument was Bunau-Varilla's own creation, but he knew it would make its way to the president. Indeed, a few days later, while sailing in the Long Island Sound during a storm, Moore told Roosevelt about Bunau-Varilla's theory. T.R. was so excited that he asked Moore to write a brief supporting the conclusions.

Since the rejection of the treaty by Colombia, the president had taken such complete control of the "Panama problem" that rumors began to circulate in Washington that he and Hay had had a falling-out. Quite to the contrary; the exhausted secretary of state had simply decided to take a vacation in his New Hampshire home, but he continued to communicate with Roosevelt through messengers. When the president received Moore's memo, T.R. was so excited he wrote a note to Hay. "I fear we may have to give a lesson to those jack rabbits."

T.R. immediately instructed the army's general of staff to prepare an invasion of the Isthmus. Reports were duly presented and tactics chosen by T.R. himself. He planned on using the railroad and the steam shovels left by the French as giant tanks to mobilize the American army. He anticipated that it would be a "brief and inexpensive war." The president was so happy with his strategy that he even drafted an address to Congress on the matter. He presented it to his cabinet and asked Attorney General Knox to render a legal opinion. Secretary of Defense Elihu Root, known for his sardonic wit, piped in, "Oh, Mr. President, do not let so great an idea suffer any taint of legality."

Dr. Herrán heard rumors about Roosevelt's invasion plan and immediately cabled his helpless government:

> Your excellency knows the vehement character of the President, and you are aware of the persistence and decision with which he pursues anything to which he may be committed. These considerations have led me to give credit and importance to the threatening expressions attributed to him.

While the army began to make preparations to execute the invasion, Bunau-Varilla arrived in Washington preaching another idea: a revolution in Panama.

To gain access to the White House, Bunau-Varilla wrote to Acting Secretary of State Francis Loomis, whose friendship he had cultivated when Loomis was ambassador to Portugal, inviting the American diplomat to dinner at his house in Paris. Loomis returned the favor; on October 9, he invited Bunau-Varilla to the State Department at 10:00 AM.

To break the ice, Bunau-Varilla told Loomis that he and his brother Maurice had recently bought *Le Matin*, France's leading newspaper. As editors, they had made the crucial decision to publish the incriminating letter that triggered the celebrated Dreyfus case and the downfall of the French Republic. Impressed, and knowing that T.R. would love to hear the story of the Dreyfus scandal directly from the man responsible for uncovering the key evidence, Loomis suggested to Bunau-Varilla that he present *Le Matin*'s compliments to Roosevelt. Loomis asked, "Do you know [Roosevelt] personally?"

Two hours later, at noon, Bunau-Varilla and Loomis were at the White House. Bunau-Varilla explained to the president how he had recognized the forged signature of Captain Alfred Dreyfus. His brother Maurice had obtained a copy of the alleged letter from Dreyfus admitting selling secrets to the Germans. Maurice showed the letter to Philippe, who had been Dreyfus's friend and classmate at the Ecole Polytechnic. When Philippe saw the letter, he compared it to an old note from Dreyfus and found the difference in handwriting not only obvious, but astounding. The brothers decided to publish both letters in *Le Matin*. The ensuing scandal led to the reopening of the investigation and the conviction of the anti-Semitic officers who had forged Dreyfus's signature.

Bunau-Varilla seized the first opportunity to introduce his favorite subject, Panama.

"Mr. President," he said, "Captain Dreyfus has not been the only victim of detestable political passions. Panama is another."

T.R. became suddenly interested, "Oh yes, that is true, you have devoted much time and effort to Panama, Mr. Bunau-Varilla. Well, what do you think is going to be the outcome of the present situation?"

"Mr. President, a revolution."

"A revolution?" Roosevelt allegedly asked, surprised.

"A revolution," Bunau-Varilla answered with certainty.

According to Bunau-Varilla, Roosevelt then turned instinctively towards Mr. Loomis, who remained impassive, and said in a low tone, as if to himself, "A revolution! Would it be possible? But if it became a reality, what would become of the plan we had thought of?" After a long pause, a surprised Roosevelt again turned toward Bunau-Varilla, "What makes you think so?"

Bunau-Varilla described Isthmian activity, Panamanian's discontent with Bogota, and the "special indications" he had received from Panamanians about their willingness to revolt. According to Bunau-Varilla, when he left the White House, he had single-handedly changed Teddy Roosevelt's plans for an invasion and convinced him to pursue a revolution in Panama. Evidence indicates, however, that Cromwell had been working towards the same goal behind the scenes.

Contrary to what the conspirators led everyone to believe, Cromwell did not leave the United States for Paris in mid-September. On October 7, the *New York Herald* Washington correspondent telegraphed his paper. "William Nelson Cromwell called on President Roosevelt today. Mr. Cromwell declared this afternoon: 'The Panama Canal will be built, and by the United States.' He would not say what new development had made this possible." He also went to visit the president two days before the meeting between Roosevelt and Bunau-Varilla that allegedly changed T.R.'s mind.

Influenced by the lobby of Cromwell and Bunau-Varilla, Roosevelt abandoned the idea of an invasion of Panama and decided to pursue a local secession from Colombia. On October 9, T.R. wrote to his friend Dr. Albert Shaw, editor of *Review of Reviews*, describing how he felt about the prospect of an Isthmian revolt:

> Privately, I would say that I should be delighted if Panama were an independent State, or if it made itself so at this moment; but for me to say so publicly would amount to an instigation for a revolt, and therefore I cannot say it.

Assured that Roosevelt was on board, Bunau-Varilla went back to New York to inform Amador. On the train from Washington, he concluded that although the T.R. was ideologically behind them, in practical terms Amador was a "childish dreamer hoping to obtain from the United States six million dollars and her military support." However, Bunau-Varilla knew that without the money or the military support, Panamanians would not revolt. The biggest problem was raising the money. As he pondered the resolution of this problem, suddenly "the light flashed" in his head.

Upon his arrival in New York on October 15, he immediately summoned Amador to suite 1162 of the Waldorf Astoria. He told the old doctor that the Panamanians needed no guns or ships to carry out the revolution. Panamanians would simply declare Panama City and Colón independent, propelling the Colombians to send troops to regain the territory. The United States would prevent their landing to protect the railroad, to "maintain free transit across the Isthmus" and to enforce the "no fighting within gunshot distance of the railway" policy as provided under the 1846 treaty. The rest of the country would be liberated later. Bunau-Varilla claimed his idea was original; however, it mirrored the plan published by Cromwell's press agent Roger Farnham in the *World* in June and discussed just a few weeks earlier by Cromwell's partner Edward Hill and Panama Railroad Company superintendent Herbert Prescott; that is, it bore the imprint of Cromwell.

Amador rejected the plan. He expected a firm assurance of financial and military support from the United States, not a vague promise to keep Colombian troops from landing. Also, the 1846 treaty provided that the United States had to put down any rebellions in Panama to guarantee "the rights of sovereignty and property which [Colombia] has and possesses over said territory." In other words, the treaty obliged the United States to quash the Panamanian revolution, and Amador had no guarantee from any American official that it would not do it.

"His attitude was sullen," recounts Bunau-Varilla. "Evidently his mind had for some months been accustomed to brooding over the idea of a contract with the United States, such as novelists imagine. He saw himself associated with the President and the Secretary of State of the powerful Republic, and disposing of her millions for a common enterprise."

Amador insisted that they should at least be given enough money to pay off the Colombian troops stationed in Panama.

"I admit it," Bunau-Varilla replied, "but $6,000,000 will not be necessary for that. There are 500 men. Let us put $20 — $100 if you like — for each man. This makes $50,000."

"It is not enough," said Amador.

"Let us put $100,000 if you like."

Amador admitted that $100,000 would be sufficient. (Coincidentally, Cromwell quoted $100,000 to Duque as the amount needed to carry out the revolution.)

"Well, Doctor," Bunau-Varilla said, "it is a small sum. I shall probably be able to borrow it in a New York bank."

"What if you don't succeed?" Amador retorted.

"Well, I shall give it out of my own pocket," the Frenchman boasted. "I can make such a sacrifice as that."

In addition to the diminished sum, Amador adamantly opposed liberating only Panama City and Colón. He claimed that conspirators had cattle ranches throughout the country that would be confiscated by Colombia if they were not liberated. Bunau-Varilla retorted that once the independence of the Isthmus was assured and the treaty ratified, "you will have $10,000,000 with which you can wage war and conquer the rest of the province." (The figure of $10,000,000 refers to the fee that the United States would pay Panama upon ratification of the treaty.)

Amador was not convinced. Growing impatient, Bunau-Varilla

stood up, "Dr. Amador," he said, "if you wait to close your eyes, you will see nothing. You came on the 23rd of September in despair to ask me for support. Today, October 15, I offer it to you. If you refuse it, well and good. I have nothing more to say."

They separated coldly. Amador met with Joshua Lindo that night to discuss alternatives. Amador did not want to go forward unless he had explicit assurances from a high-ranking American government official. Lindo argued that Bunau-Varilla's plan had most likely been conceived in the White House.

According to Bunau-Varilla's version of the story, he was awakened early the following day by two discreet knocks on the door of his hotel suite. In the hallway, he found Amador looking pale and haggard.

"Have you slept?" Amador asked Bunau-Varilla, by way of greeting.

"Very well," he answered. "And you?"

According to Bunau-Varilla's recollection of the conversation, Amador sat down and replied, "Not one second. But I have been thinking, and I have discovered that I am nothing but a fool. I have understood, pardon me, I shall obey."

"This is what I call a sensible speech," Bunau-Varilla exclaimed.

He told Amador to prepare to leave for Panama on October 20. That same evening, Bunau-Varilla took a train back to Washington to secure the United States support that he had prematurely guaranteed. He called on Hay, who had recently returned from his vacation. At 3:00 PM the following day, the secretary of state received him at his house in Lafayatte Square. Hay feigned ignorance about the plans for a revolution, while probing Bunau-Varilla for his general views on Panama. At one point Bunau-Varilla slyly remarked, "There comes a moment when one has to stand still and await events."

"These events," Hay asked, "what do you think they will be?"

"I expressed my sentiments on the subject some days ago to President Roosevelt. The whole thing will end in a revolution. You must take your measures, if you do not want to be taken yourself by surprise."

"Yes," said Hay, "that is unfortunately the most probable hypothesis. But we shall not be caught napping. Orders have been given to naval forces on the Pacific to sail toward the Isthmus."

Hay then brought up a popular novel he had just read, *Captain*

Macklin, written by his friend Richard Harding Davis (Hay himself was a failed novelist). The story followed the adventures of a West Point cadet and a Frenchman who went to Honduras, started a revolution, and became leaders of the country. Hay described the protagonists, "The young, ambitious American, and the old French officer, who as head of the army displays in all his acts the generous disinterestedness of his race, are both charming types of searchers after the 'Ideal.'" He gave Bunau-Varilla a copy of the book. "Read this volume, take it with you."

Bunau-Varilla was delighted. The gift, he surmised, represented the subtle password from Hay to go ahead. The noble Frenchman searching for the 'Ideal' was Bunau-Varilla, the man on whom the revolution depended.

A confident Bunau-Varilla returned to New York and, on October 17, met Amador one more time in suite 1162 of the Waldorf Astoria, which now was "the cradle of the Panama Republic." He assured Amador of U.S. protection and promised $100,000 once Panama City and Colón had been declared independent. But there was a catch.

"I venture to say that, because nobody knows better than I the final aim, which is the completion of the Canal and the best way to attain it, it will, therefore, be necessary to entrust me with the diplomatic representation of the new Republic at Washington."

Amador, who had been listening with enthusiasm, suddenly became sullen. "This cannot be done," he explained, "the self-conceit of the Isthmians would be hurt by the choice of a foreigner for their first representative abroad."

"A battle royal will be fought at Washington," answered Bunau-Varilla. "Let him wage it who is best equipped to win the victory."

"But could not a Panamanian be appointed whose obedience I would guarantee?" asked Amador. "You would direct his acts and his words."

"No, my dear Doctor," Bunau-Varilla replied, "a solution of that order is of no value when on one word, on a single act, in a single minute, may depend success or the reverse. Absolute liberty of decision and of action must be employed by him who commands. But this is only my advice. If it is not yours, or that of your friends, follow your personal inclinations. In such a case, you may still count on me to do everything in my power to help you, but at the same time I must tell you that I do not accept any responsibility if you do not follow the line providing the maximum quantity of favorable chances."

According to Bunau-Varilla, Amador listened with a distressed air, but replied, "Well, I shall try to carry your point."

"Nothing remains," Bunau-Varilla added enthusiastically, "but to make the model of the flag!"

Amador did not share Bunau-Varilla's enthusiasm. He took his leave but returned to the Waldorf Astoria only a few hours later, worried by the question of the ambassador in Washington, but Bunau-Varilla summarily told him that he would not budge on his demand. According to Bunau-Varilla, Amador accepted his demands.

That same day, Amador sent a letter to his son explaining the revolution scheme.

October 18, 1903

Mi hijito:

I received your telegram that you are not coming, as they have refused you permission . . . The reason for your coming was for you to meet Bunau-Varilla, to whom I have spoken of you. He said that if all turns out well, you shall have a good place on the medical commission, which is the first that will begin work; that my name is in Hay's office and that certainly nothing will be refused you.

The plan seems to me good. A portion of the Isthmus declares itself independent and that portion the United States will not allow any Colombian forces to attack.

An Assembly is called, and this gives authority to a Minister to be appointed by the new Government in order to make a treaty without need of ratification by that Assembly.

The treaty being approved by both parties, the new Republic remains under the protection of the United States, and to it are added the other districts of the Isthmus which do not already form part of the new Republic. And these also remain under the protection of the United States.

The movement will be delayed a few days—we want to have here the Minister who is going to be named so that once the movement is made he can be appointed by cable and take up the treaty. In 30 days everything will be concluded.

We have some resources on the movement being made, and already this has been arranged with a bank.

As soon as everything is arranged I will tell B.V. to look out for you. He says if you do not wish to go he will look out for a position for you in New York. He is a man of great influence.

A thousand embraces to Pepe and my remembrances to Jenny and Mr. Smith.

Your affectionate father,
AMADOR

Raoul was so excited about his father's campaign that he had asked his superiors' permission to join his father in New York. When they denied his request, confident that the revolution would take place, he deserted his post and went to New York to await his appointment as Panamanian consul. Before he left, a friend heard the Army doctor screaming from the inside of his new sports car, "Look out for a shakeup in Panama in a few days. The old man has been down to see Roosevelt and Hay, and he's got the money and backing to pull the thing off."

Although Raoul Amador's statement that his father went to Washington "to see Roosevelt and Hay" was never proven, other evidence suggests that Cromwell took the doctor to secretly see Roosevelt before he left for Paris. Allegedly, the two traveled in a compartment of the *Congressional Limited* in the middle of the night, and Cromwell drafted Panama's manifesto on the way. They met Roosevelt at the White House at midnight and conferred with him until daylight. They took the train back to New York without leaving a record of their visit. Senator Morgan received news of such a visit the next morning, and the conductor of the *Congressional Limited* also confirmed it. U.S. government records also provide evidence (or rather nonevidence) of these secret meetings. There is a curious "gap" in which the whereabouts of the president are unaccounted for fifteen minutes, and between October 10 and November 5, the Hay papers, Roosevelt's letters, and the Panama Canal file of the Roosevelt papers are peculiarly empty of correspondence. Once the revolution appeared to be a fait accompli, Cromwell took off for Paris on October 15. Before he left, he wrote to Roosevelt approvingly, "Your virile and masterful policy will prove the solution of this great problem."

Back at the Waldorf Astoria, on Sunday the 18, a beautiful autumn day, Bunau-Varilla and his wife set out on a horse-drawn carriage for the Bigelow estate at Highland Falls on the Hudson. First, they stopped at Macy's on 34 Street to pick out a few yards of silk. When they reached the Bigelow estate, Mrs. Bunau-Varilla went down to the basement with Mrs. Bigelow to sew the Panamanian flag that her husband had designed. Upstairs, Bunau-Varilla proceeded to write Panama's manifesto. The following day, October 19, one day before Amador sailed for Panama, Bunau-Varilla summoned the doctor back to his Waldorf Astoria suite for their last meeting.

Bunau-Varilla presented to Amador the "revolutionary kit." Amador found the flag to be "perfect." It resembled an American flag, but for the white Bunau-Varilla substituted yellow to characterize the Spanish and Colombian flags, and instead of white stars distributed over the blue jack, he had two yellow suns united by a white band. These suns, explained Bunau-Varilla, represented "the two continents as the stars in the American flag represent the states of the Union."

They discussed the last-minute details. Amador insisted that he needed fifteen days from the moment he arrived in Panama in order to carry out the revolution, but Bunau-Varilla was adamant that it must take place sooner.

"You leave tomorrow, the 20th, you arrive the 27th. Within two days you can act."

"Yes, if I were alone," replied Amador, "but you do not know our friends. Conference after conference will be necessary."

"The longer you wait, the more chances that Colombia will find out and have time to send troops to Panama," responded the Frenchman. "I give you up to the 3rd of November as a final limit for action. If you have not accomplished the revolution on that day or before I shall consider myself free of all responsibility for further events." (Cromwell had also chosen November 3 as the day for the revolution.)

Bunau-Varilla gave Amador the exact wording for a cable from the Panamanian government appointing him minister plenipotentiary of

Panama with powers to ratify the canal treaty. He told Amador to send it as soon as independence was declared. "Only upon receipt of that cable," Bunau-Varilla explained, "I will send $100,000 to the new Panama government and see that military protection from the United States be extended to the republic."

Finally, Bunau-Varilla gave Amador a Lieber code with which to communicate. The purpose was to keep Bunau-Varilla informed of any Colombian military movements in the Isthmus, and for Bunau-Varilla to communicate the U.S. government plans, and avoid interception by the Colombian government. The conspirators could make entire sentences by arranging senseless code words in any order. Below is the actual text of the code that Jones (Bunau-Varilla) gave Smith (Amador).

Message	*Code Word*
Two days	Ton
Four days	Heavy
Five days	Powerful
All the friends approve plan and we are proceeding to carry it out	Sad
Enthusiasm	Faithful
Discouragement	Great
Met troops disembarking or disembarked	Tradition
One hundred	Rabbit
One hundred and fifty	Cat
Two hundred	Lion
More than two hundred	Tiger
The great number of troops prevents us making the movement	Elephant
This cable is for Jones New York	Fate
This cable is for Smith Panama	Obscure
Tell me if anything had happened which obliges them not to follow plans agreed upon	Content

Message	Code Word
Nothing occurred which necessitates modification	Boy
Something has happened which compels abandonment of all idea of movement	Heaven
We have issued the declaration of independence with the six declarations without changing a word	London
Repeat your cable where occurs the word X, in order to be perfectly certain	Pius X
I repeat the word X perfectly correct	X plus
I think it is extremely dangerous to refuse that which the United States deems	India
I think that to arrive at our ends it is necessity to show some resistance	Japan
It is impossible to resist longer; you accept	China
Here is that which they desire to change	Mongolia
I think these changes extremely advantageous and that they should be accepted	Indochina
I think these changes acceptable	Manchuria
I think it can not be accepted	Liberia
Accept everything that you think best	Arabia
Do not be worried by the delay, all is well	Canada

Amador added more code words in his own handwriting to the version he got from Bunau-Varilla.

Message	Code Word
The movement will take place within	United
Days	River

Message	Code Word
One	Kentucky
Two	Ohio
Three	Mississippi
Four	Hudson
Five	Missouri
Meet minister on the wharf	Abrupt
Pablo Arosemena	Accuse
J. A. Arango	Absurd
Tomás Arias	Accent
Federico Boyd	Account
They do not accept the plan	Accord
I have received of B. V. the $4,000	Adult
I have received from B. V. the balance up to $100,000	Advent
The minister will negotiate loan	Adept
This work in your cable to Maduro means that it is for me	Obscure
Cables with this work are for B.V. transmit them (to him)	Fate
Minister sailed from Colón the 3	Three
Minister sailed from Colón the 10	Ten
Minister sailed from Colón the 17	Seventeen
Minister sailed from Colón the 24	Twenty-four
Minister sailed from Colón the 1st of December	First

José Agustín Arango got the Bunau-Varilla list and added more coded words.

Message	Code Word
Tomorrow at daybreak the movement will take place	Galveston
We have great hopes of good result	Mobile
The movement is effected with good success without casualties	Safe
The movement is effected with losses of life of small importance	Serious

Message	Code Word
The movement is effected with loss of life of grave importance	Grave
From 1 to 10 killed or wounded	Belgium
From 10 to 20 killed or wounded	France
From 40 to 80 killed or wounded	Turkey
More than 80 killed or wounded	Russia
We have taken several Colombian warships	Take
Warship *Bogota*	Wood
Warship *Padilla*	Crowd
Warship *Boyaca*	Female
Warship *Chucuito*	Small
They have left for the Cauca	South
Rendered useless	Spoiled
They are in Buenaventura, or absent from Panama	Laugh
We have news of the arrival of Colombian forces	News
The Pacific	Good
The Atlantic	Bad
One day	Word

In addition to the Bunau-Varilla-Amador code, Panamanians devised a code to communicate among themselves. Thus, Lindo and Amador wrote the following code on the back of a Hotel Endicott stationary.

Message	Code Word
The plan is accepted; minister will start	Abete
Ask Bunau-Varilla for the $4,000	Abbot
Ask Bunau-Varilla for the balance up to $100,000	Ably
Send the 50 revolvers, not very large ones, with 1,500 cartridges; must be handy, but not Smith & Wessons	Abode
Send 500 Remington rifles and 500,000 cartridges	Wry

Message	Code Word
Movement delayed for lack of arms	Truble
Movement delayed for six days	Sintruble
B. V. agrees to the delay	O.K.

Curiously, these lines were written and crossed out by Amador:

Message	Code Word
For the $100,000 loan they charge 5-10 per cent	5-10 per cent

The codes reveal that the plan was so thorough that they even had a code for changing it ("Boy"). Only the question about the minister in Washington was left open (note the entry, "Minister has arrived," with names of Panamanian conspirators). More importantly, the finances of the revolution had yet to be arranged, and a loan was contemplated (notice the crossed out "For the $100,000 loan they charge 5-10 per cent").

With these instructions, Amador left for Panama on the morning of October 20. When he boarded the ship, he gave the "revolutionary kit" to James Beers's son, who put it in the safe. After Amador left, Bunau-Varilla immediately began to look into procuring the $100,000 he had promised. He thought of approaching J.P. Morgan or Isaac Seligman for a loan, but feared that they would speculate on the French shares (he might not have been aware that they were already doing so). On October 26, $100,000 was deposited into Bunau-Varilla's personal account at the Heidelbach, Ickelheimer & Co. Bank in New York. He later argued that he got the money from his broker, who loaned it against a pledge of Bunau-Varilla's own securities. However, the money was wired from Credit Lyonnais on October 23, just three days after Cromwell's arrival in Paris. The president of Credit Lyonnais was Maurice Bo, also president of the Compagnie Nouvelle. One month after Bo's election as president of the Compagnie Nouvelle on December 24, 1901, Cromwell was reinstated as general counsel.

As soon as Cromwell arrived in Paris, he began to make the arrangements for the transfer of the concessions to the United States. His confidence that the U.S. deal would be consummated was so high that he convinced the stockholders not to sell, despite a lucrative German offer to buy the company.

Bunau-Varilla also felt assured that his plans had the backing of Washington. As he strolled through the streets of New York, he read dispatches from the *New York Times* describing the unusual movements of warships leaving San Francisco, Guantánamo, and Jamaica, bound for Panama. To predispose American public opinion in favor of the eventual revolution, he asked his friend Edward Mitchell of the *New York Sun* to write an article about the Bogota government's oppression of Panama for decades and alleging that Panamanians were justified in seeking independence. Mitchell answered that he would comply, but only after the elections on November 4. Bunau-Varilla replied, "On the fifth, it will be too late."

"Why?" Mitchell asked.

"Because," Bunau-Varilla replied in a hushed tone, gripping the editor's hand, "on that day Colombian tyranny will have ceased to exist as well as the Colombian sovereignty on the Isthmus."

Mitchell turned pale and was momentarily speechless. He clasped Bunau-Varilla's hand and replied with emotion, "The article shall appear tomorrow."

With this, Bunau-Varilla felt that all the pieces were in place. "I built the subtle diplomatic structure," he bragged, "as a bridge is built: that is, by calculating its various elements. I have made diplomacy as if it were by trigonometry." Now, all he had to do was to wait for the Panamanians to do their part.

6

Seducing the Patriots

WHEN AMADOR ARRIVED in Panama on October 27, he feared that his conspirators would berate him for his thwarted plans. He had gone to New York to obtain money and U.S. military support, but returned with neither. He took Bunau-Varilla's "revolutionary kit" out of the safe box and hid the flag, wrapping it around his waist like an exotic cummerbund. He rushed to catch the first train across the Isthmus to meet his collegues that same evening.

The inner circle met at Federico Boyd's house at 7:00 that night. Amador reported that although Cromwell had disappointed them, Bunau-Varilla had promised American support. When asked if he had personally gotten assurances from Hay or Roosevelt, his honest reply disappointed many of the conspirators.

Amador reported that Bunau-Varilla would send $100,000 when Panama City and Colón declared their independence, but his cohorts complained that this was not enough money, and that in any case, they would need it before the revolution started in order to bribe the Colombian troops. Amador explained that only Panama City and Colón would secede and receive United States protection, and that Bunau-Varilla insisted on being the first ambassador to Washington. Again, the would-be revolutionaries grumbled with discontent.

Finally, Amador unfurled the makeshift Madame Bunau-Varilla flag. That gesture did it. The conspirators began to protest violently across the board. Tomás Arias made a strong speech, arguing that many of the conspirators owned large estates outside Panama City, which Colombia would seize. As expected, the group objected to appointing a foreigner as an envoy.

To appease his partners, Amador suggested that Bunau-Varilla was probably a secret service agent acting as a liaison between the U.S. government and Panama. He took a few conspirators in private and told them that he had met Hay and T.R. The discussion dragged on for hours, with Amador asking them to trust him. Finally, Arango decided to go ahead, and soon, the others followed.

Initially, they had chosen November 28, the anniversary of Panama's independence from Spain, as the day for the revolution. But Amador insisted that it had to take place by no later than November 4, only eight days away. When the others protested, he told them that Bunau-Varilla insisted on the date. In a frenzy, they began their preparations.

Carlos Mendoza agreed to draft a new declaration of independence; Maria de la Ossa, Dr. Amador's young, energetic, and beautiful wife, offered to sew a flag that her son would design (they did not like Mrs. Bunau-Varilla's offering). José Gabriel Duque also joined the party; even though he had betrayed them in Washington, he assured them that he was faithful to the revolution and won their confidence. Duque volunteered to transform the fire brigade, which he headed, into a makeshift army of the revolution. The 287 volunteers began at once to gather rifles for the military operation. Most importantly, Amador and Arango took on the dangerous task of securing the support of the police force and of the Colombian troops, who had already begun to suspect that a revolt was being planned at Amador's house.

The Amador residence became the hotbed of the revolution. The conspirators entered the three-story whitewashed limestone building through a small door and walked through a narrow alleyway that led to an interior patio, where the strategy sessions were held. Groups of volunteers sewing the flag and composing the national hymn labored in the upstairs rooms or in the wide balconies that looked out onto the patio. At the front of the house, guards stood on the second-floor balcony keeping eagle eyes out for the police.

Despite careful planning, the traffic going in and out and the carriages and horses parked on the narrow cobblestone in front of the house soon drew police attention. The officers reported to the mayor of Panama City that "suspicious and perhaps incendiary meetings were transpiring" inside the Amador residence. The mayor, Francisco de la Ossa, Mrs. Amador's brother, told his sister that unless she put an end to the meetings and whatever else her husband was up to, he would have him arrested.

Mrs. Amador decided to reveal the conspiracy to her brother. "Kneel down, Francisco, and swear to me by the memory of our mother that you will not reveal what I am about to tell you!"

Francisco did and became a full-fledged conspirator. The next challenge was the police chief, who happened to be Arango's nephew, but he refused; instead, they got the deputy chief to neutralize the police force.

The next step was to confront the head of the Colombian military forces in Panama. The conspirators thought that since Bogota had not paid the troop's salary for three months, they could easily bribe them. The tactic, however, was mined with perils if the troops refused. Arango and Amador thus carefully approached General Esteban Huertas. Small of stature (no more than five-feet-four-inches tall), with a dark, sullen face, Huertas had had a distinguished career in the Colombian army. A precocious child, he ran away from his home to join the army when he was only eight years old; by the time he was fourteen, he was a second-class sergeant and had received numerous decorations for bravery under fire. On December 1900, while fighting in the civil war, he fired his cannon so many times that it glowed red hot, overheated, and backfired, mangling his right arm. He immediately got up and ordered, "Put in another cannon ball, for nothing has happened!!" The doctor who amputated his lower arm wanted to use anesthesia, but Huertas replied, "Just give me a shot of brandy and you may cut away as you please!" He returned to battle in a few hours, but gangrene set in, and he lost the remainder of his right arm. From then on, he wore a wooden prosthesis, but he became an expert shooter with his left hand. For his bravery, in November 1902, at the age of twenty-six, the petite soldier was promoted to general.

The conspirators knew that General Huertas loved Panama. He had married the daughter of a distinguished local merchant who bore him a son on October 5. To scare him, the conspirators circulated a rumor that the twenty-seven-year-old general was going to be sent to the volatile and dangerous Colombian interior. Under this pretext, Arango called on him during the child's baptism in Cathedral Park. Arango feigned sadness to know Huertas would be leaving, especially since he had just had a child. Arango denounced the Colombian government, telling Huertas that Bogota was tyrannical toward its troops and the people of Panama. Huertas agreed with Arango, but said that he would remain loyal to his Colombian superiors. Arango replied, "You have no superiors. You are a Panamanian now and they will try to send you away to Colombia's interior. If you leave you will never come back to your wife and child. Please stay." Huertas nevertheless maintained that he had to obey Bogota's orders. Arango left him, planning to approach him again later.

Arango then approached another high ranking Colombian officer, General Tascón, with the same story. However, unlike Huertas, Tascón flatly refused to cooperate and threatened to turn the would-be revolutionaries. To get rid of him, the conspirators spread a rumor that Nicaraguans had invaded the province of Veraguas on the western Caribbean coast of Panama. They hoped that Tascón would set out with his men to the site of the fake invasion; by the time he returned, Panama would be free.

Governor José de Obaldiá heard the rumors of the Nicaraguan invasion and immediately dispatched Colonel Tascón with a hundred men to the site. Although Obaldiá had been living in Amador's house, the conspirators had not let him on the details of their plans in order to protect him. Throughout this period, he had been sending "quieting dispatches" to Bogota regarding Isthmian activities. Not realizing that this rumor was a fabrication, on October 25, Obaldiá made the critical mistake of cabling the governor of the department of Cauca in Colombia: "Nicaraguan invasion has disembarked north of Veraguas . . . I have sent forces to attack them."

Obaldiá's report of the fake invasion spread quickly. Samuel Boyd, brother of conspirator Federico Boyd and a correspondent for the *New York Herald*, wired the news to his paper to alert the United States to send troops. The Bogota foreign office heard about the invasion and immediately cabled Dr. Herrán in Washington, asking for a report on the American government's intentions. The Colombians still expected the United States to send an army to quash the invasion and protect Colombia's sovereignty under the 1846 treaty.

Herrán did not respond. Weary of Panamanian discontent, on October 28, the Bogota foreign office cabled Obaldiá with unusual promptness, to tell him that a ship with reinforcements had departed Barranquilla and would arrive in Colón in a few days. They also asked Obaldiá to summon two Colombian gunboats mooring in the bay of Panama, the *Bogota* and the *Padilla*, and send them to Buenaventura—a port halfway between Panama and Ecuador—to pick up more troops and artillery.

The warships did not have enough coal for the trip to Buenaventura. Unaware that the Panama Railroad Company was aiding the Panamanians, the captains of the ships approached the tall, silver-haired Colonel Shaler and requested the coal to make their journey. Colonel Shaler sent the Colombian commanders to see Prescott, who in turn sent them to talk to Captain Beers. Beers claimed that he was ill and told the Colombian captains that the decision whether or not to provide the coal fell in the lap of the attorney for the Panama Railroad Company, José Agustín Arango.

By this time the Colombians were irate. Arango calmly told them that unfortunately all of the coal was stored in Colón and had been requisitioned by the steamship company. He recommended waiting for the *Pacific Mail*, which "will arrive from San Francisco in a few weeks." During the meeting, someone slipped a note to Arango telling him that the captain of the *Padilla*, General Rubén Varón, had—for $35,000 pesos—agreed to support the revolution. Arango excused himself and returned a few minutes later with the happy news that coal had been found on one of the wharves, but only enough for one boat, the *Padilla*.

In the meantime, the news that the Colombians had dispatched troops caused panic among the conspirators. They were expecting a bloodless revolution, not a war with Colombia that, without weapons, they could not win. Tomás Arias thus scoured the city's narrow cobblestone streets searching for Amador. When he found him, he screamed, "You are an old man, Arango is an old man, and you do not care if you are hanged. I do not like to be hanged!" Other conspirators followed and defected.

A worried Amador called an urgent meeting at his house. He assured the conspirators that even if Colombia sent troops, the United States would prevent their landing. But this time the conspirators wanted more than Amador's words. They told him that unless they saw U.S. warships in Colón or in the Bay of Panama by November 3, they would abandon the revolution.

On the morning of October 29, a desperate Amador cabled "Tower" (Joshua Lindo's code name) in New York:

"FATE NEWS BAD POWERFUL TIGER URGE VAPOR COLON, SMITH."

Bunau-Varilla was at the Waldorf-Astoria when Lindo came running with the cable. He deciphered the first few words from the code he had written.

FATE: This cable is for Bunau-Varilla
NEWS: Colombian troops arriving
BAD: Atlantic
POWERFUL: Five days
TIGER: More than 200

Although the last three words, *Urge vapor Colón*, did not belong to the code, Bunau-Varilla guessed that Amador wanted him to send a tug-of-war to Colón. He surmised that Amador needed to prove to the rest of the conspirators that he would deliver the military force that he had promised. Unless he performed, Bunau-Varilla concluded, the revolutionaries might forsake the movement. "It was not information which was transmitted to me, it was a test to which I was being submitted. If I succeeded in this task the Canal was saved. If I failed it was lost."

The following morning, October 30, Bunau-Varilla left for Washington. He saw Francis Loomis at his home and informed him that a revolution was erupting in Panama. Unless the United States sent troops it would regrettably be caught off guard, just as it had been in 1885, when failure to land marines to suppress a local rebellion led to the destruction of Colón. Loomis responded very formally that the United States could not commit any troops.

The following morning, Bunau-Varilla sat on a bench in Lafayette Square hoping to catch Hay as he left his house and make a pitch.

Instead, he "bump[ed] into Loomis" again (Bunau-Varilla had a knack for showing up at the very places where people would pass.) This time, Loomis was much more cooperative.

"I have thought over what you said to me yesterday; this is really fraught with peril for the town of Colón."

Bunau-Varilla concluded that Loomis' words could have but one interpretation: "A cruiser has been sent to Colón." He received additional assurances the following morning, November 1, when he read in the *New York Times* that "the American cruiser *Nashville* left this morning with sealed orders. Her destination is believed to be Colombia." He surmised that the ship was sailing to Colón from Kingston, Jamaica. Given the five-hundred nautical miles between the two cities, if the ship sailed at ten knots per hour, he calculated that it would arrive in Panama within two and a half days, on the morning of November 2. He thus sent a telegram to "Jones" (Amador), containing only one word: "BOY." Its translation: "Nothing has happened which required modification."

Later, President Roosevelt and Secretary Hay both claimed that they sent the *Nashville* to Colón purely as a precaution to protect the railroad in case of an uprising in Panama, but that at that time they had no plans to aid the insurgency. The evidence indicates, however, that Roosevelt had spent months secretly preparing for the military operation in Panama.

On October 16, Roosevelt received a report from two recent graduates of West Point who had supposedly returned from a four-month commission in northern Venezuela and Colombia; the officers, Captain Humphrey and Lieutenant Murphy, in theory stopped in Panama purely "as an unpremeditated incident of their return journey." The young officers reported that while they were visiting:

> A revolutionary party was in the course of organization, having for its object separation of the State of Panama from Colombia, the leader being Dr. Richard Arango, a former governor of Panama; that when they were on the Isthmus arms and ammunition were being smuggled into the city of Colón in piano boxes, merchandise crates, etc., the small arms received being principally the Gras French rifle, the Remington, and the Mauser; that nearly every citizen in Panama had some sort of

rifle or gun in his possession, with ammunition therefor; that in the city of Panama there had been organized a fire brigade which was really intended for a revolutionary military organization; that there were representatives of the revolutionary organization at all the important points on the Isthmus; that in Panama, Colón, and the other principal places of the Isthmus police forces had been organized which were in reality revolutionary forces; that the people on the Isthmus seemed to be unanimous in their sentiment against the Bogota Government.

Before they saw Roosevelt, the two officers were said to be so excited that they considered resigning from the army to join the revolution, and they planned to approach J.P. Morgan to ask for a $100,000 loan to pull it off. (J.P. Morgan and the sum of $100,000 resurface again.) Not coincidentally, Captain Humphrey's father was staying at the Hotel Endicott in New York a few doors from Amador.

The officers' report, however, contained gross misstatements of facts. For example, in mid-October, the conspirators in Panama were still awaiting Amador's return from the United States; "representatives of the revolutionary organization" were not present "at all the important points on the Isthmus" as only a handful of men even knew about it; and no one was smuggling weapons.

More importantly, the report contained an amazing wealth of military intelligence about the interior of Panama that could not be compiled on a four-day jaunt to Panama. The report included every cove in the country where Colombian and American ships could land; existing ports; breakwaters; available timber; and even the number of mules "that may be obtained in numbers and in localities and in one week's notice, as follows: Pedregal, 100; Puerto Mutis, 30; Mensabe, 50; Aguadulce, 50; Chepo, 10; Chorrera, 10; Panama, 50." Just one piece of information in the "unpremeditated report" might have taken merely a few weeks to gather: a topographical survey of each of the twenty-five stations along the Panama railroad route. It described the best way to transport artillery from Colón to Panama City by railroad and by foot along the track lines (the intended use for the mules), and the best spots to place artillery in order to command the cities of Panama and Colón. In short, Roosevelt had sent the officers on a four-month reconnaissance trip to Panama and had gotten all the information needed to wage a war. Surprisingly, no one in Panama saw these gentlemen traveling around the country taking an inventory of mules and timber.

Roosevelt was also personally directing the movement of warships to get them within striking distance of Panama. On October 15, seventeen days before the revolution, Admiral Glass of the Pacific squadron received an order to proceed from San Francisco to Acapulco instead of Hawaii, and on October 22, he was told to sail for Panama. Sailing at 10 knots per hour, the ship would arrive on November 3 or early on November 4 to the Bay of Panama. In the Caribbean, on October 22, the *Boston* was ordered to sail to Nicaragua, while on October 24, the *New York Herald* reported under the column "Movement of Navy Vessels" that the *Dixie* had left League Island Navy, Philadelphia, transporting 450 marines for Guantanamo, Cuba. On October 28, the *Nashville*, under Commander John Hubbard, sailed from Kingston to Colón, under sealed orders.

Not even the ships' captains knew their mission. Admiral Glass had to stop for refueling and engine problems and thus arrived late; he had not been told that he needed to proceed with all speed. Only Teddy Roosevelt had the whole picture. With only one year in office, the former colonel of the First Volunteer Cavalry Regiment in the Spanish-American War was again doing what he would later describe as the most exciting job of his life: leading a war.

In the meantime, Cromwell was in Paris making his own preparations. He drafted documents, got consents, met with the board of the Compagnie Nouvelle, and arranged everything for the eventual transfer of the concessions to the United States. The lawyer may also have been arranging the purchase of the shares of the company from its shareholders by the American speculating syndicate. On October 28, Dr. Herrán cabled a warning to his government: "Mr. William Nelson Cromwell, with general powers of attorney for the Panama Canal Co. in this country, is at present in Paris conferring with the directors of that enterprise. I have been informed that he is occupied in organizing the American syndicate to which I have made reference."

In Panama City, upon receiving Bunau-Varilla's cable, Amador convinced the patriots to continue with the preparations for the revolution. On November 1, a prominent Colón merchant, Porfirio

Meléndez, traveled to Panama City to meet with Arango and Boyd. They met for several hours in room 11 of the Hotel Central. Meléndez agreed to lead the revolution in Colón, but warned that he needed to enlist an army to overcome the loyal one hundred fifty-man Colombian police force in that city. Arango suggested "hiring" three hundred Panama Railroad Company employees stationed in Panama City. Meléndez would take them to Colón to work supposedly "at higher wages for the United Fruit Company," and enlist them instead. He agreed to the plan and returned to Colón.

Amador made another pitch for Huertas's support. He sent a messenger asking the "little general" to meet him at the Hotel Central, which became the revolutionaries' preferred meeting place when the Colombian troops placed Amador's residence under surveillance. Owned by U.S. Vice Counsel Felix Ehrman, a prominent local banker, the hotel occupied the southern block of Cathedral Plaza. Its interior patio had been the site of a great banquet honoring Ferdinand de Lesseps when the French hero visited the Isthmus. Three floors of large rooms, each with its own balcony, faced the streets in four directions; from their rooms the conspirators could keep an eye on movement throughout the city.

A nervous Amador met Huertas in the lobby of the hotel. They shook hands, and Amador asked Huertas to follow him up to room 11. According to Huertas, once inside the room, he abruptly asked, "What is the reason for our meeting, Doctor?"

"General, I am to communicate to you an important development." Amador got jittery, muffing his words.

Huertas interrupted, "Calm down and speak clearly. I've got to get back to my barracks soon."

Amador dove into it. "General, don't be upset if I talk to you about a crime. Can you keep a secret?"

"You can trust me."

"General, the issue is the independence of Panama. The independence is in accord and counting on support from the Boyds, Ariases, Obarrios, Arangos, and others. There is more to it, General. American boats will come to support us and the United States government will recognize us. But what we need is you, for you are the one man who can follow this thing through. We are awaiting your reply in order that we may achieve independence. Think of your future, your wife, your son, and your friends. You are already a Panamanian. Remember, in Colombia we are not loved. General, your decision is urgent."

Huertas was silent and pensive. After some time, he replied, "This is very serious. I will think it over."

At 5:00 that evening they tried again to convince the reclusive general. Amador sent Pastor Jiménez, Huertas's friend, to see him at the barracks. To assuage the general, Jiménez told him that people "look up to him" (although physically that would have been almost impossible), and that he had an obligation to help Panama because of his wife and child. According to the diminutive general, he replied, "*Compadre*, rest easy, I will probably give you many surprises."

Huertas then asked Jiménez to arrange a meeting with General José Domingo Diaz, a retired general who had fought during the civil war and a popular citizen of Panama. They met secretly at 7:00 that night at Diaz's brother's house. Huertas and Diaz spoke at great length; Huertas asked him if he would sacrifice his honor as a military officer for a revolutionary cause.

"General, I will give my life and my people's lives for our independence," Diaz replied.

"General Diaz, you are not alone. I have the weapons and I too love Panama a great deal," Huertas added.

When Huertas got back to his barracks, Jiménez was waiting nervously. Smiling, Huertas said, "What are we doing, *compadre*? Be calm. Panamanians may have a free country."

The following day, November 2, at 10:00 AM, Huertas got a message from Governor Obaldiá requesting his immediate presence at the Government House. When Huertas arrived, he found Obaldiá sitting down at his desk and Amador standing next to him. Obaldiá told Huertas that he had joined the revolutionary movement (although he later claimed that he never did). Amador appealed to Huertas's love for Panama and for his family. They warned him that Colombian forces under General Juan Bautista Tovar had left Barranquilla and were on their way to Panama for the purpose of relieving him of his command. They warned him that he would probably be taken back to the troubled, war-stricken Colombian interior and would never see his friends or family again. Suddenly, Huertas became worried (he did not know that the Colombian troops had been sent only to avert the fake invasion). Amador then offered Huertas $65,000 dollars in gold to support the revolution. Huertas kept silent and left without making any commitment.

As November 2 dawned, many last-minute details were covered. Maria Amador finished sewing the flag; lawyers polished the declaration of independence; Colonel Shaler agreed to direct the railroad in Colón while Prescott would be in Panama City; all rolling stock (i.e. train carriages that could be used by the Colombians to transport troops to Panama City) were moved to the Pacific terminal; Duque and Diaz would lead the fire brigade, which would blow bugles and fire a skyrocket when the revolution began on November 4; those not sympathetic to the cause would be seized in their beds at 5:00 AM; sometime in the afternoon, the brigade would gather people at Cathedral Park to hear the declaration of independence.

In Bogota, the extraordinary session of the Colombian Congress adjourned without ratifying the treaty. Marroquín sent a cable to Herrán instructing the United States to maintain order if rebellion broke out in Panama. In Washington, the State Department assured Herrán that the United States would only intervene in Panama to maintain the "free and uninterrupted transit." Hay sent a cable to Arthur Beaupré, the American charge d'affairs in Bogota, telling him that he could leave Bogota if he wished to avoid personal jeopardy. In France, Cromwell duplicitously gave an interview to the Parisian *Journal* in which he advised waiting another year for the situation to stabilize in Colombia.

One crucial element was still missing. Throughout the day, the conspirators in Colón were looking to the sea for signs of the American ships that had been promised by Bunau-Varilla. Success depended on their arrival; without them, the great undertaking would be quashed, and all of the conspirators would be executed. As the hours of the day passed and no ships showed up, "disappointment may have gradually invaded all hearts." Suddenly, at almost sunset, a column of smoke rose to the north east. Little by little the smoke thickened, the hull of a ship emerged above the horizon, and soon the Stars and Stripes were fluttering in the Bay of Limón.

It was the U.S.S. *Nashville*, anchoring at 5:30 PM, with forty-two marines. Commander Hubbard went ashore to find Colón quiet. For him, the landing was routine; he had been in Colón only two weeks earlier. With nothing else to do, he went back to his ship to await further instructions.

Colonel Shaler immediately wired Prescott in Panama City to tell the revolutionaries that the ship had arrived. The news caused great celebration. For the Panamanians, the ship's arrival was the sign that the United States and Bunau-Varilla could be trusted.

However, the celebration did not last very long. At about midnight, the *Cartagena*, a Colombian gunboat, arrived in the Bay of Limón, carrying three generals and about five hundred *Tiradores*, or expert riflemen. Nobody expected the ship to arrive that night, or to be carrying that many troops. At once, the alarming news reached Panama City. With Huertas still undecided and the Panamanians still uncertain about the United States' resolve to wage a war against a country it was supposed to protect, the patriots panicked and rapidly began to abandon the revolution.

7

Hamlet Revolution

By 6:00 AM ON NOVEMBER 3, Amador was already milling about the streets on an empty stomach, agonizing over how to keep the conspirators from deserting. He had heard about the *Cartagena*'s arrival from Herbert Prescott. Amador prayed that the United States would uphold its part of the bargain and prevent the Colombian troops from landing. By 8:30 AM, however, the worst possible news came from Colón.

At daybreak, Colonel Hubbard boarded the *Cartagena* and mistakenly ascertained that the Colombian troops had come to relieve the Panama garrison. The *Cartagena*'s commander, the fifty-year-old stalwart General Juan Tovar, told Hubbard that he was going to disembark at daybreak. Unaware of his mission, Hubbard did not object. He later said that "inasmuch as the independent party had not acted and the Government of Colombia was at that time in undisputed control of the Province of Panama, I did not feel, in the absence of any instructions, that I was justified in preventing the landing of these troops."

Hubbard should not have let them. President Roosevelt had gone to great lengths in sending the two military officers to gather intelligence in order to prevent Colombian troops from landing. Further, on November 2, acting secretary of the navy, Charles Darling, had dispatched orders to keep the Colombian troops from landing, but November 2 fell on a Sunday and the cablegram did not reach Hubbard before he boarded the *Cartagena*. By 8:30 AM, the troops were disembarking. Colombia now had five hundred handpicked riflemen and three generals in Colón, a force for the revolutionaries to reckon with.

When the conspirators in Panama City heard that the invading troops had disembarked and that the Americans had done nothing, they panicked. Tomás Arias and others again scurried through the narrow cobblestone streets looking for Amador. They found him still wandering in the alleys. Angrily, they told him that they would have nothing to do with the revolution and returned to their homes.

Amador went back to his house and lay down in the hammock on his interior patio. He, too, was ready to quit; the revolution was over. When his wife, Maria, saw him, she ordered him to get up and practically kicked him out of the hammock. "We have all gone too far to give up now. Soldiers or no soldiers, the fight has to go on!"

Amador rose reluctantly. With Maria leading, the two walked out to the streets to summon their fellow conspirators to an urgent meeting at Herbert Prescott's house. Prescott and Shaler had explicit orders from Cromwell not to aid the revolution, but these orders were changed now that the revolution was in danger. Cromwell later acknowledged that he was "in constant communication with the Isthmus" and with his partners in New York "giving advice and instructions."

At Prescott's house, Maria de Amador concocted the plan to deal with the intimidating situation. (Years later, the male conspirators would deny her role in an attempt to shore up their own prestige.) First, she suggested separating the Colombian generals from their troops. Colonel Shaler, already in charge of the railroad depot in Colón, would send the generals by train to Panama City, leaving the troops behind. Once in Panama City, the generals would be summarily dealt with (one plan was to put sleeping pills in their wine at lunch). Without their generals, the troops would be bribed to go back to Barranquilla. If they refused and tried to take the railroad rolling stock by force, Prescott would blow up the train before it arrived in Panama City, while Huertas and his men arrested the soldiers.

In Colón, as soon as Colonel James Shaler learned that the Colombian troops were disembarking, he took control of the situation. Tall and slender, with bushy silver hair and white eyebrows, his position as general superintendent of the Panama Railroad Company gave him enormous prestige and power, especially since many conspirators, including Amador and Arango, worked for him. ("All questions are referred to him for decision," wrote a *New York Tribune* reporter, "his dictum has the force and effect of law, and his advice is consistently accepted and followed.") Originally from Kentucky, he was a veteran of the American Civil War and had lived in Panama for more than a decade. Although he was seventy-eight years old—older even than Amador—he was buoyantly active, and boasted that "I'm too young to think about quitting work." A bachelor, he lived in a bleak, rambling bungalow amidst a coconut grove on the Colón waterfront. The bungalow was a man's world, filled with books, newspapers, billiard and pool tables, and male servants. Although he had stayed out of the planning of the revolution as instructed by Cromwell, now that the Colombians were disembarking, he had no choice but to assume his role.

Inside the barnlike wooden railroad depot, Colonel Shaler dispatched orders to the employees, placing them on high alert to protect the railroad trains. He summoned Porfirio Meléndez to his office. The two agreed to approach the Colombians, tell them that everything was quiet in Panama City, and encourage them to re-embark and return to Cartagena. If the Colombians insisted on going to Panama City, only the generals would be allowed; the revolutionaries would worry about the troops later.

While Shaler and Meléndez discussed their plans, the *Cartagena* sailed menacingly within feet of the *Nashville* and docked at the wharf. General Tovar was the first to disembark, followed by General Ramon Amaya, General Francisco Castro, and Colonel Eliseo Torres. Several Colón officials awaited on the dock to render military greetings, including General Pedro Cuadras, the prefect of Colón. For several minutes, the Colombian army, with its multiplicity of generals, colonels, and captains, each dressed in a gaudy yellow, blue, and gold uniform dazzling in gold laces, resplendent medals and accoutrements, shone like peacocks in the barren wooden dock of the Panama Railroad port.

Meléndez approached the Colombian generals as they reviewed the Colón regiment. He told them that the Nicaraguan invasion report had been fabricated and that everything was quiet in Panama City; he encouraged them to get back on their ship and go home. As they were talking, they were interrupted by José Segundo Ruiz, port captain from the Bocas del Toro province on the Caribbean border with Costa Rica. The agitated Ruiz told General Tovar that on October 10 the captain of a Norwegian vessel anchored in Bocas' Admiralty Bay had told him "that he knew for certainty that a separatist movement was planned in Panama and that it was openly favored by the United States." General Tovar took the prefect, General Cuadras, aside and inquired about the rumor. Cuadras told him he was unaware of any revolutionary movements in Panama or Colón. Tovar remained suspicious.

At the railroad station, Colonel Shaler detected the general's apprehension and ran to the wharf. He told Tovar that Governor Obaldiá was awaiting his arrival and had requested that they go immediately to Panama City. He added that he had arranged a special luxury train to take them, but they needed to leave at once as the hour fixed for its departure had already passed. Tovar hesitated.

"I pointed out to him," Tovar later recounted, "that it was not possible for me to accept his invitation, as it was necessary for me to take the proper measures for the disembarkation of the troops I had brought with me and because I wished to take them with me to Panama."

Shaler insisted and walked Tovar and the other generals to the railroad car, assuring them that he would send the troops over in a special train to be dispatched at 1:00 PM.

"I found no justifiable reason to persist in my refusal," recalled Tovar, "all the more so as I had been sent to Panama to assist the government against a reported invasion from Nicaragua, and that I had not the slightest idea that a barrack uprising was planned."

General Tovar left Colonel Eliseo Torres in charge of the Colombian troops and boarded the special luxury train with Generals Castro and Amaya. When it was ready to depart, an apprehensive Amaya got up, turned towards Tovar and said, "Let me remain here with my soldiers, I cannot go."

"No, you mustn't leave me here all alone," Tovar responded.

When General Amaya was ready to disembark, Shaler blew his whistle to signal the train to depart. The train pulled out at full steam, carrying the Colombian generals out of Colón. Shaler rushed back to his offices and telephoned Prescott to inform him that the generals would arrive in Panama City at 11:00 AM. He said that he would try to keep the troops calm, but he warned that they might attempt to take a train by force.

Once the generals were gone, the port captain, Ruiz, approached Colonel Torres, and, pointing to the *Nashville*, said, "That warship is here for no other purpose than to support the separatist movement which is about to break out." Torres ignored him, and a frustrated Ruiz left.

Shortly thereafter, while visiting the offices of Oscar Malmros, the U.S. consul in Colón, Commander Hubbard received the cablegram from Assistant Secretary Darling. Sent by mistake to another ship in the bay, it was one day too late when Hubbard got it. It said:

NAVY DEPARTMENT

WASHINGTON, D.C., NOVEMBER 2, 1903

SECRET AND CONFIDENTIAL. MAINTAIN FREE AND UNINTERRUPTED TRANSIT. IF INTERRUPTION THREAT-ENED BY ARMED FORCE, OCCUPY LINE OF RAILROAD. *PREVENT LANDING OF ANY ARMED FORCE WITH HOS-TILE INTENT, EITHER GOVERNMENT OR INSURGENT, EITHER AT COLON, PORTO BELLO, OR OTHER POINT.* SEND COPY OF INSTRUCTIONS TO THE SENIOR OFFI-CER PRESENT AT PANAMA UPON ARRIVAL OF *BOSTON.* HAVE SENT COPY OF INSTRUCTIONS AND HAVE TELEGRAPHED *DIXIE* TO PROCEED WITH ALL POSSIBLE DISPATCH FROM KINGSTON TO COLON. *GOVERNMENT FORCE REPORTED APPROACHING THE ISTHMUS IN VES-SELS. PREVENT THEIR LANDING, IF IN YOUR JUDGMENT THIS WOULD PRECIPITATE CONFLICT* [Emphasis added].

Darling, Acting

The cable was almost identical to the plan proposed in June by Cromwell. Though he was in Paris during this time admittedly he "called upon the American government to protect the property of the canal and railroad and to apply the clauses of the treaty of 1848, which guaranteed the free and interrupted transit across the Isthmus."

When Hubbard received the cable, he realized the mistake he had just made letting the Colombian troops disembark and ran back to the railroad station to prevent disembarkation, but he found the troops already on the wharf. He conferred with Colonel Shaler, who filled in Hubbard on the details of the revolution and the day's events. They discussed the best way to deal with the menacing Colombian troops. Shaler told him he had already decided not to transport them to Panama City unless ordered otherwise by Governor Obaldiá.

Shaler knew that his decision was in stark defiance of the 1846 treaty. The railroad was required to transport the Colombian troops unless violence was threatened on the railroad lines. If the revolution failed, his refusal to transport the troops would be grounds for forfeiting the railroad concessions to Colombia, an outcome that Cromwell had ordered them to avoid. On the other hand, if Shaler transported the troops to Panama City, they could easily quash the poorly armed rebellion and preserve the sovereignty of Colombia. The Colombian *Tiradores* outnumbered Duque's fire brigade two to one, and Hubbard's troops ten to one. Most likely, the Panamanians would abort the rebellion if the troops managed to get to Panama City.

Hubbard remained in Shaler's office "until it was sure that no action on my part would be needed to prevent the transportation of the troops." He then went back on board the *Nashville* and prepared his men in case the Colombians got violent. Shaler would simply have to raise the U.S. flag over the depot, and Hubbard's men would disembark within minutes. Once on board, Hubbard sent a cable to Acting Secretary Darling, saying,

> Railway company has declined to transport these troops except by request of governor of Panama. Request has not been made. It is possible that movement may be made tonight at Panama to declare independence in which case I will * * *

(Critics of Roosevelt later claimed the dispatch was mutilated here because it revealed that the U.S. government knew of the revolution before it occurred.)

After Hubbard left, Shaler sent for Meléndez to discuss how to deal with Torres's troops. Unaware of the other conspirators' plot, they decided that if the Colombian soldiers forced their way onto the trains, Shaler would instruct the soldiers to place all arms in the rear coach. Then, at a particular high point between Colón and Panama City, one of Meléndez's men would pull the coupling pin, and the coach would coast to a standstill. The conductor would run the train to Culebra, the highest point on the Isthmus, and abandon the troops without their weapons in the middle of the jungle. In Colón, when the *Cartagena* docked to get coal and water, Meléndez would invite the captain and officers to have a beer at a local pub. The gunboat would then be boarded by thirty men from the "United Fruit Co." army under Captain Achurra, one of Meléndez's lieutenants.

To inform the other conspirators of their plot, they sent Meléndez's teenage daughter, Señorita Aminta Meléndez, to Panama City on a fast freight train with two letters. (The ride of Aminta Meléndez later received much acclaim throughout Latin America as a courageous act on behalf of freedom and independence. Some historians claimed the timid teenager hid in the engine room, but in fact she rode comfortably to Panama City in one of the passenger cars.)

In Panama City, as soon as Prescott received Colonel Shaler's message that the Colombian generals were arriving at 11:00 AM, he rushed to Amador's house and exclaimed, "now or never is the time to act!!!" Amador called for his carriage and ordered his driver to take him to the Chiriquí barracks, where he was going to face Huertas.

At the seawall, Amador told Huertas that Colombian troops had arrived in Colón and were on their way to Panama to relieve him of his command. "Huertas, what you are today you owe to Panama. From Bogota you can hope for nothing. I am old and tired of life; it is of no importance to me to die. If you will aid us, we shall reach immortality in the history of the new Republic. Here you will have four American war ships. There will be the same number in Colón." (That turned out to be entirely accurate.) "You and your battalion can accomplish nothing against the superior force of the cruisers, which have their orders. Choose here, glory and riches; in Bogota, misery and ingratitude."

Huertas paused for a moment. Then, holding out his hand, he said, "I accept."

Huertas's decision was not as impulsive as it seemed to Amador. According to Huertas's own memoirs, he had decided to join the revolution the previous night, but had not told anyone. His *compadre*, the portly Pastor Jiménez, had called at around 10:00 PM to take him to see Arango and General Nicanor de Obarrio, the Colombian prefect in Panama, in a secret rendezvous in San Juan de Dios. The two tried to convince Huertas to join the conspiracy, but Huertas would not commit. "You are my very good friends, and you will know in a very few hours what I will do. Have no fears. Arango, you will remember what I said to you October 5; you will be the first to know."

General Obarrio replied, "And you, General, should know that tomorrow I am resigning as prefect, for we must fight."

On the carriage back to the barracks, Pastor Jiménez pleaded one more time, "My friend, please swear to me that you will be with us."

"Do not be concerned," Huertas replied, "for I will be the only one hurt or dead in this affair. So off and buy the iodine and the bandages for my recuperation, and if it comes to pass, buy the coffin for my funeral."

Jiménez left Huertas at his house. At about 1:50 AM, Huertas loaded his revolver, strapped a belt around his waist, the point of the bayonet scabbard clearing the ground by not more than a few inches, and left the barracks. As he walked down First Street meditating on his dilemma, he ran into a young officer who told him that Colombian troops had arrived in Colón. Convinced the troops had come to relieve him, Huertas said to the officer, "Go see General Diaz and tell him that I say the following: The sick man is very sick, and we will be the doctors to cure him. Let him get his medicine ready, for I am preparing my medicine chest."

Huertas walked inside a cantina owned by an Italian friend, who was surprised to see the little general so late at night, "What are you doing here? This is rare. How can I help?"

"I need twelve mules and carts," answered Huertas. "Go quietly."

At 3:00 AM, the two took the mules and carts to the Chiriquí barracks and loaded them with rifles and ammunitions. At 5:20 AM, Huertas took a coach to the rendezvous point, where he found Diaz with members of the fire brigade. Diaz looked straight into Huertas's eyes, "I know the sick person is very sick, but there is no worry, for I will give my blood so he will live."

Huertas returned to the barracks. At 6:30 AM, he received a telegram confirming the *Cartagena*'s arrival. To him, this proved what the conspirators were saying, that Colombian troops were coming to relieve him. At 8:00 AM, General Obarrio came to see him and asked about the validity of the rumors in Colón. Huertas's resolve was no longer in question.

"Yes, my friend," said he. "These generals have brought troops. They will arrive at 11:00, and if need be, I will meet them with bullets."

At approximately 10:30 AM, after his short meeting with Amador at the seawall, Huertas, as head of the Colombian regiment, marched down to the Panama railroad Pacific station to receive the Colombian generals arriving from Colón. Before leaving the barracks, he ordered a lieutenant to keep an eye on the Colombian gunboat *Padilla* mooring in the bay. Its commander, General Varón, had pledged to help the revolution and had been given the coal that he had requested from Shaler. Huertas told the lieutenant that if the gunboat tried to raise anchor and leave, he was to prevent it, with gunfire if necessary.

Huertas marched down Avenue A to the crowded, commercial Avenida Central. The streets were bustling with merchants and shoppers, but when they heard rumors about disturbances, store owners quickly closed their shops. As Huertas passed in front of the Hotel Italia, he saw Amador standing on a corner, and they nodded to each other.

Generals Tovar, Amaya, and Castro arrived at the Panama City railroad station at 11:30 that morning. If they had any lingering doubts about the real state of affairs in Panama, they were assuaged by the enthusiastic reception they received at the train station. A band played patriotic hymns and dozens of children and onlookers waved the Colombian flag. A large delegation of prominent citizens greeted them, including Governor Obaldiá; Vice Counsel Felix Ehrman, owner of the Hotel Central and of the Ehrman Bank; Dr. Amador's son; Obaldiá's secretary, Julio Fábrega; Demetrio Brid, president of the Panama City municipal council; and Eduardo de la Guardia, treasurer of the Department of Panama.

Huertas drew his troops up for review and the police force rendered military honors. The generals boarded Governor Obaldiá's elegant carriage and, preceded by Huertas's regiment and a long procession of officials, they drove to the Government Palace, where a banquet in their honor was held. Tovar later wrote that "there was nothing that did not show the greatest cordiality and give me the most complete assurance that peace reigned throughout the department."

Governor Obaldiá reported to General Tovar that the invasion of Nicaragua had no foundation and that all was perfectly quiet in Panama. At about 1:00 in the afternoon, Obaldiá ordered his carriage to take the generals to a hotel near the *Comandancia General* so they could take a siesta.

In the meantime, Amador was busy notifying the conspirators that the revolution had to take place that very evening, instead of on November 4 as originally planned. General Diaz and Duque would gather a crowd at Cathedral Plaza, where the manifesto and declaration of independence would be read. The fire brigade would distribute rifles and imprison any civilian or military person who opposed the independence movement.

News that a mass meeting was scheduled to be held in Cathedral Park at 6:00 PM spread rapidly throughout the city, even though few knew what was going to happen. A Colombian officer, General José Nuñez Roca, heard the rumors, and at 1:30 PM woke up the generals from their siesta. He told Tovar that his arrival had created great excitement and alarm throughout the city, and that a public demonstration was about to erupt. While Nuñez relayed the news, a messenger arrived with a note from Dr. José Angel Porras, a local Panamanian who was loyal to the Colombians, saying to Tovar, "Trust no one." Tovar immediately left the hotel, walked down to the *Comandancia General*, and assumed control.

Tovar demanded to know why his troops had yet not arrived from Colón. Aides told him that Shaler had refused to dispatch them unless Governor Obaldiá gave orders for their embarkation. Tovar sent two messengers to the governor's offices to order the troops' immediate dispatch. The aides returned with assurances from Governor Obaldiá that all the necessary orders had been given and that the troops would arrive that afternoon.

The generals then went to the Chiriquí barracks to inspect the armory. Huertas waited for them at the gate. Tovar carefully checked the quarters and the ammunitions and asked the troops about the situation in Panama. Everyone answered that everything was quiet, but Huertas reminded him that the troops had not received a penny in months. Tovar curtly answered, "They shouldn't worry of that any longer; a great convoy is coming."

Upon hearing this response, Huertas couldn't hide his anger. Tovar's statement confirmed his fears—Colombian troops had come to relieve him of his command and take him away from Panama.

General Tovar demanded to inspect the seawall. Built in 1675, the wide stone seawall housed b*ovedas*, or galleons, inside of which, for centuries, Spanish conquistadores stored the gold brought from the Inca empire before transporting it to the Atlantic on its way to Spain. On top of the wide seawall, dozens of cannons once protected the city from pirates and buccaneer attacks. In recent years, the seawall had been converted to a military outpost for the Colombian army. While on top of the wall, General Tovar inspected the ammunition and gave instructions as to how best to defend the position in case of attack. He saw the Colombian gunboats *Bogota* and *Padilla* mooring on the Bay of Panama and sent instructions to get them within striking distance of the city. Tovar's tour was interrupted by Obaldiá's secretary, Julio Fábrega, who brought the news that Colonel Shaler refused to dispatch the troops until the Colombians settled an outstanding debt with the railroad company.

Colonel Shaler had invented this excuse to placate Colonel Eliseo Torres, the ranking officer in charge of the Colombian troops, who was becoming impatient. He had called upon Shaler and the American consul in Colón several times demanding that his troops be transported to Panama City. At first, Shaler reiterated the promise made to Tovar to send the troops on the afternoon train. When afternoon arrived, Shaler told him that company regulations prohibited furnishing transportation unless paid in advance. Torres had no money, but he demanded credit for the Colombian government. Under the terms of the railroad concession, Shaler could not refuse credit to Colombia, but he got around it by stating that regulations required that all credit requests had to be approved by the governor of the province, Obaldiá.

When Tovar heard the news from Fábrega, he exploded and ordered him to tell Obaldiá that he was personally responsible for the money. Tovar demanded the troops be sent immediately. (Tovar had brought with him $65,272 in gold because the Bogota government had informed him that the departmental treasury had no money and the troops had not been paid in months.) Fábrega left, but Tovar no longer trusted Obaldiá. He sent two officers with Fábrega to make sure that Obaldiá obeyed his orders.

Huertas realized that he needed to take the generals away from the seawall. Stocked with ammunition, even a small group of men from this strategic spot could wreak havoc on Panama City. He asked the generals if they were hungry and suggested a walk to the *Comandancia* to have lunch.

At lunch, according to Huertas, Tovar cast a suspicious eye on Huertas. He asked the little general to accompany him to the hotel to have a glass of champagne. Huertas sensed that this was a trap and demurred, saying, "I am not in proper dress."

"It doesn't matter; we will wait," Tovar replied.

"I am tired and have to attend to some matters at the barracks. Tonight we will do it."

Huertas took his leave. Undetected, Amador had been hiding in the battalion's dressing room to make sure that Huertas truly supported the rebellion.

A short time later, the two officers came back with a personal note from Governor Obaldiá expressing "great surprise at the procedure of Colonel Shaler." The note assured Tovar that the department did not owe anything to the railroad company and that, in any case, the troops would be dispatched that afternoon. Still not satisfied, General Tovar sent General Amaya to the Government House to impress upon Obaldiá the necessity of transporting the troops immediately. Amaya offered Obaldiá money to pay the railroad company, but Obaldiá told him he didn't needed it, and again assured Amaya that the battalion would be in Panama City by 5:00 PM. General Amaya returned to the headquarters, but not without noting that the governor's mind was "not at ease."

When Amaya got back, he found a government secretary informing an alarmed Tovar that a revolution was about to break out and that he did not believe Governor Obaldiá could control it. Eduardo de la Guardia, treasurer of the province of Panama, arrived at that moment to salute the generals. Cornered and pressed for information by the Colombians, he confessed that a rebellion could begin at any moment and assume alarming proportions. De la Guardia broke down and revealed the secret plan: he said he did not believe Governor Obaldiá had given any orders to bring the troops over from Colón, that the governor would not give any orders to suppress the threatened uprising, and that Huertas's battalion and the departmental police had joined the revolution.

Tovar had had enough. He dispatched two officers to the railroad office to check if Obaldiá had sent the telegrams. On their way back, they were to warn Obaldiá that if the police did not maintain order, Tovar would personally head a Colombian battalion and execute anyone involved in a rebellion. After issuing swift orders to close up the headquarters, Tovar left with Generals Amaya and Castro for the Chiriquí barracks to confront Huertas and his men.

In the meantime, messengers throughout the city secretly carried word to friends and relatives to meet in Plaza Santa Ana at 5:00 PM. Arango, Carlos Mendoza, and Eusebio Morales, head of the Liberal party in Panama, met at Mendoza's house to make the final changes to the manifesto and declaration of independence. There, Arango learned that Arias and other conspirators had cowered and could no longer be counted on for support. Arango thus sent his son Belisario to reassure Amador that even if others deserted, he and his sons would go to the end, even if it cost them their lives. Belisario found Amador at the Chiriquí barracks talking to Duque about last-minute arrangements for the uprising.

They agreed that a skyrocket signal would be launched from the cathedral tower at 5:00 PM. The fire brigade would take over the armory and seize the Colombian armaments for distribution to the revolutionaries. Led by General Diaz and Duque, the revolutionaries would make their way to Cathedral Plaza and from there to the barracks. With the help of General Huertas and his men, they would imprison the Colombian generals and loyalist officers.

Duque immediately set out for the armory with his men, and Amador and Belisario went to update Prescott. On the way, they bumped into General Huertas who was racing to be at the barracks before the Colombian generals arrived. Amador told Huertas that the plan was to imprison the generals while at the barracks, but Huertas disagreed, claiming that this would lead to too much bloodshed. Also, he did not know if his troops would support the Panama cause or remain loyal to Colombia. Huertas had approached some of his men that morning, telling them, "The generals will try to kill me. Will you side with me? Will you fulfill my orders with sacrifice? Whoever of you will not accompany me, stand." No one stood, but no one vigorously pledged support either. Afterwards, Huertas approached one of his subordinates, the young and valiant Captain Marcos Salazar, and the two met under a palm tree in Cathedral Plaza. When Huertas asked Salazar to support the revolution, Salazar also remained silent.

Instead of the barracks, Huertas proposed to arrest the generals during a band concert in their honor at 8:oo that night. There, the generals would be separated from their troops, and the other officers could be imprisoned later. Amador agreed.

Belisario Arango run to tell everyone that the hour had changed and stopped on the house of Felix Ehrman on the way. Ehrman was the highest ranking U.S. authority in the Isthmus, as Consul Arthur Grudger was still with his family in North Carolina. Ehrman had been kept well-informed of the day's events. While he conferred with young Arango, Herman Grudger, son of the U.S. consul general, arrived with a cable from Acting Secretary of State Loomis.

> November 3, 1903
> Ehrman, Panama:
>   Uprising on Isthmus reported. Keep department promptly and fully informed.
>
> Loomis, Acting

In Washington, Loomis had learned of the uprising from William Curtis, Cromwell's partner, and from press dispatches.

Loomis wanted to verify the news in order to make his report to President Roosevelt, who was on his way back from Long Island where he was voting in the elections. (Loomis's cable would later cause much controversy as it indicated that the United States knew about the revolution prior to its execution.) Young Grudger went back to his father's office with Ehrman's response to Loomis, "No uprising yet. Reported will be tonight. Situation is critical."

Belisario Arango sought General Diaz and Duque to tell them that the hour for the revolution had been changed, but he found General Diaz in Plaza Santa Ana surrounded by a large crowd of revolutionaries. General Diaz would not hear of any delay. He and his brother, Pedro A. Diaz, marched to the Cathedral Plaza where the fire brigade was distributing weapons. Diaz then led the crowd to the Chiriquí barracks.

When the Colombian generals arrived at the Chiriquí barracks, they found Huertas and his officers sitting on benches on the seawall. General Tovar took Huertas aside and told him that a mob was making its way to the barracks. He ordered him to prepare a garrison to restore order and to place marksmen along the seawall. Tovar then told Huertas that he was under his command.

An embittered Huertas answered that people were restless, upset, and resentful of Colombia. Tovar again said, "Don't worry. A great convoy is coming," referring to the *Tiradores*. The statement made Huertas even more resentful.

By now, the little general knew for sure that the Colombians did not trust him. Earlier, he had learned that the generals had received an anonymous letter telling them to assassinate Huertas in order to stop the revolution. Also, during lunch, one of Huertas's subordinates overheard the generals saying that they were going to hang everyone involved in the revolution, including Huertas, who would be hanged "from the tallest tree in Cathedral Plaza."

A captain interrupted Tovar to report that an armed mob was arriving at the rear of the barracks. General Amaya went out to confirm the report and came back exclaiming: "We must act!"

According to Huertas, he turned his back on Amaya to face Tovar. As he turned, out of the corner of his eye, he saw Amaya signal Tovar to shoot him. Tovar nodded slightly. Pretending that he had not seen the signal, Huertas addressed Tovar. "General, let me go prepare artillery for what may happen."

Huertas told Tovar that he needed to change his coat and left for the guardhouse. When he entered it, he found Amador in hiding waiting for him. "Do it, do it now!" Amador yelled.

Huertas protested that he had been taken by surprise since this was not what they had agreed to do earlier. Amador insisted that it was now or never. Huertas looked out the window and saw the crowd arriving outside the barracks. He went to his room, got his sword and revolver, and called upon Captain Salazar. When Salazar arrived, Huertas told him that the time had come. Salazar looked at him but left without a word.

Salazar ordered the guards to affix bayonets to their rifles. They marched toward the generals, acting as though they were going out for patrol duty to restore order, as the Colombian generals had ordered. Salazar led the armed guards to the right of the seawall. As they neared the generals, the group of fourteen split into two rows, one of which passed in front and the other behind the generals. Suddenly, Salazar yelled. The soldiers lowered their bayonets and hemmed the generals in.

"Generals, you are my prisoners!" shouted Salazar.

"By whose orders?" replied Tovar.

"General Huertas!"

Tovar charged at one of the soldiers but the others thrust a dozen bayonets against his body. He stopped struggling and called on Salazar not to be a traitor. "Do you not recognize the Supreme Commander in Chief of the Colombian Army?" he bellowed.

Salazar laughed. "I don't think that I have yet had the pleasure of meeting him."

Tovar called on the sentinels and soldiers to defend Colombia and stop this treachery. He was met with jeers from the soldiers. Tovar then cried out, "Huertas, Huertas, where is Huertas?"

Huertas came out of the guardhouse and declared that he was in control. He ordered the sharpshooters and troops guarding the barracks to lower their weapons, but they were hesitant, talking amongst themselves. Huertas then raised his gun and fired a bullet in the air, and shouted, "I order you to rest arms now!"

Cautiously, the guards began to lower their guns. In the excitement, General Castro escaped. Huertas yelled, "Find that coward and bring him to me immediately!" A lieutenant arrived a few minutes later with Castro, who had taken refuge in a toilet stall. As Salazar led the prisoners away, Huertas beseeched the frightened troops to stand firm and remain loyal to the independence movement. He sent an emissary to tell the revolutionaries that he had taken the generals prisoner.

When the armed revolutionaries arrived at the barracks, General Diaz approached Huertas and said, "You have saved us; we owe you our freedom."

Huertas replied, "I owe it to you, your friends, and the people accompanying you."

The crowd outside the Chiriquí barracks swelled to several thousand. Led by the Diaz brothers, Francisco de la Ossa, young Belisario Arango, and a number of fire brigade volunteers, they led the generals and loyal Colombian officers to the jailhouse, walking over the seawall, across Cathedral Park, and up Avenida Central to the police headquarters. Thousands watched, leaning over the balconies, crowding the sidewalks, and cheering, "Viva el Istmo libre!" "Viva Huertas!" "Viva el Presidente Amador!" Those with rifles fired them into the air.

On Avenida Central, they ran into the two officers that General Tovar had dispatched to the telegraph office. As expected, they had not found any of the telegraphs that Governor Obaldiá had supposedly sent to Shaler. When the officers saw their generals in handcuffs, they took out their guns but were stormed by a mob, disarmed, and taken prisoner along with their commanders.

Amador was at Prescott's house when he learned that the Colombian generals had been arrested. Prescott sent a prearranged message to Meléndez in Colón: "The chicken soup is about to begin." It was 5:49 PM.

Amador went to Vice Counsel Felix Ehrman's to deliver the first official statement of the new Panamanian government, informing the United States government that "Panama had severed her bonds with Colombia and that a provisional government of three consuls would at once be formed." Ehrman dispatched a cable to Acting Secretary Loomis.

Panama, November 3, 1903

Uprising occurred to-night; no bloodshed. Army and Navy officials taken prisoner. Government will be organized to-night, consisting three consuls, also cabinet. Soldiers changed. Supposed same movement will be effected in Colón. Order prevails so far. Situation serious. Four hundred soldiers landed to-day, Barranquilla.

In the meantime, Arango, his son Agustín, and Antonio Valdéz went to the Government Palace to formally relieve Governor Obaldiá of his command. Since Obaldiá was also a conspirator, this was merely a formality, arranged for his protection. When they arrived, they found him sitting serenely in the drawing room waiting for them. After Obaldiá handed over the keys of the departmental treasury, Valdéz and young Arango told him he was now under arrest and took him to Amador's house, his prison. The conspirators even went so far as to summon a photographer to take a picture of a very "resigned prisoner" sitting comfortably in one of Mrs. Amador's wicker chairs.

A short time later, Arango, Amador, Boyd, and Arias met in the archbishop's house at the corner of Cathedral Plaza. Arias had joined the revolution in the last few hours after witnessing the other's resolve to fight. They agreed that Arango, Federico Boyd, and Tomás Arias should form the provisional government. Amador would be the republic's first minister in Washington, entrusted with the important task of negotiating the canal treaty. Carlos Arosemena and a young lawyer, Ricardo de la Espriella, would help Amador negotiate the treaty.

They drafted two letters to Colonel Shaler as superintendent of the Panama Railroad Company. The first informed him that independence had been declared, that "it will in the future be known as the Republic of the Isthmus" (they had no plans yet to liberate the rest of the country), and that it had sufficient military force to protect the railroad. (The letter echoed a draft that Shaler himself had written and sent to Prescott the night before.) The second letter instructed Shaler to deny transportation to the Colombian troops "because the junta of government would see itself obliged to use its armed forces to attack the trains bringing over soldiers at whatever point in the railroad line." The letters were signed "Your faithful and obedient servants José Agustín Arango, Federico Boyd and Tomás Arias, the Government de Facto."

After drafting the letters, the leaders went out to Cathedral Plaza, where a large crowd cheered them. Arango gave the letters to Prescott, who delivered them on horseback to the telegraph office.

The municipal council of Panama City met in Cathedral Park under the presidency of Demetrio Brid, the editor of the English edition of Duque's *Panama Star & Herald*. The council recognized as the de facto government a junta comprised of José Agustín Arango, Federico Boyd, and Tomás Arias. Brid then read the manifesto and the declaration of independence and fixed 2:00 PM the following day for the formal proclamation of independence. When the people learned that their new republic would be called "the Republic of the Isthmus," they vigorously protested and demanded that the name be changed to "the Republic of Panama." The junta agreed and signed the documents.

Though both the manifesto and the declaration of independence were allegedly written by Dr. Eusebio Morales, the manifesto bore the stamp of the draft prepared in New York first by Cromwell and later by Bunau-Varilla and referred to in the Amador-Lindo-Bunau-Varilla code. It said in part,

> The far-reaching act which the inhabitants of the Isthmus of Panama have just *executed by a spontaneous movement* is the inevitable consequence of a situation which had daily become graver. Long indeed is the recital of the grievance that the inhabitants of the Isthmus have suffered at the hands of their Colombian brothers [Emphasis added].

The language resembles the U.S. Declaration of Independence, stressing grievances suffered at the hands of the former sovereign as the cause for independence. However, in the case of Panama, independence was sought not only because Bogota was neglecting the province, but because Panamanians wanted a separate nation. Similarities with the U.S. version are evident throughout the Panamanian declaration.

> The Isthmus of Panama has been governed by the Republic of Colombia *with the narrow mindedness which was once shown to their colonies by European nations*; the Isthmian people and their territory were a source of fiscal resources and nothing more. The contracts and negotiations regarding the railroad and the Panama Canal and the national *taxes collected on the Isthmus have netted to Colombia tremendous sums* which we will not detail here, not wishing to appear in this recital as being animated by a mercenary spirit, which never has been nor is now our purpose [Emphasis added].

Of these large sums the Isthmus has not received the benefit of a single road, between its towns nor a public building, nor a single college; neither has it seen any interest displayed in advancing its industries, nor has the most infinitesimal part of those sums ever been applied toward its prosperity.

The passage quoted above is reminiscent of the Boston Tea Party, the famous tax protest over tariffs leading up to the American revolution. The reality is that taxes were not a significant burden imposed by the central government, which had been rendered ineffective by twenty years of civil war. Note also the reference to the "Isthmus" and the "Isthmian people," left over from the original plan worked out in New York. The declaration goes on to assail Colombia for rejecting the Hay-Herrán treaty in order to hurt Panama.

There were a few public men who expressed their adverse opinion on the ground that the Isthmus of Panama alone was to be favored by the opening of a canal under a treaty with the United States, and that the rest of Colombia would not receive direct benefits of any sort.

This oversimplification of an opponent's view is vintage Bunau-Varilla. In truth, Colombians rejected the treaty because they wanted more money, not to punish Panama. The declaration ends with a pledge to form a new republic where "finally, civilization and progress shall find perpetual stability" and where everyone possesses "a happy future devoid of troubles or dangers."

The junta asked its fellow councilmen if they were willing to pledge their allegiance to the new republic, even if it led to the ruin of their "interests and lives and even the future of their children." Before anyone had time to answer, a shell soared through the air. A loud explosion shook every wall. The bombardment by the Colombian gunboat *Bogota* had begun. That afternoon, its commander, Colonel Martinez, a loyal Colombian officer, had issued an ultimatum that if the Colombian generals were not released, he would commence fire. Panic spread through Cathedral Park as people ran for shelter. For nearly half an hour the firing continued, with five to six shells exploding.

Huertas's battalion on the Bovedas seawall counterattacked with its own shells. After about an hour, the *Bogota* finally withdrew and hid behind Pericos Island in the Bay of Panama. The only victims of the bombardment were a Chinese man sleeping in Salsipuedes street and a donkey in the slaughterhouse. (The shell that killed the Chinese man was recovered by Obarrio and later given as a gift and memento to Prescott.) The other Colombian gunboat, the *Padilla*, stayed out of the skirmish as promised by its commander, General Varón.

Fearing that the *Bogota* would make her way up the coast to the nearby city of Penonomé to pick up reinforcements, Huertas dispatched a messenger in a small canoe to warn the ship's commander that "this movement is supported to overflowing by the Americans."

After everything had quiet down again, at 10:00 PM, Council President Demetrio Brid cabled President Roosevelt:

> A SU EXCELENCIA EL PRESIDENTE
> DE LOS ESTADOS UNIDOS
>
> Washington:
>
> The Municipality of Panama is now holding a solemn session and joins in the movement of separation of the Isthmus of Panama from the rest of Colombia. It hopes for recognition of our cause by your Government.
>
> Demetrio H. Brid

The patriots awaited the expected recognition for hours. Well after midnight, Felix Ehrman was roused from bed by a cable from the State Department intended for Commander Hubbard. It read, "Make every effort to prevent Government troops at Colón from proceeding to Panama." The cable did not say a word about the requested recognition. Its curt and sober tone, lacking any congratulations or even a reaction to the day's events, implied to the Panamanians that as far as Washington was concerned, nothing had happened in Panama until all the Colombians troops had left Colón.

Ehrman awakened Shaler in Colón who promised to pass the message to Hubbard. Minutes later, the young Dick Prescott, under instructions from his brother Herbert, cut off all telephone communication between Colón and Panama City. The elder Prescott had intended to leave one wire running to his house and had given his younger brother a diagram showing which wire not to cut, but in his excitement Dick Prescott cut them all. Unable to communicate, the conspirators had no choice but to wait until morning to deal with the menacing Colombian troops in Colón.

Don Seitz, Joseph Pulitzer, and Joseph Pulitzer Jr. on the *Liberty* (from *Joseph Pulitzer, His Life and Letters*)

"Unpleasant." Cromwell, Morgan, and Taft worried about scattered evidence. (from *The Untold Story of Panama*)

William Nelson Cromwell (Culver Pictures)

Philippe Bunau-Varilla (Culver Pictures)

Stamp used as proof of active volcanoes in Nicaragua (from *Panama: The Creation, Destruction, and Resurrection*)

William Nelson Cromwell at the Chelsea Piers (Bettman/Corbis)

Theodore Roosevelt and Senator Mark Hanna in Buffalo
(Culver Pictures)

Theodore Roosevelt in action (Culver Pictures)

Senator John Tyler Morgan
(Library of Congress)

The News Reaches Bogota, from the *New
York Herald* (Culver Pictures)

J.P. Morgan (Corbis)

J.P. Morgan holding the globe
(Corbis)

John Hay (Culver Pictures)

Now Watch the Dirt Fly, from the *Globe*
(Culver Pictures)

Bunau-Varilla (to the left) and Secretary Hay (to the right) in
Hay's office moments before signing the Hay-Bunau-Varilla
Treaty (from *Panama: The Creation, Destruction, and
Resurrection*)

Panama City

Legend

1. Chiriquí barracks
2. Bovedas
3. Cathedral Plaza
4. Cathedral
5. Government House
6. French Panama Canal Co.
7. Hotel Central

8. Ehrman Bank
9. Archbishop Palace
10. Amador House
11. To Avenida Central
12. Avenida B
13. Avenida A

Plaza Cathedral, Panama City (Culver Pictures)

View of Las Bovedas and Chiriquí barracks (Culver Pictures)

Manuel Amador Guerrero (from *Panama: The Creation, Destruction, and Resurrection*)

Esteban Huertas
between followers
(Conte Porras
collection)

Founding fathers of Panama. Seated (left to right): José Agustín Arango,
Dr. Manuel Amador Guerrero, and Federico Boyd. Standing (left to
right): Nicanor de Obarrio, Carlos C. Arosemena, Manuel Espinosa,
Tomás Arias, and Ricardo Arias (Conte Porras collection)

The *Nashville* in the Bay of Límon (Conte Porras collection)

Streets of Colón (Earl Harding collection)

Colombian soldiers marching in Panama (Conte Porras collection)

French Panama Canal bonds sought by the Wall Street speculators. (from
Los Títulos Valores del Canal Frances, Bolsa de valores de Panama)

8

Birthday of Bribery

Bʏ ᴅᴀʏʙʀᴇᴀᴋ ᴏɴ Nᴏᴠᴇᴍʙᴇʀ 4, Colonel Torres and his five hundred *Tiradores* had seized the dock demanding to be transported to Panama City and were ready to forcibly take over the railroad trains. If the Colombians got to Panama City with their five hundred expert riflemen, three Colombian generals, at least two ships in each ocean that could pick up reinforcements within a day, they could easily defeat the poorly armed Panamanian fire brigade.

The revolutionaries in Panama City divided their forces into two regiments, the "First Isthmian" made up of Colombian soldiers who had joined the revolution, and the "Second Isthmian," members of the fire brigade and volunteers. The regiments numbered about twelve hundred men. However, if the secretary of the navy's instructions were to be followed, Shaler had to deny them access to the railroad track. Panamanians decided to send H.L. Jeffries, a short, stocky American mercenary, who had fought in revolutions from Mexico to Peru and boasted the rank of general of the Colombian army, to lead a battalion of seventy men to cross the Isthmus by foot through the dangerous jungles of the River Chagres.

The junta cabled Porfirio Meléndez and instructed him to inform Colonel Torres "that the people as a whole approve the movement; Generals Tovar and Amaya are prisoners, as well as all their aides, and resistance is entirely useless; that desirous of avoiding bloodshed, the junta of Government offers to provide rations and will give them passage for the return to Barranquilla." They also told Meléndez to offer Torres a bribe if he would leave.

Ironically, in Bogota, the Colombian government reposed peacefully, faithful that the United States was going to uphold Colombian sovereignty on the Isthmus under the terms of the 1846 treaty. The Colombian foreign office thus cabled Herrán on November 2: "Congress has adjourned without legislating about the canal. Reiterate to the Secretary of State declarations in telegram of September 8. Advise him to maintain order on the Isthmus and safety of traffic."

After receiving the cable from the junta, Meléndez went to the railroad station to relay the instructions to Colonel Shaler. Shaler feared Torres would become violent, but Meléndez insisted on talking to him. Meléndez went over to the dock, engaged Torres in casual conversation, and enjoined him to have a drink at Astor House away from his troops. Meléndez broke the news: the generals had been taken prisoner; the United States supported the independence of Panama; and American warships in the harbor had been sent by Washington. Meléndez offered him money if he would leave with his troops. At first, an agitated Torres refused to believe him, but when Meléndez convinced him, the colonel exploded and swore that he would kill every American in Colón unless the Colombian generals were released immediately.

Colonel Torres went back to the wharf to prepare his troops, but Shaler intercepted him with a letter from Hubbard.

TO THE GENERAL OFFICER COMMANDING
THE TROOPS, COLON.

Sir:

   The condition of affairs at Panama, I am advised, is such that a movement of the Colombian troops now at Colón to that neighborhood must bring about a conflict and *threaten that free and uninterrupted transit of the Isthmus which the Government of the United States is pledged to maintain.* I have therefore the honor to notify you that I have directed the superintendent of the Panama Railroad at Colón that he must not transport on his line troops either of the opposite party [Emphasis added].

Torres ranted and raved again and rushed off to see the prefect, General Cuadras. He ordered Cuadras to tell the American consul, Oscar Malmros, that he would burn down Colón and kill every American if the revolutionaries did not release the generals. Cuadras tried to calm Torres, but he persisted, threatening to take over the railroad station also. Cuadras advised Torres to take the money offered by Meléndez and return with his men to Barranquilla, but Torres would have none of it and insisted once again that the prefect carry his message to the American consul.

When Malmros heard about Torres's threat, he and his vice consul ran to the railroad station to confer with Shaler. They decided to call Commander Hubbard ashore by raising the American flag over the flagpole. Within minutes, Hubbard had disembarked.

The four of them took Torres's potential arson very seriously. At that time Colón was a shantytown of wooden houses that would burn like a dry forest if set ablaze. The Americans had seen this happen in 1885, when a canal laborer, Pedro Prestan, started an uprising to protest the Compagnie Universelle's inhumane treatment of black West Indian workers. While a fugitive, Prestan threatened to burn down the city of Colón unless conditions improved, but the American officers disregarded the danger, thinking that he was bluffing. Prestan followed through, and the city burned to the ground in a matter of hours, killing many Colón natives and several foreigners, including Americans. If Torres carried out his threat, the consequences would be unthinkable. The United States would be accused of instigating a fire that would likely lead to the deaths of hundreds of people, American citizens among them.

Hubbard thus ordered the evacuation of all U.S. citizens from Colón. The men were told to take refuge in the shed of the Panama Railroad Company, a stone building that could be transformed into a barracks, while the women and children went on board the German steamer *Marcomia* and the Panama Railroad steamship *City of Washington*, both of which were ready to sail if necessary. Hubbard re-boarded the *Nashville* and ordered the landing of "such body of men, with extra arms for arming the citizens as the complement of the ship would permit."

At 1:30 PM, forty-two marines docked at the wharf and immediately fortified the railroad station. When Torres saw the Americans, he ordered his troops to surround the marines and the station. The situation became very tense. Both sides loaded their rifles, ready for the worst. One false move, one scream, one alarm, and fifty years of pleasant American-Colombian relations could be over. With more than ten times the men, the *Tiradores* would easily massacre the Americans. On board the *Nashville*, Hubbard sent a cable to the Department of the Navy asking for reinforcements. He knew, however, that even if reinforcements were sent, they would not reach the Isthmus for days. He ordered the *Nashville* to get closer to the jetty and to aim its cannons at the Colombian troops.

With the situation at a standstill, Hubbard received a cable from Assistant Secretary Darling reporting that a gunboat was shelling Panama City. He instructed Hubbard to "send immediately battery 3-inch field gun and 6-pounder with a force of men to Panama to compel cessation of bombardment" (the bombardment had actually occurred the night before, but Hubbard had no way of knowing whether it had started again). With the Colombians surrounding the American troops, Hubbard could not obey the orders. He replied immediately, "I have landed force to protect the lives and property of American citizens against threats Colombian soldiery. I am protecting water front with ship. I cannot possibly send to Panama until things are settled at Colón."

The *Nashville* drew closer and trained its guns on the *Cartagena*. When the *Cartagena*'s captain saw the menacing American warship approaching, he decided that discretion was the better part of valor and set off full-steam for Barranquilla, leaving his troops behind. Hubbard made no effort to detain the *Cartagena* because of the conflict on shore.

At the railroad station, the Colombian troops did not move. "For about one and a half hours their attitude was most threatening," Hubbard recalled later, "it being seemingly their purpose to provoke an attack. Happily, our men were cool and steady and, while the tension was very great, no shot was fired."

At around 3:15 PM, Torres finally called on Shaler. He told him that he did not want any violence, that he was well-disposed toward Americans and that they had misunderstood his intentions: all he wanted was his generals' release. However, if General Tovar ordered him to leave for Barranquilla, he would obey. He thus proposed sending the sheriff of Colón over to Panama City to get instructions from Tovar.

Shaler and Meléndez agreed to Torres's request on the condition that one of Meléndez's men go along with the sheriff. Shaler requisitioned a special train to take the emissaries, but when it was ready to depart, Meléndez's man did not show up. Torres proposed sending one of his own lieutenants to escort the sheriff; for lack of a better alternative, Meléndez reluctantly agreed, and the envoys left for Panama City.

Soon thereafter, several American officers of the Panama Railroad Company arrived on a freight train offering their services. Shaler armed them with rifles and organized them into a company, "Black's Legion," to protect the railroad station. When Torres saw the Americans arming themselves and fortifying the station, he approached Commander Hubbard with a proposition: if Hubbard returned the American marines to the *Nashville*, Torres would take the Colombian troops to Monkey Hill, an outpost outside of Colón. The local police would safeguard the city until the sheriff returned from Panama City. After consulting Shaler and Malmros, Hubbard agreed. Colonel Torres then withdrew to Monkey Hill, outside of Colón, where he remained until the following morning.

Immediate disaster had been averted, but it was a temporary reprieve. The only real way out of the impasse was to convince General Tovar to order Torres to go back to Barranquilla with the troops. Tovar's command, thus, became the wild card that would make the difference between war and peace.

Throughout the day in Panama City, Amador scrambled to get the money to pay off the Colombian officers who had assisted the revolution. At daybreak, General Varón sailed the *Padilla* threateningly close to the seawall, making people fear that he was about to attack, but to their relief, he raised the new Panamanian flag. Varón came to collect the $35,000 pesos he had been promised for keeping the *Padilla* quiet while the *Bogota* bombarded the city.

The provincial treasury did not have enough money to pay him. During the night, $22,000 pesos in silver coins were taken out on a mule-drawn market cart to pay off soldiers, leaving the treasury vaults empty except for legal documents (i.e., vouchers, promissory notes, and advances on salary). Amador sent a cable to Bunau-Varilla that morning asking for the 100,000 dollars that he had promised in New York, but had received no response. Amador thus sought a temporary loan from Felix Ehrman. During the early hours of November 4, eight boxes of Colombian silver pesos were taken out of the Ehrman Bank and carried to the Government House.

With the money secured, Amador went to the Chiriquí barracks to meet the Colombian battalion at around 8:00 AM. Huertas had his men gathered and was trying to hearten them to stand firmly by the revolution, but they were frightened. They were mostly teenage boys, some as young as ten years old (Huertas was a veteran who had spent twenty-two of his thirty years in the military). They carried obsolete Springfield rifles, were uneducated and illiterate, and knew nothing of the art of war. "The soldiers are barefooted as is the rule in the ranks," wrote one reporter, "and the only resemblance to uniform was a worn and soiled cap." Amador helped Huertas encourage his men.

> Boys, at last we have carried through our splendid work. The world is astounded at our heroism. Yesterday we were but slaves of Colombia; to-day we are free. Have no fears. Here we have the proof [holding up a sheet of paper with the American coat of arms] that our agent in the United States, Señor Bunau-Varilla, gave us. Panama is free! . . . Free sons of Panama, I salute you. Long live the Republic of Panama! Long live President Roosevelt! Long live the American Government!

Amador then sent a paymaster to the Government House to bring boxes full of coins. Huertas then addressed his men.

> Soldiers, owing to the exertion of Dr. Amador and myself, we got the United States to recompense your efforts. The money which is denied us by the Government of Bogota we have here.

[This was a reference to the fact Colombia owed each soldier about fifty dollars in back salary.]

> We have money. We are free. The [American] cruisers which are here remove all our fears. Colombia may battle with the weak, but

she holds her peace in the presence of the United States. . . . The *Tiradores* battalion, which is in Colón with ammunition, cannot withstand us. We are more numerous and have more arms. The railroad is at our orders and the port of Colón is well guarded by the cruisers of the Americans, who, in case of a fight, will land men to back us up. Do not fear. We are free and powerful. Colombia is dead. Long live independent Panama. Long live Dr. Amador. Long live the American Government!

Each soldier received fifty dollars in gold. After Amador paid them, he left to join the second session of the municipal council that started at 2:00 o'clock.

The council meeting opened with prominent Panamanians castigating the Colombian government. Demetrio Brid read the new declaration of independence again, the council recognized the junta's authority, appointed a cabinet, and drafted another cable asking the United States for recognition of the new government. It also requested recognition from the consuls of England, France, Germany, the Netherlands, Italy, and every Latin American country. Most of these countries had named local prominent citizens as their representatives in Panama, and, as it turned out, every consul member, save three, was an active revolutionary, including Felix Ehrman; J. A. Arango, consul of Guatemala; Federico Boyd, consul of Spain; J. G. Duque, consul of Cuba; Pedro Arias, consul of Brazil; and Jeromino de la Ossa, consul of Chile and Honduras. Earlier, they had signed a supposedly unbiased petition pleading the Colombian generals "to leave in order to avoid a bloodshed."

Amador was called away from the meeting by an urgent message from Prescott. He told Amador of Colonel Torres' latest threats to take the rolling stock by force. Amador decided to send an armed force to Colón to assist Shaler. Prescott went to the station to tell Shaler, who warned him that State Department and Department of the Navy orders prohibited transporting Panamanian troops. Shaler told him that recently Torres had expressed an interest in negotiating, and that he had sent messengers to get instructions from Tovar. Prescott went back to tell Amador, and the doctor decided to make a pitch to Tovar before the emissaries arrived.

The Colombian generals had been confined in a windowless basement cell in the police headquarters near Avenida Central. Around 5:00 PM, Amador called on General Amaya, his friend of many years. Amaya later recalled Amador's plea:

> You must understand that those who started this movement are not insane. The United States has fully entered into this movement, and the Panamanians are not alone, as in every event they will back up our actions. Not another Colombian soldier will ever disembark again on any of the coasts of the Isthmus, and our independence is guaranteed by that colossus.

Amaya refused to cooperate. Amador then sent for General Tovar, with whom he was even more explicit about the U.S. support. He told Tovar that the United States had sent $250,000 to the Panamanian government to meet its first expenses (this was a lie; Amador was probably trying to bribe the general). He asked Tovar to order re-embarkation of the Colombian troops to avoid bloodshed and warned him that several American warships had arrived to guarantee the success of the revolution. Tovar refused to be swayed. He later recalled,

> I answered Señor Amador, that I would take no account of what he had just told me, as my duty and the duty of the army I commanded was sufficiently clear; and that in consequence no human force could drag me from the order that he desired.

While Amador was conferring with Tovar, the emissaries from Colón arrived. They gave Tovar the note from Torres requesting instructions, along with a letter signed by ten distinguished native and foreign ladies of Colón pleading Tovar to avoid bloodshed and calamity by ordering his troops to leave. Amador urged Tovar to give the withdrawal order, but Tovar again refused. He would not tell Torres to evacuate, or not to evacuate, for that matter. Torres, he said, knew what to do. "I was satisfied with [Torres's] conduct and confident that he would always do his duty, and that in consequence I had no doubts as to the determination he would make."

When the junta learned of Tovar's refusal to cooperate, Dr. Federico Boyd and Tomás Arias went to see him. Boyd and Tovar got into a bitter argument and Boyd stormed out. Arias continued to plead in vain, until he left to join a large crowd honoring Huertas.

More than a thousand people gathered at the Chiriquí barracks. They sat the little general on a chair, raised him up onto the shoulders of several men, and paraded him through the main streets of the city. Walking alongside him were Felix Ehrman, who was carrying an American flag, and Amador, carrying the new Panamanian flag. A large crowd waving American flags followed, but a sudden downpour put an end to the parade. Huertas, Amador, Ehrman, the junta, and about fifty other people retired to the Hotel Central, where Huertas was soaked with dozens of bottles of champagne. This was the last activity of November 4.

At sunrise on November 5, Colonel Torres brought his troops down from Monkey Hill and planted them on the outskirts of Colón. When Commander Hubbard found out, he immediately ordered his troops to disembark and surround the railroad station. American and British women and children again were told to board the *Marcomia* and the *City of Washington*.

Hubbard and Malmros protested to Torres that he was breaching the deal reached a day earlier and strongly advised him to withdraw to Monkey Hill in order to avoid bloodshed. Torres replied that the mosquitoes had forced them down from Monkey Hill (this might have seemed a feeble excuse to Hubbard, but mosquitoes were a genuine menace). Torres reiterated his respect for Americans, but warned that he intended to occupy Colón unless General Tovar sent instructions to the contrary.

A little before noon, the emissaries returned from Panama City. Torres and his troops marched to the railroad station to await the expected orders. When the emissaries told him that Tovar had refused to give any orders, he didn't believe them and began to yell that he was going to burn Colón unless the Colombian generals were brought over immediately. Hubbard again put his troops on high alert, but the Colombians did not assume the threatening posture of the previous day.

Porfirio Meléndez approached Torres. He again offered a sub-stantial bribe plus the expenses of the trip if Torres would leave (the amount increased by the hour). While the negotiations continued, the steamship *Jennings* arrived in the Bay of Limón carrying General Pompilio Gutierrez, one of Colombia's most distinguished soldiers, who was on a special mission to Panama.

Meléndez sent one of his men on board to tell Gutierrez that the independence of Panama had been established and that an over-whelming American force now protected the new republic. Gutier-rez became so thoroughly convinced of the futility of any effort on his part that he decided to stay on board. The emissary, however, con-vinced him to disembark to talk to Torres. They met at the offices of the Royal Mail Steam Packet Co., a British company. Torres asked his senior officer to take command of the *Tiradores* regiment, but Gutierrez refused. He advised Torres to return to Barranquilla, but like Tovar, he would not give him any orders. Gutierrez re-boarded the *Jennings* and "went away convinced of the uselessness of making any effort."

With neither Tovar nor Gutierrez assuming command, the deci-sion now rested entirely on Tores's shoulders. He gave an ultimatum to bring over the Colombian generals from Panama City, or he would take Colón by force. Shaler, Malmros, and Hubbard decided that the best way to avoid an armed confrontation was to bring the gen-erals to Colón. Once there, they would try to convince them all to leave. They cabled Prescott and told him to send the generals as soon as possible.

In Panama City, just before dusk, a large group of armed soldiers escorted Generals Tovar, Amaya, Castro, and the other Colombian prisoners from the police headquarters to the railroad station, where they mounted a car. However, Panamanian troops were not allowed in the trains to guard the prisoners. Prescott thus asked Tovar to give his word that he would go to Colón as a voluntary prisoner, that he would not try to escape, and that he would depart for Colombia imme-diately. Tovar summarily refused to cooperate and insisted on going to Colón as a prisoner or returning to the police barracks. An argu-ment between Prescott and Tovar ensued; Tovar accused Prescott and the United States of treachery against Colombia, a friendly nation. Prescott telephoned Colonel Shaler, who put Hubbard on the line. Hubbard told Prescott to send the generals with a "civilian escort."

Prescott organized a garrison of young Panamanians dressed in civilian clothes but armed to the teeth and put them on a train in front of the generals. Just as they were departing, Shaler called again, this time with great excitement in his voice. He and Porfirio Meléndez had just succeeded in persuading Torres to leave for a price of $8,000 dollars. To hasten his departure, Shaler said he would pay Torres the money using the Panama Railroad Company's funds, provided that the junta would reimburse the company immediately.

Prescott took a carriage to Cathedral Plaza where he found Amador, Boyd, and Arango, and gave them the good news. Amador told him that the treasury did not have any money to pay back the railroad company, but promised he would try to borrow it from a local bank. Prescott rushed back to the station, telephoned Shaler, and told him that he had the money in his possession. Shaler informed him that the Colombian troops had already begun to board the *Orinoco*, a steamer owned by the Royal Mail Steam Packet Co.

Torres's payment consumed all of the money in the Panama Railroad Company's safe and did not leave enough even for the troops' passage, another one thousand pounds sterling. The agent of the *Orinoco* approached Shaler, "Now, how about paying for all these people we are taking back?"

Shaler answered, "We have not got any money, but you take them over and it will be all right."

"That cannot be done; it is against company regulations."

Shaler told him that he would personally vouch for the money. The agent, however, required a second person, so Commander Hubbard volunteered—the two American officers became guarantors of the Panamanian junta.

The *Orinoco* took away 2 commanders, 21 officers, 438 soldiers, and 13 civilians. Just before it sailed, two cases of champagne were sent on board for Torres, compliments of Colonel Shaler. Meléndez gave Torres half of his payment in two sacks of $20 dollars gold pieces and handed the rest to the purser of the *Orinoco*, with instructions to give it to Torres when they were far out to sea. Meléndez then signed a draft for $8,000 on behalf of the Panamanian junta payable to the Panama Railroad Company.

While the Colombian troops were re-embarking, the U.S.S. *Dixie* arrived in the Bay of Limón. Hubbard requested the landing of troops, and forty marines disembarked immediately in nineteen boats. When the captain of the *Orinoco* saw the new American warship, he raised anchor and left the bay at full steam. Hubbard then yelled over the megaphone: "Situation under control!"

The *Dixie* anchored at 7:05 PM. Commander Hubbard boarded the ship to report to his superior, Commander F.H. Delano, who ordered the withdrawal of the *Nashville*'s troops and replaced them with men from the *Dixie*. Delano then relieved Hubbard of his command.

Out at sea, Torres got drunk on champagne and boasted to his men, who partook of humbler spirits, that he had been given $8,000 dollars and that he was going to Jamaica with it. His men, irritated by his boasting, tossed him overboard and divided the cash among themselves.

That night, a crowd gathered at the house of Porfirio Meléndez to celebrate the independence of Panama. They nailed a Panamanian flag to a pole outside the house. The following day, November 6, the Republic of Panama was formally proclaimed in Colón. Meléndez, Shaler, a number of officers from the *Dixie* and the *Nashville*, leading merchants, foreign consuls, together with a large crowd gathered at the prefecture. The vice president of the municipal council read a resolution adhering the district of Colón to the Republic of Panama. Meléndez made a few short remarks and read the manifesto and the declaration of independence. He then called on Major William Murray Black, from the U.S. army, to run the new Panamanian flag up the flagpole. As the flag flung its folds to the breeze, the crowd cheered: "Viva la Republica!" "Vivan los Americanos!" (Years later, Major Black would be severely criticized in the Senate for the act that he performed.)

Tovar and the other generals stayed in the new republic until November 12, when they were freed on the condition that they leave immediately. They returned to Colombia on the Spanish steamer *Leon XIII*.

As forecasted by Cromwell's press agent Roger Farnham in midsummer, the revolution had escaped conspicuous publicity thanks to competition from the election news. On November 4, the *New York Herald* dedicated almost its entire front page to the election of Democratic candidate George B. McClellan as mayor of New York city. Buried in a lower corner was a short dispatch from the *Herald*'s Isthmian correspondent, Samuel Boyd, brother of conspirator Federico Boyd.

> Cable, Panama, Colombia, via Galveston, Texas. Panama taken by Rebels, Independence declared. Successful Revolution Coup Effected, War Ships at the Port are Seized and Colombian Officials are Prisoners.

During the next few days, several U.S. warships arrived on both sides of the Isthmus to prevent a Colombian invasion of Panama. Colombia was seething with war spirit, and in every town men volunteered to subdue the rebellious province. To avoid such an attack, President Roosevelt himself took control and put a military force in Panama to prevent Colombians from landing on the Isthmus. Army officers disguised as lumberjacks and New York capitalists penetrated the Darien jungle on the eastern end of the republic, exploring and mapping rivers and trails where Colombians could hide. On the Atlantic coast, the navy had several run-ins with the Cunas Indians, who were loyal to Colombia. About five hundred Colombian troops attempted to cut through the Darien jungle, but after a few weeks of battling infernal heat, snakes, mosquitoes, and diseases, they relented and turned back.

By mid-November, Teddy Roosevelt had firm control over the Isthmus. The Stars and Stripes were everywhere. In fact, on November 7, the U.S.S. *Boston* docked in the Bay of Panama. When Vice Consul Ehrman went aboard, a firing of the guns saluted him. Huertas thought this was in his honor and responded with a gun salute from the seawall. The *Padilla*, still mooring in the bay of Panama, raised the U.S. flag.

Despite the departure of the Colombian troops and the independence celebrations, the United States had inexplicably failed to grant its official recognition to the new government. With Colombians still posing a threat, the survival of the small republic depended on America's continuous protection. The Panamanians thus turned to Bunau-Varilla to break Washington's exasperating silence.

9

Treachery

 $\mathbb{B}$ UNAU-VARILLA WAS JUST AS EAGER as the Panamanians to gain Washington's recognition of the new republic and formalize his appointment as foreign minister of Panama. On November 3, he went to the State Department on a semi-official visit and spoke to Loomis. "I come," he said, "no longer as a friend, but as the — for the moment semi-official, tomorrow official — delegate of the Republic which was born yesterday at Panama."

He asked Loomis for the "good-will," that is, the recognition, of the new republic, promising that Panama would sign the canal treaty immediately, but Loomis replied that so long as Colombian troops remained in Panama, the United States could not grant formal recognition to the provisional government.

Bunau-Varilla returned to New York on the evening of the fourth. Joshua Lindo visited him at his suite in the Waldorf Astoria with an encrypted cable from Amador saying "100,000 pesos is needed immediately" to pay the Colombian troops.

The cable did not mention the diplomatic appointment that Bunau-Varilla had requested from Amador during their last meeting in late October. Bunau-Varilla complained about it to Lindo, who allegedly replied, "You are perfectly right . . . they have said nothing to you as to your diplomatic mission. You are not bound to do anything."

After reflecting for a few minutes, Bunau-Varilla later claimed to have answered, "This is true, but they may have an urgent need of money." He gave Lindo an order to withdraw 50,000 pesos, or $25,000 dollars, of the $100,000 he had received from Credit Lyonnais in the Heidelbach Bank. Lindo immediately instructed his bank to issue bills of exchange to the Isaac Brandon & Bros. bank in Panama to meet the immediate needs of the revolutionaries for bribing the Colombian soldiers.

The following day, November 5, at 9:30 in the morning, Bunau-Varilla received another cable from Amador asking for help in obtaining the U.S. recognition and also pressing him for more money. Bunau-Varilla responded by urging the Panamanians to expel the Colombian troops in Colón and refusing to send more money until he got the promised appointment. At 11:00 that night, an ecstatic Lindo showed up at the Waldorf Astoria with yet another telegram: "The hostile troops are re-embarking. Demand from Jones (Bunau-Varilla) $100,000."

With the departure of the Colombian troops from Colón, all the American government's conditions for recognizing the new government had been met, but Bunau-Varilla was worried that the cable did not mention his appointment. "The silence of Amador as to my diplomatic powers seemed to me to be very suspicious," Bunau-Varilla later recounted with scorn. "He seemed to have entirely forgotten all about it and to have remembered only my promise to furnish the new Republic with funds."

The Panamanian junta had decided not to grant Bunau-Varilla the appointment he sought. Amador was slated to sign the treaty, but they did not want to tell Bunau-Varilla in order to procure his continuing help with the U.S. government. The conspirators erroneously believed that Bunau-Varilla was the key to recognition. They sent two messages to his hotel in Washington D.C. on November 4 and 5, appointing him "Confidential Agent near the Government of Washington to *negotiate the recognition* of the Republic and contract a loan" [Emphasis added]. However, when the cables arrived, Bunau-Varilla had already left for New York, and the New Willard Hotel did not forward the cables as he had instructed. He never saw them, but the conspirators thought that he did not respond because he was angry, and they also thought that he was responsible for the lack of recognition from Washington. In reality, Bunau-Varilla had nothing to do with the decision in Washington. Roosevelt and Hay had already decided to recognize the new republic once the Colombian troops had left Colón. While the troops occupied the city, they could not claim that the provisional government was the de facto government of the Isthmus. Cromwell was also pressing for recognition thorough his partner, William Curtis, who met with Roosevelt several times that week.

Bunau-Varilla, however, let the Panamanians believe that he was the key to recognition. On the morning of the sixth, he sent an angry cable to Amador, in which he made it seem that recognition depended on his appointment as foreign minister. He issued a warning: "I decline any responsibility in the future, if Government of the Republic prefers any other solution." Two hours later, he received another cable from the junta begging him to "press the recognition" as soon as possible.

Coincidentally, only a few hours after the Panamanians cabled Bunau-Varilla, at exactly 12:51 PM, Secretary Hay sent the following communiqué to Minister Beaupré in Bogota and to Vice Counsel Felix Ehrman in Panama:

> The people of Panama having by an apparently unanimous movement dissolved their political connections with the Republic of Colombia and resumed their independence, and having adopted a government of their own, republican in form with which *the Government of the United States has entered into relations*, the President of the United States, in accordance with the ties of friendship which have so long and so happily existed between the respective nations, most earnestly commends to the Governments of Colombia and Panama the peaceful and equitable settlement of all questions at issue between them. *He holds that he is bound not merely by treaty obligation, but by the interest of civilization, to see that the peaceful traffic of the world across the Isthmus of Panama shall not longer be disturbed by constant succession of unnecessary and wasteful civil wars* [Emphasis added].

The speed of this official recognition, only three days after the revolution, was unprecedented. When the news reached Bogota, violent crowds erupted crying "Down with Marroquín." "Very great excitement," reported Beaupré. "Mass meeting denounced him; called for a change of government. Hundreds gathered at the palace, their orator, a prominent national general, called for his resignation. Troops dispersed gatherings, wounding several. Martial law imposed. Residence of Marroquín attacked with stones."

In Panama, the news caused celebration. To the revolutionaries, Bunau-Varilla was responsible because the cable from Hay had been received only hours after they had sent the telegram asking Bunau-Varilla to intervene on their behalf. Unaware that he had nothing to do with the recognition, at 6:45 in the evening, the Panamanians sent to him the following fateful cablegram:

> The Junta of Provisional Government of Republic of Panama appoints you Envoy Extraordinary and Minister Plenipotentiary near the Government of the United States of America *with full powers for political and financial negotiations* [Emphasis added].

Bunau-Varilla now had reasons to celebrate. He and Lindo went down to a cafe in the Waldorf Astoria, where, according to Bunau-Varilla, Lindo "forced me in conformity with American customs, to share with him a bottle of champagne, in order to celebrate the new Republic." Before going to sleep that night, he sent a flowery cable to Panama accepting the "high mission" that was "entrusted to me." The new republic's minister of foreign affairs, Ricardo de la Espriella, immediately replied:

> The Government of Panama recognizes the importance and the efficacy of the services of Your Excellency, whose name will occupy a preeminent place on the first page of our history.

They had no idea that by trusting him as they did, the "first page" of Panama's history would be a very disadvantageous treaty.

Between the evening of November 6, when Bunau-Varilla received his appointment, and November 18, the Panama Canal treaty was negotiated and rushed to signature, even before the Panamanian delegation arrived in Washington. What transpired in those eleven days would incite a whirlwind of controversy and remain the thorniest issue in the relations between the United States and Panama throughout the twentieth century.

As soon as Bunau-Varilla received his appointment, he cabled Secretary John Hay to announce that "the Republic of Panama has been pleased to designate me as its Envoy Extraordinary and Minister Plenipotentiary near the Government of the United States.," He praised the administration for "spreading her protecting wings over the territory of *our* Republic" [Emphasis added]. He headed for Washington the following day, and on Sunday, November 8, he installed himself at the New Willard, ready to embark on the most important chapter of the "Great Adventure."

Bunau-Varilla called on Secretary Hay, who invited him to lunch the next day. For the rest of the day, he occupied himself writing letters to the press and senators asking for support of "my government." The lunch was held at Hay's house in Lafayette Square, rather than at the State Department because the United States had not recognized Panama officially until the president had met the foreign minister. Bunau-Varilla implored Hay to arrange the meeting with T.R. as soon as possible. They agreed it would be held at 9:30 in the morning of Friday, November 13. Bunau-Varilla would represent Panama.

Hay seemed to be in agreement, but he wanted Bunau-Varilla to clarify a report published in that morning's newspaper, stating that a special commission of Panamanians led by Amador was coming to Washington to negotiate the canal treaty. Bunau-Varilla was shocked by the news. He interpreted this action, coupled with the Panamanians' earlier refusal to give him the appointment, as a blatant maneuver to oust him. He concluded, "Amador was a party to it. I knew his childish desire to sign the Treaty. He had evidently refused for that reason to assume the office of President of the Provisional Government, which belonged to him by natural right. All this clearly indicated that it was the beginning of a plot against me."

"Mr. Secretary of State," Bunau-Varilla told Hay, "the situation harbors the same fatal germs—perhaps even more virulent ones—as those which caused at Bogota the rejection of the Hay-Herrán Treaty. There the only enemies were the intrigues of the Colombian politicians. The same elements will be found at Panama."

Drawing analogies to the Colombian senators, Bunau-Varilla prescribed the tactics that he and Hay would use to defeat the "enemy," that is, the Panamanians he supposedly represented. "It is necessary to leave the enemy no time to perfect his plans. It is necessary to strike, to strike again, to keep on striking, and to win the victory, before the foe has time to block the way."

When the secretary asked him what they should do about his appointment, Bunau-Varilla answered emphatically, "So long as I am here, Mr. Secretary, you will have to deal exclusively with me."

As soon as he got back to the New Willard, Bunau-Varilla sent an angry telegram to Minister Ricardo de La Espriella in Panama asking for an explanation and claiming that the news of Amador's mission to Washington had made "a very bad impression" on Hay, "as it would be contradictory to my mission."

The following morning, November 10, de la Espriella sent a cable confirming that a commission was sailing for New York that day, but not "to discuss and sign Canal Treaty, all things that exclusively concern Your Excellency." The following day, de la Espriella sent another cable reiterating Bunau-Varilla's authority; together, they provided Bunau-Varilla with enough evidence to prove that his appointment remained intact.

Not wanting to rely entirely on Bunau-Varilla's words, Hay sought confirmation of his appointment from Felix Ehrman. On November 10, Ehrman informed Hay that the party led by Amador was "on the way to Washington to *arrange* in satisfactory manner to the United States *the canal treaty*." However, he contradicted himself the next day with another cable that read, "I am officially informed that Bunau-Varilla is the authorized party to sign treaties. Boyd and Amador have other missions and to assist their Minister."

The source of Ehrman's second cable is a mystery, causing some to speculate that it may have been fabricated by Bunau-Varilla or even by the State Department, since the instructions that Amador and Boyd carried with them clearly specified that Bunau-Varilla was nothing more than an intermediary. Addressed to Bunau-Varilla, the instructions read:

> You will have to adjust a Treaty for the Canal construction by the United States. But all clauses of this Treaty will be discussed previously with the delegates of the Junta, M. Amador and Boyd. *And you will proceed in everything strictly in accord with them* [Emphasis added].

In case Bunau-Varilla refused to limit himself to an intermediary role, Amador and Boyd had the power to negotiate directly with Washington. Clearly the Panamanians saw Bunau-Varilla as a liaison between Panama and the United States, not as someone with authorityto sign the treaty. However, the Panamanian junta directed Ehrman and Foreign Minister de la Espriella to send cables confirming Bunau-Varilla's powers only because they wanted his continued support until Amador's delegation reached Washington, at which point they would strip him of his power. Like Marroquín, the Panamanians thought that they could play a game and outsmart their foreign cohorts, and like Marroquín, they would be sadly surprised.

Bunau-Varilla learned that the commission had sailed on the mail steamer *City of Washington* on November 10. He calculated it would take about six or seven days for the ship to dock in New York City and another day for the delegates to make it to Washington D.C. He immediately set out to accomplish his "high mission" before the Panamanians arrived.

The first thing Bunau-Varilla did was to pay a "flying visit" to the offices of J.P. Morgan & Co. in Wall Street. In a glass-enclosed alcove, he met the renowned Morgan himself. Bunau-Varilla asked the old financier to make a loan of $100,000 to the new republic guaranteed by his deposit of $75,000, the balance of the money he had received from Paris. In consideration, Morgan would be appointed financial agent for Panama with the exclusive right to cash the $10,000,000 indemnity that Panama would receive when it signed the canal treaty. In less than an hour, Bunau-Varilla claimed he had a deal. (Considering that Morgan was a member of Cromwell's Americanization scheme, most likely the deal had already been arranged).

Bunau-Varilla left from New York to Washington for his official meeting with President Roosevelt. On the way, he learned that Marroquín had offered to ratify the Hay-Herrán treaty by presidential decree without the need for congressional approval if the United States would quash the rebellion in Panama. General Rafael Reyes, the Conservative party presidential candidate, had been given a diplomatic mission to win Panama back. He had sailed from Cartagena to Panama accompanied by Generals Pedro Nel Ospina and Jorge Holguín, both ex-presidents of Colombia. Reyes was one of the most respected Colombian leaders, and the Panamanian government feared the effect of his charm and powers of persuasion if he arrived on the Isthmus.

De la Espriella sent a cable to Bunau-Varilla asking him to

arrange for an American warship to block the Reyes mission at the mouth of the Magdalena River. Bunau-Varilla knew this was impossible and cabled back suggesting instead to request diplomatic papers from Reyes before he was allowed to disembark in Panama. When the Reyes mission docked in Colón, U.S. Admiral Coghlan boarded the French steamer *Canada* and asked Reyes for official papers. Since Reyes did not have such papers, he was told that he could not land. A committee of Panamanians met with him on board the steamer, but Reyes saw that his mission in Panama would be useless and decided to sail for Washington.

In the meantime, Cromwell had sailed back to the United States. His brief admits that "he sailed on November 11 for the United States, to be present at a conference previously arranged with the special delegates of the new Republic of Panama on their arrival in New York." Cromwell sent his senior partner, William Curtis, to meet with President Roosevelt and Senator Hanna because he was concerned about Bunau-Varilla's actions. The new ambassador had such a lust for interviews to magnify his own importance that he was causing quite a stir in Washington. A letter Bunau-Varilla sent to Senator Morgan, intending to win his support for Panama, had created a scandal. Members of the diplomatic corps were not supposed to lobby Congress directly, so many senators thought that Bunau-Varilla was trying to bribe Morgan. Some congressmen suggested throwing Bunau-Varilla out of the country, a punishment for political impropriety that only two ambassadors had received in the whole of the nineteenth century. Even President Roosevelt became concerned. William Curtis, Cromwell's senior partner, recalled that in the meeting with Hanna and T.R., the president turned to him and said in his vigorous way, "Do you know Bunau-Varilla?"

"Yes," Curtis answered.

"I wish you would tell him to shut up and not talk so much."

Senator Hanna laughed. "I barely think that message will be effective. You say to Mr. Curtis that you desire him to say to Bunau-Varilla that the President of the United States requests him to avoid public interviews and public discussion of this matter, and I have no doubt he will readily comply."

Roosevelt repeated the senator's words. "Please say to Bunau-Varilla that the President of the United States desires him to discontinue his interviews and public utterances on the subject."

President Roosevelt then stood up, leaned over toward Senator Hanna, and said, "Senator, in the language of our boyhood, I think we should be permitted to 'skin our own skunk.'"

When Curtis told the president that the Compagnie Nouvelle was not responsible for Bunau-Varilla's appointment, Roosevelt replied, "Nevertheless, all I can do is exact justice between man and man."

The president's suggestion to downplay his celebrity may never have gotten to Bunau-Varilla, who continued his "high mission" unconcerned that he had become a buffoon, the laughingstock of the press. To the Frenchman, this all seemed a small price to pay for the greater goal, a canal treaty that would vindicate the "glory of France."

> It seemed to me as if I were in the position of the legendary hunter, who in the middle of the Indian forest had placed himself in a cage surrounded by the carcasses of sheep to attract the wild beats. He could peacefully enjoy the spectacle of the exasperated and powerless tigers gnashing their teeth against the steel bars of the cage.

On Friday, November 13, the long-awaited day arrived. At nine in the morning, Bunau-Varilla left the New Willard for the State Department, where Secretary Hay was waiting to accompany him to the White House. Bunau-Varilla brought with him his frail-looking, asthmatic son Etienne so that the boy "might witness history in the making." Upon arriving at the State Department, he left Etienne outside in the carriage. Hay insisted on taking a historic photograph with Bunau-Varilla before going to the White House. They sat beside a neatly arranged desk with a world map on the background. Hay, upright and expressionless, his hands on his lap, looked off to the distance, while a confident Bunau-Varilla, his arm resting against the edge of the desk, looked straight into the camera. He was in control.

When they went out, they found Etienne watching the people passing by. Bunau-Varilla introduced him to Hay, who, according to Bunau-Varilla, "had the charming idea of taking him to the White House to witness the ceremony." Bunau-Varilla gladly consented. He took a seat in Hay's carriage, leaving Etienne to follow them in his own carriage.

Once at the White House, they were led to the Blue Room, where diplomatic receptions were held. Etienne quietly and "modestly sat down at a little distance" from his father and Secretary Hay. A few minutes later, the president entered, followed by his secretary, Mr. Loeb.

Bunau-Varilla bowed. After shaking the president's hand, he read a flowery discourse in French saying that by accepting him as the minister plenipotentiary of Panama "you admit into the Family of Nations the weakest and the last-born of the Republics of the New World." He assured the president that "the highway from Europe to Asia, following the pathway of the sun, is now to be realized." Roosevelt then gave a short statement. After the last word, according to Bunau-Varilla, Roosevelt asked, "What do you think, Mr. Minister, of those people who print that we have made the Revolution of Panama together?"

Bunau-Varilla responded, "I think, Mr. President, that calumny never loses its opportunity even in the New World. It is necessary patiently to wait until the spring of the imagination of the wicked is dried up, and until truth dissipates the mist of mendacity."

Etienne, consumed by curiosity, rose from his chair and drew near, attracting the attention of the president. Secretary Hay smiled and said, "I have now, Mr. President, to introduce you to Monsieur Bunau-Varilla Junior."

According to Bunau-Varilla's memoir, Roosevelt's face "brightened with an affectionate smile, and he was on the point of kissing on both cheeks the child," when Bunau-Varilla interrupted.

"I brought him," he said, "as the representative of the generation, which, more than our own, will reap the fruit of the work you have accomplished this morning."

The ceremony was over. Not one word of Spanish had been spoken, not one Panamanian was present or even invited. To the press, which covered the most minute details of this "sudden and unexpected entrance of the new Republic into the Family of Nations," the whole event seemed an *opéra comique*. The *New York Times* denounced the apparent corruption in the affair; the Sunday edition contained a cartoon entitled "The Man Behind the Egg," in which Bunau-Varilla, in a top hat, clutched French canal stock in one hand and with the other held a candle marked "intrigue" to hatch an egg with the Panama chick for Roosevelt. Etienne got a considerable share of the publicity, which pleased his father, but which "considerably roused" the frail child because the reporters gave his age as ten years, when he was in fact thirteen.

Before they left the White House, Bunau-Varilla reminded Hay of the urgency of signing the treaty. "Not one minute [is] to be lost," he said. He saw "two clouds rising above the horizon": the Amador mission on its way from Panama and the Reyes mission on its way from Bogota.

"To prevent any injurious action on their part," he told Hay, "it [is] necessary that on their respective arrivals, they would be met not with arrangements for the signing of a treaty, which they might defeat, but with definitive and accomplished facts. Success [is] more than ever the price of rapidity of movement."

Since the Panamanians were expected to arrive in only five days, Bunau-Varilla did not have much time. For two anxious days, he did not hear from Hay. On the evening of Sunday, November 16, he received at the New Willard a manila envelope labeled *confidential* and a note that read:

Dear Mr. Minister:
    I enclose a project of a Treaty. Please return it to me with your suggestions at your earliest convenience.

Hay

It was essentially the Hay-Herrán treaty with a few minor modifications. Bunau-Varilla stayed up all night reading the draft, sleeping only between midnight and 2:00 in the morning. By dawn, he had decided that it would not do.

"I [am] thus led to the conclusion that the indispensable condition of success was to draft a new treaty, so well adapted to American exigencies, that it could challenge any criticism in the Senate."

From the Hay-Herrán treaty, he decided to leave intact first, the principle of neutrality of the interoceanic passage; second, the rigorous equality in the treatment of all flags, whether American or non-American, from the point of view of the charges and conditions of passage; third, the attribution of the indemnity of $10,000,000 to Panama; and last, the protection of Panama. Every other concession that Concha had demanded would be deleted. The share of sovereignty attributed to the United States in the canal zone would be extended from six to ten miles. More importantly, instead of listing the attributes of sovereignty that the United States would receive inside the Zone, he decided to grant a "concession of sovereignty *en bloc.*" That is, Panama would have no rights in the canal zone, as if it were not Panama's territory. The concession, instead of being granted for a hundred years and renewable, would be "leased for perpetuity."

Bunau-Varilla's decision was an act of treachery. As a representative of Panama, he had a duty to negotiate the best deal for the country, but he did the opposite. At the very least, he could have simply signed and sent back the treaty as Hay had drafted it. His fear that Congress might reject it was unfounded, since a treaty with similar terms had already been approved by the U.S. Senate only six months earlier.

Shortly after breakfast, Frank Pavey, an eminent New York lawyer and friend of Bunau-Varilla, arrived at the New Willard. They installed a stenographer in an adjacent suite, and Bunau-Varilla began to dictate his draft of the treaty. Pavey, according to Bunau-Varilla, "corrected the literary imperfections, polished the formulas, and gave them an irreproachable academic form."

Bunau-Varilla stepped out only once around noon. He ran to the State Department to tell Hay that he was drafting a new treaty more favorable to the United States. Hay did not object. Bunau-Varilla went back to his hotel suite and continued working until ten o'clock that night, finishing the draft only twenty-four hours after he had begun.

He made two copies and rushed to Hay's house on Lafayette Square, but he found the large mansion in darkness. Not wanting to disturb the secretary's sleep, he decided to try again first thing in the morning. At around 10:00 AM on Tuesday, November 17, he sent Hay the draft of the new treaty with a letter promising that if the secretary did not like his draft, he would sign the one Hay had originally sent to him.

That same morning, the Panamanian delegation of Amador, Boyd, and Carlos Arosemena docked at the Chelsea Piers aboard the *City of Washington*. They were besieged by the press, but Bunau-Varilla had sent a cable advising them not to speak to reporters. Joshua Lindo welcomed them and led them to Cromwell's press agent, Roger Farnham. Farnham informed them that his boss would be arriving from

France aboard the *Kaiser Wilhem der Grosse* at around noon, and asked them to stay and confer with him as "previously arranged."

The meeting was a grave error for the Panamanians. Had they gone straight to Washington, they would have arrived before Bunau-Varilla had time to sign the treaty to the detriment of Panama. Instead, Roger Farnham escorted them to the Fifth Avenue Hotel, where they waited another day to meet with Cromwell.

Cromwell and the Panamanians conferred for several hours, allegedly on financial matters and other issues facing the new republic. By the end of the meeting, the Panamanian patriots had appointed Cromwell fiscal agent, general counsel, and representative of Panama in the United States. The fact that Cromwell had allegedly insulted Amador and endangered the lives of Panamanian patriots did not seem to have deterred them from this appointment.

Some commentators have argued that Cromwell was working in concert with Bunau-Varilla to delay the Panamanians' arrival in Washington. Yet, when Bunau-Varilla heard that the Panamanians had met "the lawyer," he concluded that Amador was trying to enlist Cromwell's help to oust him, thereby fulfilling Amador's own "secret ambitions" to sign the treaty. Amador, Bunau-Varilla concluded, was endangering the "delicate fabric and the precious mechanism" of his work for "personal satisfaction." He decided to act rapidly. "I had to shield, from the nefarious influence of these passions and of these interests, the realization of the supreme event," that is, the signing of the Hay-Bunau-Varilla treaty.

Despite Bunau-Varilla's urgency, Hay did not answer his call on Tuesday. "It was with anxiety that I awaited a summons from the Department of State during the day," recalled Bunau-Varilla. "It did not come. Mr. Hay made me no sign."

By ten o'clock that night, Bunau-Varilla could not take the suspense any longer and decided to send Hay a note.

> Dear Mr. Secretary:
> I have not heard from you to-day, and did not dare to appear to be urging you.

I cannot refrain from respectfully submitting to you that I would like very much to terminate the negotiation and to sign the Treaty to-morrow.

I feel the presence of a good deal of intrigues round the coming Commission and people hustling towards them who will find great profit in delaying and palavering and none in going straight to the end.

I beg, therefore, dear Mr. Secretary, that we should fulfill our plan, as originally laid, to end the negotiations now.

I am writing to the Commission to stay in New York to-morrow and to leave before evening. In any ease I would be thankful to you to see me to-morrow or to-night if this should be convenient to you.

Hay replied immediately. "Please come to-night if you prefer. . . . Or to-morrow at nine here, if you like it better."

Bunau-Varilla left at once for Lafayette Square. The two men held a "long conference together" in which they discussed the basic tenets of the Bunau-Varilla treaty. Article III contained the controversial clause.

The Republic of Panama grants to the United States all the rights, power and authority within the zone . . . which the United States would possess and exercise if it were the sovereign of the territory . . . to the entire exclusion of the exercise by the Republic of Panama of any such sovereign rights, power, or authority.

In contrast, the Hay-Herrán treaty provided:

The rights and privileges granted to the United States by the terms of this convention shall not affect the sovereignty of the Republic of Colombia over the territory within whose boundaries such rights and privileges are to be exercised. The United States freely acknowledges and recognizes this sovereignty and disavows any intention to impair it in any way whatever.

The difference was crucial, since the new clause ceded the land to the United States. As historian David Howarth later said, "How could the Canal Zone be said to belong to Panama, if neither the government nor the people of Panama had any rights there, or any prospect of ever receiving their rights again till the end of time?"

During the meeting, in addition to discussing the controversial clause, Hay told Bunau-Varilla that some important Republican leaders insisted on paying Colombia part of the $10,000,000 indemnity as reparation for wresting away Panama. Bunau-Varilla strongly disagreed, claiming that to do so would amount to an admission of wrongdoing. Besides, he added, Colombians would be insulted by the token sum, as they had lost a lot more than money in Panama. Seeing that Hay was still hesitant to sign, Bunau-Varilla issued another warning.

"So long as the delegation has not arrived in Washington, I shall be free to deal with you alone, provided with complete and absolute powers. When they arrive, I shall no longer be alone. In fact, I may perhaps soon no longer be here at all."

Hay decided to proceed. This was the most controversial decision of his eminent career and turned him into an accomplice in a grossly unjust act. However, the temptation to put an end to the Panama issue was irresistible. Since the revolution began, he had been working himself to exhaustion. The covert events, from secret orders to warships in Colón, to the Frenchman with the waxed moustache arriving to his house in the middle of the night had created more intrigue and suspense than all the unpublished novels he had written. He was also wholly satisfied with the treaty. He later confided to Senator Spooner that the new treaty was "very satisfactory, vastly advantageous to the United States, and we must confess, with what face we can muster, not advantageous to Panama. . . . You and I know too well how many points there are in this treaty to which a Panamanian patriot could object."

The following day, Wednesday, November 18, Hay invited Secretary of Defense Elihu Root, Attorney General Knox, Secretary of the Treasury Leslie Shaw, and several leading Republican congressmen to a lunch at his house to explain the treaty and get their consent. After the lunch, he rushed back to the State Department. Just a few hours before the Panamanian delegation arrived in Washington, he sent Bunau-Varilla the following cable: "Will you kindly call at my house at six o'clock today?"

When Bunau-Varilla arrived, reporters were gathered at the State Department entrance. Bunau-Varilla did not yet know the purpose of Hay's invitation. The reporters flanked his carriage and asked him if he was coming to sign the treaty.

"You seem to be much better informed than I am. Why do you suppose that?" he answered.

"Well," they said laughing, "scarcely five minutes ago the head of the Treaties Bureau at the Department of State entered Mr. Hay's house. Now you arrive."

According to Bunau-Varilla, Hay received him with great solemnity, repeatedly using the word "Excellency" to address him. "I have requested you," Hay told him, "to be so good as to keep this appointment in order to sign, if it is agreeable to Your Excellency, the Treaty which will permit the construction of the Interoceanic Canal."

Bunau-Varilla answered, "I am at the orders of Your Excellency to sign either of the two projects which, in Your Excellency's judgment, appears best adapted to the realization of that grand work."

"The one that appears best adapted to that end," replied Mr. Hay, "not only to myself, but also to the Senators, who will have to defend it in the Senate, is the one Your Excellency has prepared. In its text we have not found it necessary to make the slightest modification, save for an insignificant question of terminology on one single point."

In Article II, Hay wanted to use instead of the words *leases in perpetuity* the phrase *grants to the United States in perpetuity the use, occupation and control.* He also suggested that to preserve the neutrality of all the flags they would state that the canal would be operated in accordance with the stipulations of the Hay-Pauncefote treaty with England.

"If Your Excellency agrees to it, the Treaty will now be read and we will then sign it."

Bunau-Varilla eagerly suggested that "the reading be abridged as far as possible," as time was of the essence, since he knew the Panamanians delegation was arriving anytime. At 6:30, the group was ready to sign.

"Did you bring your seal, to put it upon the document?" asked Hay.

"I did not expect this event," answered Bunau-Varilla. "I am taken by surprise."

"Well, this is very curious," replied Hay. "It is exactly what happened to Lord Pauncefote two years ago; as it is exactly two years today that we signed the Hay-Pauncefote Treaty. . . . I then proposed to him to use as a seal the signet ring which Lord Byron wore when he died at Missolonghi, the ring I am now wearing. That is what he did. I now offer you either the same signet ring or another with my family arms. Which do you prefer?"

"The share which Your Excellency has in the accomplishment of this great act determines my choice. I shall be happy that the Treaty, due to your generous policy, should bear at the same time your personal seal and that of your family."

At exactly 6:40, they dipped the pen in an inkwell that had once belonged to Abraham Lincoln. Bunau-Varilla signed first in a small, controlled hand, and Hay followed with a wild, large stroke. According to Bunau-Varilla, Hay then took the pen and offered it to Bunau-Varilla. "This is just what Your Excellency should keep, in memory of this Treaty which you have devised."

"We separated not without emotion," Bunau-Varilla recalled, and "I hastened back to my hotel to wire the news of this all-important event to my Government."

Back at the hotel, he received a dispatch from New York announcing the delegates' arrival in Washington at 9:00. Bunau-Varilla set out immediately for the train station where he "greeted the travelers with the happy news."

10

The Rape of the Isthmus

W<small>HEN</small> B<small>UNAU</small>-V<small>ARILLA</small> <small>SAW</small> <small>THE</small> Panamanian delegation at the railroad station, he called out, "The Republic of Panama is henceforth under protection of the United States. I have just signed the Canal Treaty!"

According to Bunau-Varilla, Amador nearly fainted. Federico Boyd was livid, and Panamanians later claimed that he spat in Bunau-Varilla's face.

The three met the following day at the New Willard Hotel. The angry Panamanians insisted that Bunau-Varilla had acted without authority. They showed him the instructions they had brought, but according to Bunau-Varilla, he got "some amusement to embarrass" them by showing the cable from Foreign Minister de la Espriella, describing the passive role they were coming to play. In any case, he told them, all of this was "ancient history." The treaty had been signed.

Boyd insisted on starting fresh negotiations with the State Department. Bunau-Varilla responded, "Cherish no illusion, Mr. Boyd, the negotiations are closed. It belongs now exclusively to the Senate of the United States, and to the Government of Panama, either to accept or to reject this Treaty."

He then reminded them that they had no authority over him. "According to this correspondence you have come to hold yourself at my disposal if I meet with any difficulty which I should be unwilling to settle alone. . . . You have, therefore, neither in law nor in fact any reason for intervening, so long as I do not ask for your advice."

Bunau-Varilla insisted that the treaty had to be ratified by Panama before Colombian General Reyes arrived on November 28. He ordered Amador and Boyd to use their authority as the official delegation of Panama to ratify the treaty immediately, but Amador and Boyd vehemently refused.

Bunau-Varilla took them to see Hay at the State Department, hoping that the secretary could convince them. At the meeting, Hay supported Bunau-Varilla's suggestion, asking Amador and Boyd if they had the powers to ratify the treaty, but both claimed that it had to be sent to Panama.

"I detected a slight tension on the expressive face of Mr. Hay," recalled Bunau-Varilla. "Evidently he was hurt by the lack of promptitude on the part of the delegates to meet him halfway on so important a subject. This attitude displeased me also very much, and I wondered at that moment if the era of difficulties was really ended, as I had thought."

In the corridor outside Hay's office, Bunau-Varilla confronted Amador and Boyd and "made it clear to the delegates that their lack of good grace had left a decidedly bad impression." He directed them to request a special power from the provisional junta to ratify the treaty, since sending the treaty to Panama would take too long. Amador and Boyd again refused.

When Bunau-Varilla returned to the New Willard, he found William Nelson Cromwell waiting for him. An angered Cromwell accused Bunau-Varilla of entangling the new republic in "financial and other complications" in order to gain recognition from other countries without authority from Panama. To Jusserand, the French ambassador, Bunau-Varilla had pledged that Panama would "protect with vigilance the French interests" and "maintain and interpret in the sense most favorable to French interests all contracts." What angered Cromwell the most was the deal Bunau-Varilla cut with England. A number of London banks had loaned the government of Colombia moneys secured by the expected $10,000,000 payment from the United States. As a result of the Panamanian revolution, Colombia would no longer be receiving the payment, and the bondholders had requested the English government to withhold formal recognition until Panama agreed to repay part of the loan. Bunau-Varilla wrote to the British ambassador on behalf of Panama offering to assume a share of the Colombian debt in proportion to the population of each respective republic. Cromwell vetoed the offer. He wanted every penny paid by the United States to go to his clients, the Compagnie Nouvelle and Panama. The two men parted with angry words.

Henceforth, Cromwell pushed Bunau-Varilla away from any financial matters dealing with Panama. Consequently, a few days later, on November 26, Bunau-Varilla wired $75,000 dollars, the balance of the $100,000 he had received from Credit Lyonnais, from his account in the Heidelbach bank to J.P. Morgan & Co. On November 25, Cromwell obtained for Panama an additional loan of $100,000 from the Bowling Green Trust Co. secured by a pledge of railroad bonds owned by Cromwell. The funds were credited to the Morgan bank, which immediately credited Lindo's bank, which in turn wired the funds to Isaac Brandon & Bros. in Panama, which then made it available to the patriots. Cromwell and J.P. Morgan, not Bunau-Varilla, were now in charge of disbursing the funds to bribe the Colombian soldiers.

To Bunau-Varilla, Cromwell's assault at the New Willard confirmed that Cromwell and Amador had teamed up to oust him. Bunau-Varilla decided it was time to take the matter out of "inexpert hands." "I resolved to obtain the ratification from the Government itself, before the arrival of the Treaty at Panama, in spite of the delegates' bad grace."

Bunau-Varilla went back to New York the evening of Friday, November 20, and on Saturday morning, he sent a long dispatch to Minister de la Espriella saying that the delegates had "caused a very bad impression" on Mr. Hay, and that their refusal to ratify the treaty was embarrassing the United States. "It puts the Government here in a rather false position before the public for having stepped forward with great haste and for not meeting the same attitude on the other side." He insisted that they had no time to send the treaty to Panama, and that Amador and Boyd should be granted powers to ratify it immediately. To facilitate an immediate decision, he cabled a draft of the treaty.

Saturday evening passed without an answer, as did the following day. All day Monday Bunau-Varilla waited anxiously "without any tidings." At last, at 10:00 PM on Monday, November 23, de la Espriella sent his reply, an unequivocal no: the treaty would have to be sent to Panama.

Bunau-Varilla was irate and determined to exact revenge. "The conflict had begun," he told himself, his next step already decided, "the country would be declared in danger."

Although Bunau-Varilla and the delegates were hardly on speaking terms, on Tuesday, November 24, at nine o'clock in the morning, he invited them to his suite in the Waldorf Astoria to seal the treaty and send it on to Panama. Etienne was the only witness to the lofty ceremony. They placed the treaty inside an envelope sealed with the family crest of John Bigelow; they wrapped the envelope in a Panamanian flag that Bunau-Varilla had made for the occasion; and they wrapped the American flag around it. They deposited the package in a safe filled with cotton and wool and took it on board the steamer *City of Washington*, which sailed for Panama at 1:30 that afternoon. Colonel Shaler was on board and agreed to safeguard the treaty.

After the ceremony, Bunau-Varilla departed hastily for Washington "to shake off the web which I felt was being woven about me." On the evening of November 25, he sent a blunt cable to Minister de la Espriella that struck fear among the Panamanian patriots.

> The coldness on the part of Panama after the signature of a Treaty which the United States justly considered as generous for Panama has caused surprise in the high spheres which, as hours are passing, degenerates into indignation.
>
> I know the extremely difficult ground of Washington. The peril may not be apparent for others, but I affirm it to be very great and that at any moment a brilliant victory may be transformed into a crushing defeat.

He demanded assurances from the junta that the treaty would be ratified immediately upon "the arrival of the document at Colón." His demands were followed by a warning:

> If the Government does not think possible to take this minimum but sufficient step, I do not wish to appear responsible for the calamities which certainly will result from this situation; *the most probable being the immediate suspension of the protection and the signature of a final treaty with Bogota in accord with the constitutional laws of Colombia in case of war*. In such case I beg Your Excellency to present my resignation to the Government [Emphasis added].

The warning was a malicious lie. Neither Hay nor Roosevelt had suggested or even contemplated withdrawing their support of Panama. Bunau-Varilla had not consulted with either of them and could not cite any evidence to support his threat. On the contrary, Roosevelt had given his unparalleled support to his "little war" despite the fallout in the press. He had sent a half-dozen ships that had besieged the Isthmus and prevented Colombian troops from landing. The Reyes mission was not considered to be much of a threat either, as Marroquín's belated promise to sign the treaty by presidential decree was viewed by Washington as another act of extortion (if he had the power to sign, why didn't he assert that power initially?). If Washington were to pull out at this crucial juncture, the pro-Nicaraguan forces in Congress would have their day, the lives of many Americans in Panama who had aided the revolution would be placed in danger, and the railroad company would lose its concession. Given Teddy Roosevelt's impulsive character, he would have found another way to secure the Panamanians' cooperation.

Panamanians, however, would not risk even the possibility that the United States could withdraw its support of Panama. Several Colombian warships carrying thousands of troops were still trying to land on the Isthmus; if the American left, Colombians would take over Panama in days, and every revolutionary would be executed. Since they erroneously credited Bunau-Varilla with obtaining Washington's recognition in the first place, the patriots were panicked by the cable.

The following day, Thursday, November 26, Bunau-Varilla received a reply from Panama:

> Your Excellency is authorized to notify officially to the Government
> of the United States that said Treaty will be ratified and signed as soon
> as it is received by the Provisional Government of the Republic.

Arango, Arias, Espinosa, and de la Espriella signed the cable. "This time I hit the mark," recalled Bunau-Varilla. "The Government of Panama was at last liberated from the morbid influence of its delegation." Overjoyed, Bunau-Varilla interrupted Hay's Thanksgiving dinner to deliver the news. Hay, however, was worried that the Panamanians would not keep their pledge. Bunau-Varilla thus wrote to Edward Drake, manager of the Panama Railroad & Steamship

Company, asking for a one-day delay in the departure of the steamer set to sail from Panama to New York on the day of the treaty's arrival. The next steamer was scheduled to depart a week later, and Bunau-Varilla did not want to give the Panamanians a full week to debate the treaty. He figured that if a ship was idling in the harbor waiting to take the document, the patriots would be pressured to ratify immediately without debate.

Bunau-Varilla's request did not actually amount to much, as delays of the steamships from Panama to New York were commonplace. However, a few days later, Edward Drake sent Bunau-Varilla a cable denying his request. Bunau-Varilla suspected that Cromwell was behind the denial, as everyone knew that he controlled the Panama Railroad Company. Bunau-Varilla was irate; he expected Cromwell to repay the favor of getting him reinstated as general counsel of the Compagnie Nouvelle in 1901. Bunau-Varilla then marched into Drake's office demanding the company obey his request. The conversation got heated and almost broke out into a fistfight, yet Drake, under Cromwell's direction, did not budge.

Cromwell had decided it was time to get rid of Bunau-Varilla. With the Frenchman having served his purpose, he had now become a hindrance for Cromwell. To get rid of him, he sent a cable to the junta urging Bunau-Varilla's dismissal, but the junta did not respond. On November 30, on behalf of Cromwell, Drake sent a second cable to Captain Beers in Panama, urging him to tell the Panamanians that Bunau-Varilla's "threats" about the withdrawal of recognition were "absolutely without foundation." The letter stated that "Mr. Cromwell has direct assurances from President Roosevelt, Secretary Hay, Senator Hanna, and other Senators that there is not the slightest danger of this."

The Panamanians, however, still feared Bunau-Varilla too much to disobey his orders. On December 1, as soon as the *City of Washington* docked in Colón, the provisional junta ratified the treaty by unanimous vote. A full day passed before they removed the treaty from its cotton safe and read a line from the original, but they blindly adopted it without modifications—a mere twenty-seven days after the revolution, and six days before the debates in the U.S. Senate began.

Senator Morgan opened the debate on December 7 with a vicious assault on the corrupt and dishonest means by which the treaty had been ratified. He accused Roosevelt of manufacturing a revolution and using military force to achieve his imperialistic goals. Republican Senator Pue Gorman announced that he was going to run against the president in the upcoming elections for just this reason.

The press also attacked the treaty. The *New York Times* editorialized that "the canal was stolen property" and that "the partners in the theft" were a "group of canal promoters and speculators and lobbyists who came into their money through the rebellion we encouraged, made safe, and effectuated."

On January 17, 1904, Pulitzer's the *World* published a scandalous exposé occupying seven of the nine columns on the front page. The headline read, "THE PANAMA REVOLUTION, A STOCK-GAMBLER'S PLAN TO MAKE MILLIONS." The *World* alleged that a gang of speculators had purchased French Canal Co. stock and then enlisted the aid of the U.S. government to wrest Panama away from Colombia and reap millions. It cited facts as yet unknown to the public about the secret conspiracy to free Panama. According to the article, the guiding spirit was Philippe Bunau-Varilla. It mentioned the names of everyone involved, with one conspicuous omission: William Nelson Cromwell. Bunau-Varilla thus surmised that Cromwell had supplied the information to the press. In fact it was Cromwell's press agent Jonas Whitley who had tipped the *World* for a hundred dollars under orders from his boss, who sought to discredit Bunau-Varilla.

Roosevelt got a chance to answer the accusations made against him in the State of the Union address in January 1904. For months, he had been rehearsing the speech. He had ordered Secretary Moody and the head of the naval war records department to find precedents for his military actions in Panama, but they reported that none could be located. During a cabinet meeting, Roosevelt offered his colleagues his account of the events in Panama to see their reactions. When he finished, he asked, "Well, have I answered the charges? Have I defended myself?"

Defense Secretary Elihu Root replied sardonically, "You certainly have, Mr. President. You have shown that you were accused of seduction and you have conclusively proved that you were guilty of rape."

It was Roosefelt's friend Oscar Strauss who gave the president his best argument, suggesting that the people of the world had a "right of passage" through the Isthmus of Panama that no government could impede, similar to "a covenant running with the land."

In his address on January 4, Roosevelt began by asserting that he had "a mandate from civilization" to build an Isthmian canal and neither the Colombian government nor any other had the right to stop the canal construction. He quoted Secretary Cass, who in 1855 said that "sovereignty has its duties as well as its rights," and that "no government should be permitted to close the gates of intercourse on the great highways of the world" or claim "that these avenues of trade and travel belong to them." He explained that Panama had been under tyrannical rule for almost a century, and that as a result the United States had been drawn into "unnecessary and wasteful civil wars" time and again.

Roosevelt dedicated most of his address to refuting reports that he had helped manufacture the Republic of Panama. He claimed he had nothing to do with the planning of the revolution and only heard about it following Captain Humphrey and Lieutenant Murphy's visit to the Isthmus as "an unpremeditated incident of their return journey." He stated that no American warships, troops, or sailors had been present when the revolution took place in Panama City. The people of the Isthmus, he explained, feared that the Colombian government's rejection of the Hay-Herrán treaty would leave the country impoverished without a canal, and so they "rose literally as one man." ("Yes, and the one man was Roosevelt," piped in Tennessee Senator Edward Carmack.)

Roosevelt maintained that only after the revolution in Panama City had been consummated did U.S. troops intervene and then only to preserve the neutrality of the railroad pursuant to the 1846 treaty. At Colón, Commander Hubbard had acted with "entire impartiality toward both sides, preventing any movement, whether by the Colombians or the Panamanians, which would tend to produce bloodshed. . . . Our action was for the peace both of Colombia and of Panama." He concluded, "I think proper to say, therefore, that no one connected with this government had any part in preparing, inciting, or encouraging the revolution on the Isthmus of Panama."

Although the debates went on for almost two more months, little objection could be made to the terms of the treaty. Even Senator Morgan, who had proposed over sixty amendments to the Hay-Herrán treaty, couldn't find fault with the Hay-Bunau-Varilla treaty. Another Nicaragua supporter, Senator Hernando de Soto Money, admitted that "we have never had a concession so extraordinary in its character as this. In fact, it sounds very much as if we wrote it ourselves." Support for the treaty was led by Spooner, and Senators Cullom and Henry Cabot Lodge, among others. The missing element this time was Senator Hanna, who was dying of typhoid fever in a room at the Arlington Hotel.

The Colombian delegation, headed by General Rafael Reyes, in a last desperate attempt, made an offer to "grant the Canal rights to the United States without the payment of a cent." At first some took the idea of a free canal enthusiastically; however, they soon realized that something was awry if a government unanimously rejected a treaty insisting on more money and then offered its acceptance for free. Reyes's offer merely demonstrated to the administration that Colombia had been trying to extort money all along. Reyes gave up and left for Paris to try to file a lawsuit attempting to block the transfer of the concessions from the French company to the United States. On February 10, Dr. Herrán closed the Colombian legation and notified Secretary Hay that he was leaving for Bogota with "crushed spirits and broken health." He never made it to his native land; he died in a New York hotel soon after.

On February 15, Senator Mark Hanna died at the age of sixty-six. Hanna's funeral was held in the Senate Chamber on February 22. As a member of the diplomatic corps, Bunau-Varilla was invited to sit in the front row of the Senate. Behind him, he recalled with obvious pleasure, "as if by a derisive trick of Fate, sat my, and Hanna's, mortal—but defeated—enemy, Senator Morgan." The following day, February 23, the Senate voted on the canal bill, and the Panama Canal treaty was ratified sixty-six to fourteen.

Hay and Bunau-Varilla exchanged ratifications ten days later, on February 25 at 11:00 PM. Each placed his signature next to the government seal. Bunau-Varilla was first, followed by Hay. They then bid farewell. It was the last time they would see each other, and it was a moving moment for the two of them. Bunau-Varilla later recalled.

It was for him and for myself one of those emotions which remain engraved in the memory for the rest of one's life. We were both of us deeply moved.

Two strokes of a pen were sealing forever the Destiny of the Great Thought which had haunted humanity during four centuries.

In an instant I beheld, focused before my eyes, the efforts of the knights of the centuries to wring from Nature its mystery, from Man its prejudices.

I thought of all those heroes, my comrades in the deadly battle, worthy grandsons of those Gauls who conquered the Ancient World, worthy sons of those Frenchmen who conquered the Modern World, who fell in the struggle against Nature, a smile on their lips, happy to sacrifice their lives to this work which was to render still more dazzling the glory of French genius.

I thought of the shameful league of all the passions, of all the hatreds, of all the jealousies, of all the cowardices, of all the ignorances, to crucify this great Idea, and with it all those who had hoped, through its realization, to give France one more glorious page in the history of humanity.

I thought of my solitary work, when I went preaching the Truth in the Highways.

I thought of the untold number of stupidities I had had to destroy, of prejudices I had had to disarm, of insults I had had to submit to, of interests I had to frustrate, of conspiracies I had had to thwart, in order to celebrate the Victory of Truth over Error and mark at last the hour of the *Resurrection of the Panama Canal.*

Despite all his thoughts and emotions, Bunau-Varilla only uttered the following words to Hay, "It seems as if we had together made something great."

He went back to the New Willard to prepare for his return to Paris. He sent a cable to the Government of Panama stating that since his mission had been accomplished, he resigned as minister plenipotentiary of Panama. He requested that any honoraria due him be used to build a statue of Ferdinand de Lesseps on the *Bovedas* seawall overlooking the entrance to the canal. The junta promptly appointed Obaldiá to replace him.

According to Bunau-Varilla, as he crossed the hotel lobby to take the message to the telegraph office, "somebody unexpectedly seized my hands to express to me his congratulations. It was the lawyer Cromwell."

On February 20, Manuel Amador Guerrero took the oath of office as the first president of Panama. Despite the fact that he was the spiritual father of the new republic, the doctor had not been a member of the provisional junta because he had intended to be Panama's first minister in Washington entrusted with the task of negotiating the canal treaty, but Bunau-Varilla had derailed those plans. With his election as president, Amador finally occupied the role that he deserved.

President Amador's inauguration took place in Cathedral Plaza before a joyous crowd. He had been elected by a national constitutional convention whose duties also included drafting the new constitution. Completed in less than a month, it resembled the constitution of the United States. Presidential terms were four years, and laws would be passed by a national legislature of *diputados* and interpreted by an independent court. Despite the general similarities, there were some peculiar differences: no president could run for more than one term or be succeeded by a member of his immediate family; habitual inebriation could lead to loss of citizenship, and the U.S. dollar was declared to be legal tender.

Amador would preside over approximately 350,000 citizens of a nation that extended from the southeast end of Costa Rica to the northwestern region of Colombia. Its borders would be a matter of controversy for years. Despite the Chiriqui's province initial hesitation to join the new republic, by February all the provinces of the former Colombian Department of Panama had acquiesced, thanks in part to the protective and menacing presence of U.S. warships patrolling the coast.

The future of Panama looked exceedingly bright. The dark ages from 1889 to 1903 brought on by the collapse of the French enterprise had ended. The renewed construction would draw thousands of workers and rejuvenate the local economy. As a physician, Amador saw advances in sanitation that would make Panama a "model for the tropics."

To express gratitude to President Roosevelt, the Panamanians presented to Herbert Prescott the first flag of Panama sewn by Señora Maria de la Ossa de Amador. Prescott passed it on to Cromwell, who gave it to Roosevelt. In presenting the flag, Cromwell ironically remarked to the president that "while the United States would never part with its historic treasure, the Liberty Bell . . . yet so fond was the gratitude and affection of the Republic of Panama to the President that they gave into his hands their most precious treasure." According to Cromwell, Roosevelt accepted the gift "in most enthusiastic and grateful terms."

There were some Panamanians, however, who bitterly criticized the patriots for hastily ratifying the unfavorable treaty. In their view, the country had sold itself to the "Great Hog of the North." Evidence of friction surfaced right away. In August 1904, not even six months after the treaty was signed, Panamanians made a formal request for interpretation regarding the rights to some islands off the Atlantic coast. Displeased by the U.S. response, Dr. Eusebio Morales, minister of public works, traveled to the United States to write an exposé for the *North American Review* on the history of Panama's revolution. When Roosevelt learned about Morales's mission, he sent various Washington politicians to his hotel. They promised that the United States would re-examine the contentious issues if he would not publish the article. Morales's bargaining tool was effective: to resolve the dispute, Roosevelt sent to Panama his new secretary of war, William Taft, accompanied by none other than William Nelson Cromwell.

It was Cromwell's first visit to the Isthmus since the revolution. During a banquet at the Hotel Central on New Years Eve, 1904, with Taft seated next to him, Cromwell gave a memorable speech in which he compared his feelings to those of Roman soldiers who "after years of absence in foreign wars . . . reentered the capital city following their victorious generals . . . bearing the trophies of their valor and the symbols of fresh conquest." He called himself a "humble soldier in the Panama cause" who was coming to greet Panama "after the years which have separated us, while I have been battling at the front for the Canal—the hope of the Isthmus, and upon the fate of which, hung its very existence." He admonished Panamanians to remain close to the United States and to himself, and he finished by declaring him-

self a citizen of Panama. During the next few days, he summarily bro-
kered a solution to the treaty dispute, and Morales destroyed the
incriminating article.

Apart from this incident, everything went as smoothly as possible,
especially when the new republic began to receive the promised
money from the United States. Not surprisingly, the Panamanians were
not the only ones clamoring to dip their hands into the vaults of the
American treasury. William Nelson Cromwell and J.P. Morgan also
sought to control the booty.

In early March, Cromwell paid a calculated visit to the offices of the
soon-to-depart Secretary of War Elihu Root. The United States was
considering paying $40,000,000 directly to the French liquidator and
$10,000,000 to Panama, but Cromwell had a different plan.

He told Root that several lawsuits had been filed in the United
States, France, and Panama by Colombia to enjoin the transfer of the
French concessions to the United States without the consent of the
Colombian government. Therefore, if the U.S. treasury itself made
the payments, the Colombians could attempt to seize the money. He
suggested an alternative: J.P. Morgan would be named "Special Dis-
bursing Agent"; his bank would pay the French liquidator and
Panama; and once payment had been made, the treasury would issue
a warrant, or authorization to get paid, on behalf of J.P. Morgan.

Root declined. He was wary of relying on Cromwell and Morgan
for such a large transaction and suggested waiting until the lawsuits
were settled. Cromwell, however, went to Treasury Secretary Leslie
Shaw and assured him of the trustworthiness of J.P. Morgan. Shaw,
in turn, consulted the president. By early April, Cromwell was drafting the agreement between the U.S. Treasury, the Compagnie Nouvelle, the Republic of Panama, and J.P. Morgan & Co. Cromwell and
J.P. Morgan now had control over the disbursement of the single largest
payment ever made.

The $50,000,000 payment for an area thirty miles long and ten miles
wide exceeded the amount paid by the United States for the com-
bined territories of Louisiana ($15,000,000), Alaska ($7,200,000) and
the Philippines ($20,000,000). Neither the press nor members of Con-

gress could fathom how the United States could pay so much for what was considered nearly worthless assets. They knew that Wall Street was reaping a huge profit, but they were powerless to stop it.

Cromwell prepared the bills and deeds of transfer, obtained the approval of the shareholders at a general meeting in Paris, and helped settle the lawsuits. On May 2, at the offices of the Compagnie Nouvelle, with Cromwell personally supervising the signatures of the documents, all the holdings, materials, and records of the Compagnie Nouvelle were formally transferred to the U.S. government.

The same day, J.P. Morgan paid to the Panamanian government the first installment of $1,000,000. They used $622,000 to pay loans requested from several banks, including J.P. Morgan, while the rest, approximately $375,000, went to the Panamanian treasury. Two weeks later, on May 19, J.P. Morgan paid the second installment of $9,000,000 to the republic. About $4,000,000 was sent to Panama for "much needed public works," and the remainder was to be invested "for posterity." The Panamanians appointed a special "fiscal commission" to manage the $6,000,000 fund, supervised by none other than Cromwell and J.P. Morgan. They bought railroad bonds and mortgages in New York real estate. The firm of Douglas Robinson, brother-in-law of Teddy Roosevelt and alleged member of the Cromwell syndicate, reviewed the applications of borrowers and the valuations of the properties for the mortgages. In short, most of the payment that Panama received remained in the United States in the hands of the alleged speculators.

By far the most important transaction that spring was the payment to the French shareholders. In early May, after Cromwell completed the transfer of the assets, J.P. Morgan traveled to Paris to personally make arrangements for the $40 million cash payment to the French liquidator. The bank shipped $18,000,000 in gold bullion from New York to Paris, bought exchange in the Paris bourse to cover the rest, and allegedly paid the entire $40,000,000 to the Banque de France. With all the payments made, on May 9, the U.S. Treasury issued to "J. Pierpont Morgan & Company, New York City, Special Dispensing Agent," a warrant for $40,000,000, the greatest sum paid out by the United States government to date. The Compagnie Nouvelle allegedly only paid the banker $35,000 for his troubles, barely enough to cover his expenses.

On June 30, 1904, the Compagnie Nouvelle pour le Canal Interoceanic shut its doors on the narrow Rue Louis-Le-Grand. The records were put under a sealed order and placed in a safe in the vaults of Credit Lyonnais to be held there for twenty years, and then destroyed.

In Panama, formal transfer took place on May 4. To the Panamanians, who remembered the horse parades, the banquets, the French flags, and the festivities when Ferdinand de Lesseps visited the Isthmus to proclaim the beginning of the work, the transfer was a total disappointment. Lieutenant Brooke and a half dozen Army officers met a representative of the Compagnie Nouvelle at 7:30 in the morning at its offices in the Grand Hotel. After being handed the keys to the storehouse and to the Ancón Hospital, the army officer signed a receipt and read a few words, and the ceremony was over. It lasted only a few minutes; no Panamanians were present. Lieutenant Brooke did not even bother to invite Amador.

The disbursement of the money to the shareholders of the Compagnie Nouvelle and the Compagnie Universelle would take years and would involve almost 100,000 claimants. The Compagnie Nouvelle, made up of primarily large investors, including Gustave Eiffel, Charles de Lesseps, and Philippe Bunau-Varilla, collected 38 percent, or $15,000,000, while the small shareholders of the Compagnie Universelle received the remaining 62 percent, or $25,000,000. Supposedly, investors got a return of about 3 percent on their original investment in the Compagnie Nouvelle and 10 percent in the Compagnie Universelle. Bunau-Varilla's firm got $440,000, plus a profit of $13,200.

All the while, mysterious developments were coming to light. Word immediately broke out in France and in the United States that Panama had been a syndicate's gamble. On February 4, 1904, the *New York Times* reported that the president of a large French national bank had said that roughly half of the money would stay in the United States. Another French banker commented, "I am surprised to hear that the fact is not generally known in America." Hutin, who had abdicated the presidency of the Compagnie Nouvelle, said that the money had never reached French shareholders "as the United States naively thought."

Despite the rumors, Roosevelt put an end to the speculation when he exclaimed "Let the dirt fly!" to start the Herculean task of building the Panama Canal. The engineering, medical, and administrative challenges and the risks of digging the canal were so great that few cared to know how the rights to build the canal had been obtained. With everyone involved keeping silent, the public thus came to believe Roosevelt's statements that the actions of his government had been "as free from scandal as the public acts of George Washington or Abraham Lincoln" and "as clean as a hound dog's teeth." In various pronouncements, T.R. alleged that in the history of the United States, there was no "more honorable chapter than that which tells of the way in which our right to dig the Panama Canal was secured. . . . Every action taken was not merely proper, but was carried in accordance with the highest, finest and nicest standards of public and government ethics."

Senator Morgan disagreed. He spent the last years of his life trying to prove that a secret speculating syndicate had committed heinous acts in Panama. In January 1906, the embittered Democrat again commenced hearings before his Committee on Interoceanic Canals. This time, the focus of his investigation was the activity of his nemesis, William Nelson Cromwell.

Unlike the other syndicate members, who quietly left the scene after the sale to the U.S. government was consummated, Cromwell's Achilles' heel was his lust for ruling Panama. It absorbed so much of his time that, admittedly, "clients of our law firm and the public came to understand and to recognize that we were not available as formerly for other professional work." Ruling a country became the passion of the orphaned boy from Brooklyn who had risen from poverty to conquer Wall Street and now owned a nation. His role became so visible that it provoked Senator Morgan again to try to put an end to Cromwell's power in Panama.

Morgan brought John Wallace, the first chief engineer of the canal, to testify before his investigating committee. Wallace claimed that he left his post "to shake Cromwell off my back." He accused the lawyer of creating a scheme to squeeze money out of the Panama Railroad Company a few weeks before the U.S. government bought it. The scheme involved having the company issue $1,000,000 in railroad bonds and then use the money to pay an extraordinary dividend to the shareholders, which indirectly included the Wall Street syndicate, leaving Uncle Sam with the debt. Wallace also told the committee that the lawyer was "in" with the new Secretary of War William Taft. By Wallace's account, Cromwell issued orders as if he were the secretary himself and had even sworn Wallace in to his post. Wallace claimed that at one point he went to see Taft and Roosevelt to complain about Cromwell's behavior, but they dismissed him "with a severity that was astonishing and unseemly."

Morgan asked Cromwell to appear before the committee to testify. Cromwell declined to answer most of Morgan's questions on the grounds that affairs of his client, the Compagnie Nouvelle, and its business, were confidential. An infuriated Senator Morgan threatened to impose sanctions under a congressional law regarding witnesses who do not divulge information. Cromwell remained impassive and repeated, "I refuse to answer."

Senator Morgan then brought a resolution before the Senate to force Cromwell to testify. The resolution passed, but Cromwell was in France when it did. Morgan died shortly thereafter. On March 22, 1906, the *New York Times* expressed its views regarding the value of further proceedings:

> But what's the use? The history of the Panama Canal is one long track and trail of scandal. There has been scandal in the remote past, in the recent past, there is some now and we fear there will be more in the future.

Without Morgan's leadership, the Senate dropped the investigation, leaving the question unanswered: Who got the money?

For years, no one made the inquiry again. As Earl Harding of the *World* wrote, "there was a long period during which intelligent discussion and honest criticism of the Panama affair was so unpopular as to be almost entirely suppressed." If a syndicate existed that speculated on canal shares, nobody knew for sure. The issue did not resurface again until October 2, 1908, when Cromwell's agent Jonas Whitley showed up in the Pulitzer building and mistakenly gave to editor Caleb Van Hamm the details of a long forgotten scam.

11

Who Got the Money?

Pulitzer sent two of his best reporters, Henry Hall and Earl Harding, to Panama, Washington, Paris, and Bogota to dig up information for his defense against Roosevelt's libel suit. Hall was particularly well-positioned to contribute to the case. Robust, witty, and resolutely determined to unmask the scandal, he had worked in Panama for several years as a reporter for José Gabriel Duque's *Panama Star & Herald* and knew everyone who had been involved in the revolution.

Roosevelt did everything in his power to keep the reporters from finding any incriminating evidence. Hall and Harding were hounded by U.S. Secret Services agents everywhere they went. The agents opened every letter in the Pulitzer building and arrested Harding in Colombia when they thought he had procured valuable documents. Galley proofs of articles on the Panama affair had to be printed as soon as copies reached the editor's desk, for fear that they might disappear.

In France, when the reporters tried to get access to the records of the Compagnie Nouvelle to conclusively determine the identity of the shareholders who received payment from the United States, French officials informed them that these records had been sealed by court order and deposited for twenty years with the Chamberlain of Seals in a vault at the Credit Lyonnais, after which they would be destroyed.

The *World* retained well-known Paris lawyers as well as an eminent British attorney and a member of Parliament to help circumvent the French secrecy law. However, when the lawyers won their case and got to the vault, they found a surprise—the records of the company had simply been "wiped off the face of the earth." The British lawyer reported,

> I have never known in my lengthy experience of company matters any public corporation, much less one of such vast importance, having so completely disappeared and removed all traces of its existence as the New Panama Canal Co. . . . So thorough has been its obliteration that only the United States government can now give information respecting the new company's transactions and the identity of the individuals who created it to effectuate this deal, and who for reasons best known to themselves wiped it off the face of the earth when the deal was carried through.

The identity of the shareholders was also lost. According to the same lawyer,

> The stock of the new company was originally registered, so transactions in it could be traced, but power was subsequently obtained to transform it into "bearer" stock, which passed from hand to hand without any record of being preserved. . . . There is nothing to show the names of the owners of the stock at the time of the liquidation of the company and who actually received their proportions of the purchase money paid by the United States. . . . No record exists here of a single person who received the money or of the proportions in which it was paid.

In short, all evidence that might have incriminated the Americans had simply vanished.

In Panama, the reporters did not fare any better, even though, as one prosecutor quipped, "Cromwell's man here was an ass and left too much evidence uncovered." A court-appointed commission traveled to Panama in June 1909 to gather testimony and evidence. Earl Harding went to the Chelsea Pier to bid farewell to the delegation leaving on the ship bound for Panama and saw Edward Hill, Cromwell's partner, boarding the ship with Assistant U.S. District Attorney Knapp sitting next to him. Harding surmised that "every bit of telltale evidence in Panama would be bottled up." Originally, Harding had not planned to go, but after the ship left, he hurried to get the next train to New Orleans. From there, he traveled on a United Fruit Company steamer that landed him in Panama a few days after the court-appointed commission began to take witness testimony.

Amador and Arango had died, but every other conspirator testified before the court. During the testimony, encouraged by the late Dr. Amador's advice that "if the American Government finds out we do not keep our political secrets, it will no longer trust us," the Panamanians stuck to one story: They had not conspired with Washington or the Panama Railroad Company. No money was used to pay off anyone; the Panamanians did not borrow any money from any Wall Street bank; and they never saw Cromwell in New York. In short, according to the *World*, they insisted that "the Panama affair had been all that T.R. had assured Congress and the American people it had been—as clean "as a hound's tooth."

Throughout the hearings, Edward Hill sat beside U.S. District Attorney Knapp and "sprinkled the record with objections" to questions posed by the *World's* counsel, Dan Fuller, and kept interrupting Fuller's examinations of the witnesses. The *World* subpoenaed the records of the Panama Railroad Company but most of the incriminating cables to and from Cromwell were missing. When the *World* tried to interview General Huertas, they were told that "he was in the interior of the country."

Given the failure to obtain any incriminating evidence in either Paris or Panama, by mid-1909, Pulitzer was almost ready to give up and face retribution from Roosevelt. His agents had not found a single document confirming the creation of a syndicate, or a receipt proving that Americans bought shares of the French canal company, or any incriminating letters from Panamanians admitting that the U.S. government played a role in planning the revolution. Afraid they would lose the case for lack of evidence, the *World's* lawyers shifted their defense to claim the constitutional right of free speech. Suddenly, however, the evidence that had eluded them for years began to appear.

The first big break came when the *World* found a 65,000-word brief from Sullivan & Cromwell claiming $800,000 in legal fees from the

Compagnie Nouvelle. The amount was an astounding sum for a law firm, constituting 2 percent of the entire $40 million paid by the United States, and the French liquidator denied the claim. The matter was submitted to arbitration before French tribunals. In support of his claim, Cromwell submitted a confidential memo describing in excruciating detail the services he and his firm had rendered to the Compagnie Nouvelle since 1896. Only twenty copies were printed, and all but two were destroyed after the arbiters rendered their decision. One night, one of those copies was mysteriously found on the desk of a Paris correspondent for the *World*.

The brief boasted of Cromwell's role in convincing Secretary Hay to thwart Colombia's demand for money from the Compagnie Nouvelle; his part in planning the Panama revolution; and his creation of the American syndicate to purchase the assets of the Compagnie Nouvelle. It ended saying that "no summary could describe in their true proportion the variety, the scope, the gravity, the responsibility, the difficulty, and the absorbing nature of the labors imposed by the exigencies of this case." Those services included "every branch of professional activity: engineering, law, legislation, finance, diplomacy, administration, and direction . . . as well as many other matters which would be impossible to enumerate—nor even perhaps would be proper so to do." Plainly put, "Messrs. Sullivan & Cromwell . . . claim that they planned everything, directed everything, and obtained everything; that nothing was done without them, nor by anybody, but themselves."

The second break came in Panama when Earl Harding had the vision to focus on Raoul Amador, the quirky young doctor and son of Dr. Manuel Amador Guerrero. The *World's* lawyer Dan Fuller did not want to use him as a witness because he had heard that "his father called young Amador *loco* and didn't trust him with anything." Fuller also explained that young Dr. Amador had earned a bad reputation in New York due to an extra-marital affair with a certain Mrs. Gresham while serving as Panamanian counsel, and this "would discredit our case if we used him a witness." He insisted that "we must have nothing to do with him."

Harding ignored the warning and began to "quietly cultivate" Raoul Amador. He was friendly and promised to show Harding his father's archives, but every time they had an appointment to go to Dr.

Amador's country house, where the papers were kept, Raoul had an excuse. The day before Harding was supposed to head back to New York, he went looking for Raoul at the country house. He met the young doctor on the way and reminded him that this was his last day in Panama, and that the world would sadly be denied the opportunity to see what old Amador had left for posterity. Apologetically, Raoul exclaimed, "I'm so sorry! I forgot! I left the key to our town house in the country!"

This time Harding had had enough. He knew that the Panamanians were reputed to nurture much jealousy toward each other, so he remarked indignantly, "Don Raoul, I'm sorry, too—for I'm forced to the conclusion that you've been filling me with plain North American bull!" Naming one of the patriots whom he knew to be a rival of young Amador, he said, "Don so-and-so [name omitted from the record] ought to know—and he's authority for the statement that your father thought you were *loco*, had no confidence in you, and never trusted you with anything!"

The trick worked. According to Harding, Raoul lost his temper and let fly a string of Spanish expletives. "You come over to my house! I'll show you whether my father had confidence in me!"

"How'll you get in without a key?"

"Come with me, I'll show you!"

They took a walk around the corner to the Amador country house, and "a thrust of Don Raoul's shoulder pushed the tropically light wooden door past its lock." Reaching up to find a hidden key, he unlocked a battered old steamer trunk and from its bottom right-hand corner pulled a packet of letters tied in a red ribbon.

"So they say my father didn't trust me! Read this letter!"

It was the *Mi hijito* letter, perfectly preserved in old Dr. Amador's careful script, written in New York two days before the doctor sailed for Panama to carry out the revolution. The letter started with a naïve "The plan sounds good to me," implying that it had been the Americans, not Amador and the Panamanians, who had planned the revolution. It showed that the United States government had plans to prevent Colombia from landing troops to put down a revolt. Only Panama City and Colón would be declared independent and brought under the immediate protection of the United States. The other districts of the Isthmus would be brought in later, as indeed they were, and "these all would be under the protection of the United States." A minister would be on hand in Washington, as Bunau-Varilla was, "to take up the treaty. In 30 days everything will be concluded." Financing of the "revolution," Dr. Amador assured his son, "already has been arranged with a bank."

As Don Raoul finished reading the letter, translating his father's Spanish into English, he turned to Harding, "Isn't that just what your newspaper has been trying to prove?"

Harding could hardly contain his excitement. Raoul also gave him other mementos of the revolution, including an invitation to a dinner in New York for all the railroad men who had helped the revolution, as well as the handwritten, unedited memoir of Dr. Manuel Amador. "He had crossed out some whole paragraphs, interlined others and corrected words and phrases in his unmistakable hand," recalled Harding. The manuscript clearly demonstrated the complicity of the Panama Railroad Company.

Afraid the evidence would disappear, Harding photographed the documents and dispatched plates and prints on the first train to Colón to be mailed to New York the next day and then showed the originals to Dan Fuller. Fuller introduced them into the court's record. He brought Raoul to the witness stand. The young doctor testified without hesitation and accused the other patriots of conspiring to hide the truth. He told the court that his father had confided to him that he would never have risked his life on the words of Bunau-Varilla, and that Dr. Amador had personally met with Roosevelt in Washington before he returned to Panama. "Father told me he did not dare risk his life and the lives of our people on any secondhand promises." U.S. Attorney Knapp didn't ask Raoul a single question. The news shocked the whole country. Raoul was ostracized by the other patriots and had to exile himself from Panama. He first moved to Kingston, Jamaica, and eventually settled in Paris, where he died in the company of his mother, Maria de la Ossa de Amador, in 1939.

As a result of Raoul Amador's testimony, the other conspirators panicked, fearing that they would be accused of perjury. Suddenly, evidence began to pour in from everywhere. The first to squeal was Tomás Arias, who gave the *World* copies of the secret codes the conspirators had used. Duque testified that Cromwell had taken him to see Hay in early September 1903 in the middle of the night so that they would leave no traces of their visit, and that Cromwell had promised him the presidency of Panama if he would instigate the revolution. The *World* also obtained previously suppressed copies of an early draft of Arango's memoirs, in which he described the role of the United States government in the planning stages. The reporters got hold of the original cable from Arango to Amador dated September 14 asking Amador to explain the meaning of the cable "Hope." Contrary to what had been said, the cable was sent eight days before Bunau-Varilla arrived in New York, and therefore suggested that Cromwell had been the one who gave Amador his hopes. Some of the lost cables from Cromwell also made an appearance, and the cover-ups and contradictions began to be revealed.

More important, the reporters pieced together how the money was spent in Panama after the revolution, revealing a massive fraud. They learned that on May 13, 1904, President Amador signed law no. 48 of the National Assembly, whereby the financial records of the first eight months of the republic were sealed. After the session, according to J.G. Duque and Eduardo Icaza, national treasurer of Panama, the receipts and accounts showing how the money had been disbursed during those first months were burned in a secret session of the National Assembly. Henceforth, the patriots resolved not to publish the country's finances. This law legalized in lump sums the expenditures through June 30, 1904, as follows:

Liquidated accounts of the extinct department up to November 3, 1904	$ 400,000
Expenditures of the junta from Nov 4, 1903 to February 20, 1904	$1,200,000
Expenditures of the junta from Feb 20, 1904 to June 20, 1904	$1,400,000
	$3,000,000

The conspirators forgot, however, that the *Official Gazette* had already published the finances of the new republic since November 1903. The lump sum accounting legalized by the National Assembly and the monthly statements published in the *Official Gazette* did not match. By comparing the two, the reporters discovered flagrant exaggerations of the expenditures legalized by the assembly.

First, the legalized account grossly exaggerated the first month's expenditures. It showed that the new republic paid $400,000 in obligations of "the extinct department up to November 3, 1904." However, the *Official Gazette* shows total expenditures for November 1903 of only $27,448.80 (of which $22,629.65 was used to pay the *Padilla's* Commander Varón on November 4).

Secondly, the patriots inflated the "army" expenses during the first six months of the republic. The disbursements published by the *Official Gazette* for the first seven months show the following apportionment:

	For the army	Other expenses of government	Cash balances
December 1903	$103,997.65	$23,808.35	$4,158.15
January 1904	204,606.70	13,681.55	1,688.10
February 1904	95,954.20	31,859.20	11,470.0
March 1904	217,051.15	115,028.20	-
April 1904	71,579.50	104,829.60	-
May 1904	132,224.30	106,264.50	11,050.6
June 1904	14,927.00	34,461.30	31,857.8
Total	840,340.50	429,932.70	-

As can be seen above, the total $840,340.50 dollars spent "For the army" is twice as much as the $429,932.70 spent on the rest of the government. According to the testimony taken by the *World*, the government did not have substantial military expenses to justify this figure. "The equipment of the army had cost virtually nothing, since the arms, according to Panamanian accounts at such time, had all been taken from Colombian garrisons." The Panamanians may have purchased some arms after the revolution, but considering that they had the protection of U.S. warships, this could not have amounted to much.

Lastly, the patriots legalized a lump sum of three million dollars for the first eight months when, according to the *Official Gazette*, the total amount spent during that period comes out to just over two million. The difference, roughly one million, equals the first lump sum payment made by J.P. Morgan to the Panamanian treasury on May 2. In short, the patriots kept for themselves the first installment received from Uncle Sam.

The most pressing question that arises, once again, is who got the money? A large portion was paid to Colombian military officers and soldiers who helped the revolution. Eduardo Icaza, the first treasurer of the republic, testified to the court that he began paying off the soldiers immediately with money lent by the local banks. In the first month alone, he said to have disbursed more than $200,000 silver coins, and another $70,000 dollars in gold. Maria Amador's brother-in-law testified that "a simple order written on any old piece of paper and signed by Huertas was enough for the fortunate one to get the money he asked for."

Most of the officers were given $10,000, although some got more, including Captain Marco Salazar and Commander Tascón, each of whom received $35,000. Huertas was paid $30,000 in silver soon after November 3. Then, on May 4, 1904, when Panama received the first one million dollars from the United States, President Amador approved law no. 60 placing at Huertas's disposal $50,000, ostensibly for a trip to the United States, France, and Germany "on a special mission to study the military organizations of those countries." Accompanied by a large party of his friends, he went as far as England and came back dressed in a flashy uniform covered with gold lace. Once the Colombian troops had been paid off, as can be seen in the table above, the military expenses of the new republic fell suddenly from $100,000 or $200,000 each month to $14,927 in June 1904 and $11,504 in July.

The American officials of the Panama Railroad company also received their pay in the spring of 1904, between $15,000 and $25,000 in silver coins. Henry Hall lamented that "considering their services, which were the principal factor, aside from warships and money, in giving the Panamanians their independence and opportunity for graft, the American railroad men were underpaid."

According to the *World*, the Panamanian "patriots" got by far the most, between $25,000 to $100,000 each. The reporters found a check from J.P. Morgan drawn in the name of Amador Guerrero for $100,000, a veritable fortune. Maria Amador's brother-in-law, Donaldo Velazquez, testified that "I am not certain of the money that Dr.

Amador took for his own use; but I know that before the independence he lived off his pay as a doctor employed in the Santo Tomás Hospital, and that he was in a very bad financial condition and it was evident after the revolution that he had enough to pay his debts, to live well, and eventually to purchase the building known by the name Bela de Ore . . . paying large sums in cash." The *World* also uncovered hundreds of J.P. Morgan drafts paid to various local "merchants" who allegedly had provided services to the government. Several of these "merchants" had been conspirators, including José Agustín Arango and José de Obaldiá.

Prompted by the scandal, in 1908, Isadoro Hasera, then minister of finance, tried to make a comprehensive accounting to the National Assembly, but President Amador stopped him, telling him simply that the first million was unaccounted for. No one else has attempted this futile task again.

Content with what they found in Panama, the *World* reporters returned to New York to try to dig up evidence on the American syndicate speculation with the French shares. In late January 1909, John Craig Hammond, a free-lance investigative reporter who had exposed several Wall Street scandals, arrived at the office of Don Seitz, the business manager of the *World*. The reporter had heard rumors about the American syndicate and told Seitz that he believed he could obtain documentary evidence.

When Seitz asked him for his sources, Hammond explained that he had been working on another financial scandal for a magazine and was bribed to drop that investigation in exchange for a much bigger story—the inside scoop on the Panama syndicate operations. He had accepted the deal and had obtained the original syndicate agreement as well as the record of how the profits had been distributed.

Seitz and Harding were ecstatic. They begged Hammond to give them the documents that had eluded them for years, but Hammond refused. He explained that he had been summoned to Washington by very powerful politicians and financiers, including Edward Harriman and several senators, who interrogated him in a conference room for hours. Hammond told Seitz that he could not hand over the documents until March 5, 1909, and then only if his action was approved by certain members of the group whose identity he had sworn to protect. When Seitz asked him the significance of the date, Hammond pointed out that on March 4, Teddy Roosevelt's eight-year reign of power would be over.

Hammond promised to deposit the documents in safe no. 1453 of the Nassau Bank on Wall Street. For months, Seitz and Harding patiently awaited the designated date. On March 5, they went to the Nassau Bank, opened the safe, and found the documents inside. No one knows how much Hammond received in return for the favor. What follows is the complete text of what appears to have been the original signed syndicate agreement:

MEMORANDUM OF AGREEMENT

WHEREAS, J.P Morgan & Co., J. Edward Simmons. James Stillman, Isaac Seligman, Douglas Robinson, Henry W. Taft, H. H. Rogers, J. B. Delamar, and others desire to purchase certain shares of the capital stock of the Compagnie Nouvelle Du Canal de Panama Company, at such terms, and upon such conditions as may be named by a committee of three persons to be selected from the parties to this agreement:

NOW, THEREFORE, we, the undersigned, for ourselves, our administrators and assigns, in consideration of the mutuality hereof, have agreed to and with each other as follows:

FIRST: To purchase as many shares of the capital stock of the Compagnie Nouvelle Du Canal de Panama Company as possible, at a price not exceeding twenty per cent (20%) per share, per par value of One Hundred Dollars ($100).

SECOND: When so acquired, to place the whole of said shares of stock in the hands of the committee herein before I referred to.

THIRD: Said stock is to be held by said committee for the benefit of the parties to this agreement, and to be disposed of at a price not less than Fifty-five (55%) per share on a basis of One Hundred Dollars ($100) par value.

The proceeds of the sale of the stock, after deducting all and any expenses in acquiring and in making the sale thereof, are to be divided pro rata among the parties to this Agreement, and according to the respective amount situated and paid in by them for the purchase of the aforementioned stock.

IN WITNESS WHEREOF, the parties hereto have set their hands and seals this twenty-fifth day of May, Nineteen Hundred (May 25, 1900)

In the presence of:

WNC (signature)	J.P. Morgan & Co.	(signature)
WNC	James Stillman	(signature)
WNC	I. Seligman	(signature)
WNC	J. Edward Simmons	(signature)
WNC	J. R. Delamar	(signature)
WNC	Vernon H. Brown	(signature)
WNC	Geo J. Gould	(signature)
WNC	Chauncey M. Depew	(signature)
WNC	E. C. Converse	(signature)
WNH	Clarence H. Mackay	(signature)
WNC	Douglas Robinson	(signature)
WNC	H. H. Rogers	(signature)
WNC	Winslow Lanier & Co.	(signature)
WNC	Henry W. Taft	(signature)
WNC	Charles H. Flint	(signature)
WNC	Edward J. Hill	(signature)

June 6th, 1901

The reporters hired a handwriting expert who confirmed that the set of initials "WNC" to the left of each of the signatures belonged to William Nelson Cromwell. The date of the syndicate's creation, May 25, 1900, coincidentally corresponds to the time when Maurice Hutin, president of the Compagnie Nouvelle, dismissed Cromwell as U.S. general counsel of the company. The parties listed were those rumored to have been involved from the beginning. Many of them, including J.P. Morgan, Douglas Robinson, Isaac Seligman, and J. Edward Simmons, had been actively involved in the Panama story before and after the revolution. (A copy of the original syndicate statement appears on pages 182–183.)

The other document provided by Hammond was a red Moroccan leather bound book. The name WINDSOR TRUST CO. appeared on the cover in gold letters. Stamped inside was the title BANKER'S TRUST COMPANY, a bank headed by E.C. Converse, another syndicate member. The sixteen pages of the book show handwritten names listed next to notations of dollar amounts, representing the investment of each person in the secret syndicate. The original subscription agreement was signed by ten men, and the rest joined later. The list of original signers were:

J.P. Morgan & Co.	$433,333
J.E. Simmons	800,000
Winslow Lanier & Co.	333,333
George J. Gould (E.H.H.T)	950,000
J.B. Delmar (misspelled)	1,333,333
Chauncey M. Depew	385,000
Clarence Mackay (see NPC)	750,000
Douglas Robinson (legal See C)	200,000
Isaac Seligman (Morton T Co see C)	1,333,333
Henry W. Taft	190,000

The names of those not on the "Memorandum" were:

C.W. Young	$385,000
F.L. Jeffries [Amador]	750,000
Nelson P. Cromwell	1,333,333
J.R. Hill	170,000
G.W. Perkins	233,000
H.J. Satterlee	200,000

"Nelson P. Cromwell" appeared in a number of press reports about Cromwell's "Americanization" scheme in 1899. When Senator Morgan asked him to identify "Nelson P.," Cromwell refused to answer. Amador had become a syndicate member, cloaked by F.L. Jeffries, the American adventurer who helped in the revolution and got as his reward a huge timber and land grant in the Bayano River valley, where the *World* reporters later found him.

The Hammond papers established the existence of a conspiracy to buy the shares, but they did not prove that the speculators purchased

MEMORANDUM OF AGREEMENT.

W H E R E A S, J. P. Morgan & Co, J. Edward Simmons,

James Stillman, Isaac Seligman, Douglas Robinson, Henry W. Taft,

H. H. Rogers, J. R. Delamar and others   , desire to purchase certain shares

of the capital stock of the Compagnie Nouvelle Du Canal de Panama

Company, at such terms, and upon such conditions as may be named by a com-

mittee of three persons to be selected from the parties to this agree-

ment;

NOW, THEREFORE ,we, the undersigned, for our

selves, our administrators and assigns, in consideration of the mutuality

hereof, have agreed to and with each other as follows:

First: To purchase as many shares of the capital stock of

the Compagine Nouvelle Du Canal de Panama Company as possible, at a

price not exceeding twenty per cent (20%) per share, per par value of

One Hundred Dollars ($100.)

Second: When so acquired, to place the whole of said

shares of stock in the hands of the committee herein before refered to.

Third: Said stock is to be held by said committee for

the benefit of the parties to this agreement, and to be disposed of at a

price not less than Fifty-five (55%) per share on a basis of One Hundred

Dollars ($100) par value.

The proceeds of the sale of the stock, after deducting all

and any expenses in acquiring and in making the sale thereof, are to be

Memorandum of Agreement (from *The Untold Story of Panama*)

devied pro rata among the parties to this agreement, and according to

the respective amount subscribed and paid in by them for the purchase

of the aforementioned stock.

IN WITNESS WHEREOF, the parties hereto have set their

hands and seals this Twenty-Fifth day of May Ninteen hundred (May 25,

1900)

In the presence of:

any shares from the French shareholders. The *World* thus subpoenaed Wall Street brokerage houses for any activity in Compagnie Nouvelle or Compagnie Universelle shares. The investigators obtained ledger sheets from the banking houses of J.&W. Seligman & Co. and Kuhn, Loeb & Co. (both members of Cromwell's syndicate), which showed, under the heading "PANAMA OBLIGATION, POOL ACCOUNT," various purchases and sales from January 1902 to February 13, 1906 (liquidation of the French accounts was not completed until June 1908). Participants in the pool account were, among others, Isaac Seligman, Otto Kahn, and Paul Warburg (he later advocated the privatization of the Panama Canal). Isaac Seligman's purchase record (a copy of which follows on p. 185) provides a clear example.

With these documents, in addition to testimony from French shareholders who had sold their bearer shares to Americans, the *World* had the evidence that it had been seeking. Earl Harding, Henry Hall, Dan Fuller and other reporters were summoned back to New York. Led by Caleb Van Hamm, Don Seitz, and old Pulitzer himself, still running his empire from the *Liberty*, the editorial room began its work, weaving the components into a coherent tale of fraud and scandal.

On May 25, 1900, William Nelson Cromwell organized a secret syndicate including, among others, J. P. Morgan, E.J. Simmons, Isaac Seligman, Douglas Robinson, and H. W. Taft. Dr. Manuel Amador made a claim in this organization at a later date.

Cromwell controlled the syndicate and had a major stake in its holdings. The purpose was to buy as much of the stock of the Compagnie Nouvelle and of the Compagnie Universelle for as little as possible. The syndicate subscribed $5 million, more than sufficient funds to buy all of the Panama stock. Once the covert investors had collected enough shares, they would concentrate on getting the United States to buy the French holdings for $40 million, the payment of which would actually flow back to them. The scheme was a gamble, but the reward enormous.

Since the collapse of the de Lesseps company, everyone believed the project was dead and that the French stock was worthless. Actually, bonds of the company were sold in France for about 3 percent

MR. ISAAC N. SELIGMAN,

In Account With J. & W. SELIGMAN & CO.

1902
Aug. 6   To 1500 Panama Canal 6% 1st Series, Separate A/c)
 "   "   " 1000   "   "   6% 2nd   "   "   ") $ 34,384.75

Oct.13   "   881   "   "   6% 1st   "   "   ")
 "   "   "   619   "   "   6% 2nd   "   "   ")   30,129.50
Nov.30   " 1475   "   "   6% 1st   "   Special A/c   23,543.26
Dec. 5   "   125   "   "   New Stock,   "   "   2,533.14
1904
Jan.11   "   175   "   "   6% 1st Series,   "   ")
 "   "   "   177   "   "   6% 2nd   "   "   ")
 "   "   "   174   "   "   5%   "   "   ")
 "   "   "   194   "   "   4%   "   "   ")
 "   "   "   150   "   "   3%   "   "   ")   11,021.74
 "   13   "   917   "   "   New Stock,   "   "   20,064.16
Apr.11   " 1000   "   "   "   "   "   "   23,942.95
Jun.29   " Delivered in Paris by Mr. Kahn on instructions)
             given by Paul M. Warburg for a/c of Isaac)
             N. S.:
             328 Panama Canal 6% 1st Series)
             146   "   "   6% 2nd   ")
             458   "   "   5%   ")   ----
             374   "   "   4%   ")
             355   "   "   3%   ")
             203   "   "   Lottery Bonds)
              60   "   "   New Stock)
1905
Sep.20   " Received from the Liquidator in Paris)
             815 Panama Canal Lottery Bonds) Spec'l A/c
 "   "   " 1353 Panama Can.Lott.Bds., Separate A/c
 "   "   "   475   "   "   "   "   A/c Warburg
 "   "   "   20   "   "   "   "   A/c Coupons
 "   29   "   11 6417 "   "   "   "   Bought of Jefferson S.   255.34
 "   "   "   802 4440 "   "   "   "   Bought of J.& W.S.& Co. 17,599.50
Oct.17   " his proportion of Paris Joint A/c)
             145 20 Panama Canal Lott.Bds.)   2,946.09
 "   "   "   2 70   "   "   "   " Bought of Isaac S.
                                               London   54.78
1903
Oct.13   " 2000 Panama Canal New Stock, Special A/c   27,020.51
May 20   " 1250   "   "   "   "   Separate   25,972.18
Aug.13   " fcs.11,000 50 abandoned call Panama Stk.,Separate   2,125.70
1905
Oct.25   "   " 11,000 E.F. Winslow, Special A/c   2,130.09

PAUL M. WARBURG.

1903
May 20   To 1250 Panama Canal New Stock   25,966.64
              Cables   12.00

1904
Feb.15   By 850 Panama Canal New Stock   18,748.78
Mch. 9   " 400   "   "   "   "   8,854.97

of their face value. Since no one would buy them, the Paris bourse did not trade them, and no one kept a record of transactions as the bonds were in bearer form.

In 1900, the syndicate sent word to the "penalized" banks of the Compagnie Nouvelle, including Credit Lyonnais, headed by Maurice Bo, to quietly buy up the bonds of the Compagnie Universelle. The speculators instructed the banks not to buy the bonds in hundreds but in fives and tens from the thousands of peasants who owned them. An eminent American lawyer who was involved in the affair described the operation:

> Agents of these men quietly bought up for several months thousands of shares of the Old Company all through the country. The small holders of the canal paper hastened to take advantage of the gift laid at their doors, for the shares for many years had been considered practically worthless by thousands of peasants.

The president of a large French bank verified the account:

> These gentlemen were engaged for many months in buying up the Old Panama shares at the cheapest rate possible. When they had enough shares or enough influence to control the fate of the Canal, they managed to bring to a successful issue the paperbacks with the American Government.

(At one point, Maurice Bunau-Varilla wrote to his brother Philippe that J.P. Morgan was interested in buying their shares.) All the bonds were supposedly purchased for about $3.5 million. The syndicate then embarked on a mission to convince the United States to buy its company.

The first hurdle was getting the Isthmian Canal Commission to recommend the Panama route instead of the Nicaragua route and to get the commission to offer a high price for the Compagnie Nouvelle's holdings. Cromwell wined and dined the members of the commission on their fact-finding trip to Paris and convinced them to offer forty million dollars for the rusting machinery and soon-to-expire concessions of the company, even though the syndicate had just bought the company for only $3.5 million. The "penalized stockholders" of the Compagnie Nouvelle who had not sold to the Americans, including Philippe Bunau-Varilla, Charles de Lesseps and Gustave Eiffel, also pushed for the scheme since they would share in the profits.

Cromwell controlled the company through these large shareholders, but because of his speculating activities, he was dismissed by a board that did not include any penalized shareholders. By January 1902, he was back in Washington lobbying, thanks to the help of Bunau-Varilla. A new administration took over the company, and its president, Maurice Bo, a penalized shareholder, began to facilitate the operation in France to make sure the plan was carried to completion.

The penalized shareholders sent Bunau-Varilla to America to help lobby Congress to approve the construction of the canal in Panama instead of Nicaragua. Some claimed that the speculators bribed many congressmen to help the Panama cause. It is certainly possible that Mark "Dollar" Hanna supported Panama under the guise of patriotism when he was actually working to help his banker, J. Edward Simmons, and the syndicate. (On the occasion of his funeral, the *Evening Post* published an inflammatory article with the following headline: "His Skin was Ever Tough, Conscience was a Word Unknown to Him.")

As a result of the lobby's whirlwind activity, Congress adopted the Panama route. All went well in Washington, but Colombia almost derailed the speculator's plot by trying to claim a large part of the forty million dollars to be paid to the Compagnie Nouvelle. For Cromwell and the American syndicate members, any money paid to Colombia meant less for them. Cromwell thus convinced Hay and Roosevelt that Colombia's president Marroquín was trying to blackmail the United States to get more money for himself and his cronies, and that Colombia's demands were "wholly inadmissible" to the United States government.

When Colombia rejected the treaty, Cromwell planned, instigated, and manufactured a revolution in Panama. Most of the revolutionaries, including Amador and Arango, were employees of the Panama Railroad & Steamship Co., whose head and representative was Cromwell. Cromwell and Bunau-Varilla convinced President Roosevelt and Secretary Hay that there was no alternative to a revolution and got the United States to violate treaty rights and international law to wrest Panama away from Colombia.

Although Cromwell superficially appeared hostile, in fact he planned all the details of the revolution, including the ruse used by the Panama Railroad Company to deny transporting the Colombian troops to Panama City that could have quashed the insurgency. During the revolution, the Panamanian patriots relied on their unlimited supply of Wall Street dollars to bribe Colombian troops to go home without fighting, while enjoying the cooperation and protection of the American railroad officials and U.S. warships sent by Roosevelt.

After the revolution was complete and the treaty hastily signed by Bunau-Varilla, it was not the secretary of the treasury who made the payments, but J.P. Morgan, who had been appointed fiscal agent for transactions between the United States, Panama, and the Compagnie Nouvelle. With his lawyer Cromwell overseeing disbursement, Morgan paid about 30 percent of the money to the penalized shareholders, who reaped a 129 percent profit for their investment (a terrible punishment for fraud). Bunau-Varilla received at least $440,000. The rest of the money, 60 percent of the forty million, went to the American syndicate members, who may have received returns on their investments as high as 1,233 percent. No records have ever been found regarding the distribution of the forty million.

The bounty did not end with the payment to the French company. Before Cromwell gave up control of the Panama Railroad & Steamship Co., he squeezed out another million by issuing bonds and then using the money to pay the syndicate a dividend, leaving Uncle Sam with the debt. In addition, he helped Amador distribute the money that Panama received from the United States. He became Panama's general counsel, fiscal agent, and representative in the United States, with discretion to decide how the new republic's money was invested. By becoming Roosevelt and later President Taft's adjutant, he ruled the affairs of the Panama Canal for more than a decade.

When the case came to trial before Judge Charles Hough in the United States District Court in New York City on January 25, 1910, the *World* was fully prepared to submit the evidence that would prove it was justified in writing the famed editorial. At the same time, however, counsel to the *World* moved to quash the indictment on the basis that the court had no jurisdiction in the matter. Many small newspapers did not want the *World* to concede that a federal libel law existed, as this would leave them at the mercy of government officials who might use libel suits to bankrupt them.

Judge Hough agreed with the *World*. On the first day of the trial, he dismissed the case, ruling there was no such thing as a federal libel law. President Taft decided to take the case to the U.S. Supreme Court in order to settle the free press issue once and for all. On January 3, 1911, Chief Justice White handed a unanimous decision in favor of the *World*, based on constitutional rights. Newspapers all over the country congratulated Pulitzer for defending the right to free speech. When a reporter asked Roosevelt for his view, his only reply was, "I have nothing to say!"

For Earl Harding, Henry Hall, and their colleagues who had spent three years digging information, the decision was a disappointment. They wanted the case to go to trial to get a chance to conclusively show the truth about the Panama scandal. They did not have to wait very long.

On March 23, 1911, during a speech at the Greek Theater at the University of California at Berkeley, before eight thousand people, Roosevelt made a fateful remark that essentially contradicted every statement he had made about Panama to date. For years, he had been denying his complicity in the Panama revolution, but he had decided to run for president again and taking credit for the canal was a political asset.

Roosevelt started his speech with a spirited call to the people of California to carry on the courage of the pioneers who had settled that state. Then his mood lightened:

> The Panama Canal I naturally take special interest in because I started it. [*laughter and applause*]
>
> There are plenty of other things I started merely because the time had come to whoever was in power would have started them.
>
> But the Panama Canal would not have been started if I had not taken hold of it, because if I had followed the traditional or conservative method I should have submitted an admirable state paper occupying a couple of hundred pages detailing all of the facts to Congress and asking Congress consideration of it.

In that case there would have been a number of excellent speeches made on the subject in Congress; the debate would be proceeding at this moment with great spirit and the beginning of work of the canal would be fifty years in the future. [*laughter and applause*]

Fortunately the crisis came at a period when I could act unhampered. Accordingly I took the Isthmus, started the canal and then left Congress not to debate the canal, but to debate me. [*laughter and applause*] [Emphasis added].

"I took the Isthmus" was a proud and boastful statement characteristic of Roosevelt, "the kind of exaggeration that he liked to make," as Secretary Root observed. It was also a misleading statement, for it dismissed the importance of Cromwell, Hanna, Amador, Bunau-Varilla, and others. At various times, T.R. had stated that he had merely "ceased to stamp out the revolutionary fuses" and also that " I took the canal because Bunau-Varilla brought it to me on a silver platter."

Nevertheless, his latest statement traveled the world like a brush fire. Riots broke out in many Latin American cities, and Colombia immediately demanded that the United States apologize and pay a sizable reparation for the "taking" and the country's loss. They implored the U.S. secretary of state to submit the issue to the Hague Tribunal. This prompted the House Committee on Foreign Affairs, headed by Congressman Rainey, to conduct yet another investigation into the events surrounding the Panama revolution. On January 26, 1912, the committee passed the following resolution:

> WHEREAS, a former President of the United States has stated that he took Panama from the Republic of Colombia without consulting Congress, the committee be directed to inquire into whether the United States should pay Colombia reparations for the alleged taking.

The committee originally intended to investigate the activities of Theodore Roosevelt, but soon it became evident that its real focus would again be William Nelson Cromwell, whom Congressman Rainey called "the most dangerous man in America since Aaron Burr." The main witness during the hearings was Henry Hall, who presented the evidence that the *World* had compiled for the court case. For almost a month, Congress listened as Hall narrated the events surrounding the Panama affair. His testimony consumes over 600 pages in the congressional record, compiled under the title *The Story of Panama*. Supported by hundreds of pages of evidence, it provides the most faithful recollection of the events that took place before, during, and after the Panamanian revolution.

On February 20, almost a month after the hearings had begun, the committee called for a recess before voting on the resolution. But friends of Roosevelt in Congress, including Henry Cabot Lodge, blocked any further deliberations. The committee never met again.

A great deal of time and money had been spent on the investigation, but the question of "Who got the money?" was never conclusively answered. Worse, it was never raised again. To critics and supporters alike, Roosevelt's statement, "I took the Isthmus," would be remembered as the best explanation of what happened in Panama in 1903, a symbol of Teddy Roosevelt's "gunboat diplomacy." Now that the president had stated his version of events, no other explanation would do. Henceforth, allegations about a syndicate that had speculated on French canal shares and fomented a revolution in Panama would be summarily dismissed. Later, even Roosevelt would deny any involvement with the American syndicate. In his *Autobiography*, he made no mention of Cromwell although he devoted an entire chapter to the Panama Canal and discussed at length Bunau-Varilla's role. In other words, not only had Roosevelt "taken the Isthmus," he also eliminated the possibility of further investigation and scrutiny about Wall Street's role in the creation of Panama.

The conspiracy and the "long track and trail of scandal" that had seemed so obvious to Senator Morgan and had consumed three full congressional investigations was thus forgotten. Historians would later question whether the issue should have been raised at all, as there was nothing illegal in risking money, lobbying, or even encouraging a revolution. Historian David Howarth offered an explanation:

> On the whole it seems likely that American speculators had made a handsome profit. It is odd that other Americans should have been surprised and incensed at the idea. There was nothing illegal about it. . . . It would have been much more surprising if nobody had taken a tempting gamble, and if no tips had ever leaked out of Cromwell's office. If

the treaty and the consequent sale had not gone through, the shares would have been valueless. If none of the $40 million found its way back to America, the American financial world had been much less shrewd than it was supposed to be.

If, however, Roosevelt, Hay, Hanna, Congress, the Isthmian Canal Commission, or any other public official had knowledge of the scheme and took action to help the American syndicate, a severe offense was committed. Though the evidence certainly seems to indicate collusion, no one will never know conclusively.

After the congressional investigation, as the scandal faded into obscurity, the evidence that the *World* had arduously collected was essentially lost. The "Memorandum of Agreement" and the bank records that proved the existence of the speculating syndicate were locked in a vault in the old Pulitzer Building on Park Row for years, until the newspaper met its end in 1919. Before the newspaper closed, Robert Lyman, one of the managing editors who had supervised the collection of evidence, called Harding, who had moved into the business world. Lyman said, "Records in the old Panama vault will be discarded unless we preserve them. Would you join me?" Harding responded to the call, and the two took a mass of material, including much of the testimony, letters, cables, and agreements that supported the assertions in the court case and the congressional investigations, and deposited them in a rented fireproof warehouse vault. The records remained there until 1937, when Lyman made his final call before he died. "Then I took over," Harding recounted in his 1959 book entitled *The Untold Story of Panama*, "and shall preserve the Panama papers until eventually they shall go to one of the libraries that have shown a special interest in Latin American history." However, many of the original agreements, copies of checks paid by J.P. Morgan to various patriots, and other incriminating documents that Harding collected are mysteriously missing from the collection and other libraries. It is suspected that many revealing photographs and documents have been purchased and taken out of circulation over the years by people who have an interest in hiding the truth.

Although the scandal has been forgotten, what happened in Panama in 1903 created both a physical and metaphorical rift between the United States and Latin American countries throughout the twentieth century. Roosevelt's "I took the Isthmus" proclamation badly blemished the reputation of the United States in the eyes of its southern neighbors. The Monroe Doctrine, which had guided the friendly relations between the United States and Latin America throughout the nineteenth century, was now firmly dead. Henceforth, as Congressman Rainey said, "in the plazas of the more important cities of the Spanish American Republics, as they sit there in the evenings, you will hear, if you listen, that they refer to the United States as the 'Great Hog of the North.'"

The "Great Hog of the North" denied any wrongdoing to Colombia for two decades. During Woodrow Wilson's tenure, the U.S. government proposed and signed a treaty apologizing to Colombia for its actions in Panama and providing a twenty-five million dollar reparation. The Colombian congress swiftly ratified the treaty, but during the U.S. congressional debates, former President Roosevelt emerged from the Brazilian jungle, where he had been suffering a near-fatal case of yellow fever, to chastise the Senate for even considering so lowly an agreement, contending that it amounted to an admission of guilt by the United States. The Senate cowered before Roosevelt's diatribe; friends of Roosevelt, including Henry Cabot Lodge, led the way for the rejection of the treaty.

Colombia had to wait until T.R. died to get justice from the United States. Roosevelt died in his sleep in 1919, a victim of the malaria and leg infection that he contracted during his vigorous expedition to Brazil. In 1922, Henry Cabot Lodge and his Republican congressmen led the charge again, but this time they advocated ratification. What precipitated their change in policy? Oil reserves had been discovered in Colombia, and American oil companies were trying to secure the rights to them.

Though Colombia had to wait two decades for reparations, Bunau-Varilla and Cromwell couldn't be happier with the course of events after Roosevelt claimed responsibility. Although in Panama Bunau-Varilla's name would always be synonymous with treachery, he enjoyed great fame and fortune in Europe, where no one doubted that he had acted purely for the "glory of France" as he had always claimed. After he signed the Hay-Bunau-Varilla treaty, he returned to Paris, where he became editor-in-chief of Paris's *Le Matin*. He did not slow his pace after Panama, but continued to absorb himself in various engineering projects. During World War I, at Verdun, he designed a system for purifying water that is still used all over the world. He also suffered the loss of his left leg.

The Grand Officer of the French Legion of Honor never forgot Panama. He was a passenger on board the first major steamer to travel through the canal. He wrote three separate accounts of what had occurred in Panama, including a five-hundred-page treatise entitled *Panama: The Creation, Destruction and Resurrection*, in which he claimed that he alone, and not "the lawyer Cromwell," was responsible for the resurrection of the Panama Canal. He lived a long life and would "stump the boulevards of Paris with the rosette of the Legion of Honor in his button hole." During World War II, this "veritable Panamanian Ulysses" became a fascist and supported Hitler, but died just days before Germany invaded his beloved France. It is not known whether he made any more than $440,000 on the Panama deal, but his heirs inherited a great fortune for which they cannot account.

The biggest winner by far was William Nelson Cromwell. Precisely how much money he made in the Panama affair is a mystery. Two full congressional investigations, more than 5,000 pages of the congressional record, and a libel suit before the U.S. Supreme Court were devoted to trying to prove he and his friends made a handsome profit in Panama, but thanks to his cunning, nothing was ever conclusively decided. As for his legal fees, Sullivan & Cromwell's bill was arbitrated from over $800,000 to just under $250,000. Although Cromwell claimed that he never charged Panama for his services as general counsel, his activities in handling Panama's constitutional fund of $6,000,000 may have paid handsomely. In November 1910, six of the twenty-eight members of the Panama National Assembly demanded that Cromwell be bonded to force him to account for the whereabouts of the fund, but the assembly refused to turn against the republic's benefactor. Cromwell continued to serve as Panama's fiscal agent until 1937, when he and J.P. Morgan turned over the constitutional fund invested in more than a hundred New York City mortgages to the Chase Manhattan Bank.

But for Cromwell, Panama meant more than money. Wall Street tycoons and robber barons at the turn of the century had created fortunes hitherto unimaginable. They built mansions that rivaled European palaces, and with their wealth bought power and prestige. Still, they could never have what kings and princes had boasted for centuries, sovereignty over a territory and dominion over a people. In Panama, Cromwell got that kind of power. Throughout the decade, he ruled Panama with an iron fist, installing government ministers and removing them, managing the country's money and its relations with the United States, and deciding the fate of the Panama Canal on behalf of Presidents Roosevelt and Taft. In retrospect, he was the real-life incarnation of Captain Macklin, the admired hero of Richard Harding Davis's popular 1902 novel by the same name about an American boy of modest means who becomes the ruler of a Central American country. Congressman Rainey's comparison of Cromwell with Aaron Burr was not far off either: Burr had sought to become emperor of Mexico.

After Panama, Cromwell spent the better part of his time in France. He received the Grand Cross of the Legion of Honor from that country for his work in resurrecting the Panama Canal. Meanwhile, his firm, Sullivan & Cromwell, flourished as one of Wall Street's preeminent law firms under the direction of his handpicked successors, John Foster Dulles and Arthur H. Dean. Cromwell died in 1948 at the age of ninety-four, leaving nineteen million dollars and no heirs.

Neither Cromwell nor Bunau-Varilla ever acknowledged the role the other played in the Panama affair. It must have appeared to each that to ignore would be more insulting than to criticize. In Panama, only Bunau-Varilla's six-month involvement would be remembered, even though it was the Fox who paved the way for the construction of the Panama Canal.

Thanks to the intervention of these two opportunists, Panamanians got the independence that they sought throughout the nineteenth century. History would have been very different if Colombia had ratified the treaty, or if Roosevelt had gone ahead with his original plans to annex Panama. He wrote, "If they had not revolted, I should have recommended Congress to take possession of the Isthmus by force of arms." But the Panamanians did revolt and got the republic that they wanted. However, their victory was only partial. Due to Bunau-Varilla's treacherous act in re-drafting the treaty, the canal became a thorny source of controversy between the United States and Panama throughout the twentieth century.

In short, only the Wall Street speculators got everything that they sought. In America at the turn of the century, these robber barons saw the synergies between three powerful forces: Teddy Roosevelt's hunger for territory in which to build an Isthmian canal; Panama's century-long quest for freedom; and Wall Street's greed. William Nelson Cromwell created a syndicate and a brilliant scheme that perfectly synthesized these forces and executed it flawlessly. In the process, the Wall Street tycoons created a nation, realized for mankind the centuries-old dream of building the Panama Canal, and then made sure that "grass grew over the episode." American capitalism functioned exactly as it was supposed to do: the plan was lavishly profitable and immensely beneficial.

Epilogue
A Chapter of Dishonor

The Panama Canal treaty became a source of controversy between the tiny republic and the United States the moment it was hastily signed. Contested issues ranged from rights over islands, ports, duties, employee salaries, and postal fees, to the amount of the yearly indemnity. However, nothing was more repugnant to Panamanians than the existence of the Panama Canal Zone.

Created pursuant to article III of the Hay-Bunau-Varilla treaty, the offspring of Bunau-Varilla's treachery, the United States acted as sovereign within the zone. To keep the Panamanians out, Americans built a tall fence and guarded it with armed military officers. Inside the fence, silver-haired G.I.'s cut the grass, kept their wooden houses freshly painted, played golf in the manicured courses, and eradicated every tropical disease. Outside the fence, West Indian blacks lived in pestilent wooden shacks on streets plagued by crime and poverty. Amador's dream of a prosperous country free from diseases, a "model for the tropics," did not materialize, except inside the Canal Zone.

Generations born after the events of 1903 could not understand why Panamanians were not allowed inside their own land, or why the United States flag fluttered atop the flagpoles. Ignorant of the means by which the republic came into being, they blamed the first patriots of selling out to the "Great Hog of the North" and strove to remove the artificial barrier between two countries and two worlds. The rest of Latin

America rallied to the cause of the Panamanians, as the fence came to symbolize the twentieth-century imperialism of the United States.

Beginning in the 1930s, Panamanians demanded a new treaty that would confer upon them greater rights than the Hay-Bunau-Varilla treaty. They proposed several amendments, but each successive American administration rejected a substantial revision. Presidential campaigns in Panama were waged on convincing the United States to ratify a new treaty. However, time and again the United States was quick to remind Panamanians that their country had come into existence as a protectorate.

When Egypt's Colonel Nasser nationalized the Suez Canal in 1956, Panamanians began to lobby for control of the Panama Canal. In 1964, riots broke out when a group of students, fueled by national pride, scaled the fence and raised the Panamanian tricolor flag over the Canal Zone's Balboa High School. The Americans responded by gunning down the unarmed students, killing nine and crippling others.

Panama severed relations with the United States for the first time in its history. Though diplomacy was restored soon thereafter, everyone in America understood that henceforth the peace and stability of the Panama Canal depended on giving up some of the liberal concessions that the United States had unjustly obtained in 1903. Many Zonians—the name given to Americans living in the Canal Zone—vehemently disagreed. One of them, Maurice Ries, wrote in the *Legion Magazine*:

> The Panama Canal is our jugular vein, our lifeline. Cut it and the United States dies. Wrest it from our control and in matters of seaborne commerce and naval defense the U.S. east and west coasts again become, as once they were, months instead of days apart. Block it and our foreign commerce strangles. Take it away from us and we have no further right to establish defenses so far to the south. The result will be that then our hemispheric relations will change, and our foreign policy must change, and no man on earth can say what might happen to his nation once that chain reaction is set in motion.

Given the entrenched American public opposition to a new treaty, it took a military threat from Panamanians to convince the United States to negotiate a new treaty.

On October 11, 1968, a young colonel named Omar Torrijos Herrera overthrew the constitutional government of President Arnulfo Arias and began a twenty-year populist reign of power that culminated with General Manuel Antonio Noriega. Obtaining a new canal treaty became the raison d'être of the populist Torrijos government. Torrijos mobilized international support and made formal demands to the United States. The Panama Canal question became a major issue in the 1976 presidential campaign. Republican candidate Ronald Reagan drew thunderous applause when he made his claim that "we bought [the] canal, we paid for it, it's ours, and we should tell Torrijos and company that we are going to keep it." Senator Samuel Hayakawa, in contrast, joked that "we stole it fair and square." How the rights to the canal were obtained had become an issue in a presidential campaign a century later.

After President Jimmy Carter's election, he immediately appointed a team of negotiators to begin the arduous work of drafting a new treaty. For him, the Panama question had become the touchstone of the new United States policy towards the Third World, in which it would try to "adjust to nationalistic aspirations instead of confronting them." He also feared a military conflict in Panama. Secretary of State Cyrus Vance, who had witnessed the 1964 uprising as Johnson's secretary of war, believed that "Panamanians would eventually resort to violence, even to the point of destroying the Canal." Although it was unlikely that Panamanians would damage the country's most valuable resource, when a reporter asked Torrijos how he would respond if Panamanians marched en mass to demonstrate against the zone, he answered, "Two courses are open to me. To smash it or to lead it, and I am not going to smash it." The Pentagon took his statements so seriously that it made contingency plans to deploy 100,000 troops in Panama if necessary.

Negotiations began on February 17, 1977, and continued for almost two years. Panamanians wanted nothing less than the immediate dissolution of the insidious Canal Zone, which had made them outsiders in their own heartland, forcing them to gaze "like the poor looking through the lodge gates at some unapproachable estate." They also insisted on administering the canal and on the removal of U.S. military fortifications in Panama by December 31, 1999. Americans, in exchange, demanded a neutrality guarantee, insisting on the right of the United States to intervene in Panama if the stability of the canal were ever threatened.

With each side compromising on some of its demands, the treaty was signed and sent to the U.S. Senate. The arduous debate occupied forty-two working days, three times as many as had been spent on the NATO treaty in 1949. Republicans led the charge against it, but the Democrats used the threat of "a military nightmare, another Vietnam," "with volunteers from all over Latin America," to claim that the United States had no choice. On April 18, 1979, the Torrijos-Carter treaty was ratified by a vote of sixty-eight to thirty-two, just one vote more than the required two-thirds majority. Panamanians also ratified it overwhelmingly by a national plebiscite, and on October 1, 1979, the fence that had existed for three-quarters of a century, finally came down.

Panama, however, will remain under the everlasting watch of the United States. The Torrijos-Carter treaty maintains the famous "neutrality clause" that has been a fixture in all U.S. treaties with the territory of Panama since 1846. Although the wording has changed, its essence has not, granting to the United States the right to intervene in Panama to defend the waterway against "any threat to the regime of neutrality," that is, "any aggression or threat directed against the Canal or against the peaceful transit of vessels through the Canal."

Aware of the clause's potential reach, the Panamanians insisted on inserting in the treaty a reservation to the effect that the clause will not be "interpreted as a right of intervention in the internal affairs of Panama or interference with its political independence or sovereign integrity." The Americans agreed to the amendment to appease the Panamanians, but everyone understands that the controlling clause is essentially the 150-year-old right to intervene in Panama.

This became evident during the 1989 invasion of Panama to oust General Manuel Antonio Noriega. Noriega himself was the consequence of U.S. policy in Panama. After the Torrijos-Carter treaty was signed, the U.S. administration ordered the creation of a strong Panamanian military capable of protecting the canal once the Americans troops departed. The Pentagon turned the small and disorganized Panamanian police force into a powerful army trained in the most sophisticated weaponry. The United States could not foresee that this army would turn against it in the hands of a despot.

In 1982, the charismatic General Torrijos was mysteriously killed in an airplane crash, and the reign of terror of former chief of intelligence General Manuel Antonio Noriega began. The stout, so-called pineapple face (thanks to his pot-holed complexion) had been an ally of the United States since the 1950s, when as a military student in Peru, he sold military secrets to the C.I.A. He continued to cooperate with succeeding American administrations by selling information during the volatile years of peasant uprisings in El Salvador and Nicaragua. At the same time, the trusted ally was playing double agent, aiding emerging arch rivals of the United States, Colombian drug traffickers.

During the Reagan administration's war against drugs, a Florida federal court issued an indictment accusing Noriega of providing the famed Medellín drug cartel with secret airfields in Panama from which to smuggle drugs into the United States. The trusted ally on the payroll of the C.I.A. now became the #1 enemy of the United States. The Reagan administration moved to impose sanctions against Panama, but Noriega reacted by publicly waiving his machete, defying United States intervention in Panama.

A brutal period in Panamanian history ensued. Noriega overthrew his own puppet government three times in less than five years. His enemies were exiled; many were killed; his military cronies sacked the public vaults; and in 1989, after two years of public defiance of U.S. sanctions, he staged a second fraudulent election, invalidating the results when his candidate overwhelmingly lost to the opposition coalition led by Guillermo Endara. He became newly elected President George H.W. Bush's personal headache. Bush himself was battling the image of a wimp, and for a while Noriega seemed invincible.

By the end of 1989, merely a decade after the second canal treaty had been signed, the relations between Panama and the United States were dismal. Prominent congressmen, such as Jesse Helms, began to advocate the derogation of the second canal treaty. But the Pentagon had another plan to regain its hegemony in Panama.

On December 20, 1989, as Panamanians were preparing for Christmas, they were awakened at midnight by bombs shaking the city. Thousands of troops from the U.S. military bases from the canal and

Fort Bragg, North Carolina, descended on Panama City to decimate Noriega's military apparatus. Operation "Just Cause" became a testing ground for President Reagan's new "Star Wars" weaponry, including Cobra helicopters and Stealth bombers, and within twenty-four hours, Americans "took the Isthmus" much like Teddy Roosevelt had done at the turn of the century.

However, the target of the invasion, General Noriega, was nowhere to be found. For the next two weeks, Americans troops exerted sovereignty over the streets of Panama City in a wild manhunt resembling General Pershing's search for Pancho Villa during the Mexican Revolution. Noriega eventually took refuge in the Vatican's nuncio, where G.I.s surrounded the building and blasted rock-and-roll at all hours of the night to break the general's nerves. On December 31, just hours before the new decade, the strongman surrendered and was flown, handcuffed, to a prison in Miami. He was convicted and sentenced to forty years in prison for conspiring to smuggle drugs into the United States.

The United States was again in control of Panama. In fact, within hours of the invasion, the plump, comical, and overwhelmingly pro-American Guillermo Endara was sworn as president of Panama inside a U.S. military base during an ironic ceremony televised only on U.S. Southern Command television.

Every Latin American country denounced the United States invasion of Panama. The American government cited the war against drugs, but skeptics pointed out that corruption and loose law enforcement, Noriega's crimes, had been characteristic of many Latin governments. Others suggested that Bush's need to bolster his image played a part in his ordering the invasion. The legal justification was given by a State Department brief delivered before the United Nations general assembly: the United States had the right to invade Panama under the Torrijos-Carter treaty to guarantee the "neutrality" of the canal.

Since John Bidlack and Pedro Herrán coined the famous phrase in the summer of 1846, it has been molded and shaped into whatever form the latest exigency required. During the nineteenth century, successive American administrations relied on it to justify seven invasions of Panama to quash local insurgencies on behalf of the Colombian government. In 1903, President Roosevelt used it to prevent the Colombian troops from using the railroad to reach Panama City, resulting in the independence of Panama. In the 1920s, American marines seized presidential election ballots and counted the votes, supposedly to avoid the factional wars that could threaten the "neutrality" of the canal. And in 1989, when Noriega threatened U.S. control over the Isthmus, the Bush administration pulled the famed neutrality clause out of the hat to justify the retaking of Panama.

Even though the Panamanians own the canal, they know that this ownership is only valid as long as it is kept open, is well-maintained and secured, and the Panamanian government is pro-American and well-behaved. Zbigniew Brzezinski, Jimmy Carter's national security adviser, told the truth when congressmen asked him what would happen if the Panamanian government decided to close the canal "for repairs." Washington, he answered, would "move in and close down the Panamanian government 'for repairs'."

Despite the rocky beginnings of the second canal treaty, after the invasion, with successive, stable, pro-American governments in Panama, the United States slowly began to withdraw its troops in anticipation of its total surrender of the canal. Finally, on December 31, 1999, in front of the stately steps of the neo-Greek Panama Canal administration building, with salsa ensembles and fireworks under a tropical rain, President Mireya Moscoso, the widow of deposed President Arnulfo Arias, presided over the formal transfer ceremony and thus cut the umbilical cord that had sustained relations between Panama and the United States for an entire century. The historical festivities were attended by dozens of foreign dignitaries and the King of Spain, but it was shunned by President Bill Clinton and his cabinet. In an election year, with two-thirds of Americans opposing the handover, no high ranking American official wanted to go down in history as the weakling who surrendered Teddy Roosevelt's canal. Former President Jimmy Carter was thus sent to finish the unpopular business he had began, and for which he may have paid dearly, at least in part, with his own failed re-election.

Today, the canal is no longer the vital waterway that it once was. Panama, however, continues to be the coveted territory imbued with the special mission because of its critical position as the crossroad of the Americas. The challenges facing the canal are no longer only the security of its waterway, but a forty-year-old civil war in Colombia; drug trafficking; corruption; money laundering; authoritarian regimes; and poor social conditions throughout Latin America.

For the first time since 1857, United States military officers will not be present in Panama to police the Isthmus. Now, therefore, more than ever, Panamanians must remember the warning that Secretary Cass issued in 1855, when he said that "sovereignty has its duties as well as its rights," and that no government would be permitted "to close the gates of intercourse on the great highways of the world." The Isthmus, in short, if not the entire country, will always have, as Teddy Roosevelt loved to say, a "covenant running with the land."

To the Zonians, the guarantee of neutrality would never be consolation for what they lost. For those born and raised in the tropical paradise that they came to view as American land, packing their possessions and leaving behind their large houses and maids to move to small family homes in Alabama or Texas, far from the Pacific Ocean that they grew to love, the de-Americanization of the Panama Canal that Jimmy Carter began would always be a terrible mistake. They felt betrayed by Washington, and worse, they felt that the good old days of "gunboat diplomacy" when the chief administrator of the United States could be trusted to further American interests abroad by any means were over.

"The past is dead," lamented one of the Zonians to the New York Times upon leaving the canal. "Teddy Roosevelt is in the ground."

Notes

1. *Scandal*

The source of the *World* scandal is Don Carlos Seitz, *Joseph Pulitzer, His Life and Letters* (New York: AMS Press 1970), 352-385; Harding, Earl, *The Untold Story of Panama* (New York: Athene Press, 1959), 48-51; and the impressive investigation by the House of Representative's Foreign Relations Committee in February 1912 into what transpired in Panama in 1903, known as *The Story of Panama: Hearing on the Rainey Resolution before the Committee on Foreign Affairs of the House of Representatives* (Washington, D.C.: Government Printing Office, 1913) (hereinafter *The Story of Panama*).

PAGE

2. "Dear, dear Jonas." Quoted in Seitz, *Joseph Pulitzer, His Life and Letters*, 352.

3. "Financiers invested." *New York World* (October 3, 1908).

3. "Lying fabrication." *New York World* (October 3, 1908).

3. "Practically the Secretary of War." *New York World* (October 6, 1908).

4. "The Campaign is over." *Indianapolis News* (November 2, 1908).

4. "What New York newspaper." Quoted in Seitz, *Joseph Pulitzer, His Life and Letters*, 356.

5. "The Panama Scandal: Let Congress Investigate." *World* (December 8, 1908).

6. "These stories need no investigation whatever." Quoted in *The Story of Panama*, 259.

6. Information about Roosevelt assigning detectives on Fairbanks can be found in Peirce, *The Roosevelt Panama Libel Case* (New York: Greenwich Book Publishers, 1959), 117.

2. Wall Street vs. Congress

Material on Cromwell's activities comes from his own lengthy brief submitted to an arbitration tribunal asking for legal fees, published in *The Story of Panama* under exhibit A. The main source for information on Bunau-Varilla is his own published recollections, in particular, *Panama: The Creation, Destruction and Resurrection* (New York: Robert M. McBride, 1920). Although both men tend to inflate their own importance, they cite important facts that have not been challenged. For the congressional debate, the source is the voluminous congressional records published in *The Story of Panama*, as well as David McCullough's masterly *The Path Between the Seas* (New York: Simon & Schuster, 1977).

PAGE

9. "Accidents don't happen." Quoted in Arthur H. Dean, *William Nelson Cromwell, 1854-1948* (New York: Ad Press, 1957), 117.

9. "Strikingly pretty" and other descriptions of Cromwell are found in David Armine Howarth, *Panama: Four Hundred Years of Dreams and Cruelty* (New York: McGraw Hill, 1966), 218-219.

9. "In striped trousers and morning coat." McCullough, *The Path Between the Seas*, 271.

9. "No life insurance could beat him." *World* (October 4, 1908).

10. "To obtain favorable consideration." Quoted in Ibid., 165.

11-12. For background information on Ferdinand de Lesseps, the French Panama canal company and its bankruptcy, see *The Path Between the Seas*.

12. For information about the voyage of the *Oregon*, see *The Path Between the Seas*, 254.

12. "Masterful mind, whetted on the grindstone of corporation cunning." Quoted in *The Story of Panama*, 94.

13. "The Nicaragua Canal project." *New York Herald* (January 30, 1902).

13-14. For information on Cromwell's first trip to Washington D.C., see *The Story of Panama*, 178-180.

14-15. The donation to Hanna is documented in Ibid., 26, 112.

15-16. Cromwell's hosting activities in Paris are documented in McCullough, *The Path Between the Seas*, 275,276.

16. "On what price." Quoted in *The Story of Panama*, 107.

17. The source of the information on the Americanization scheme is Cromwell's brief in *The Story of Panama*, 183-4, and Harding, *The Untold Story*, 10.

17. Information about the creation of the American company can be found in *The Story of Panama*, 108, and Harding, *The Untold Story*, 10-11.

18. Rumors of a secret syndicate are documented in Harding, *The Untold Story*, 11,12.

18. Information on Cromwell being fired can be found in *The Story of Panama*, exhibit K, 636, and Harding, *The Untold Story*, 11-12.

19-20. Information on Bunau-Varilla's background can be found in McCullough, *The Path Between the Seas*, 276-279.

20. "Preach the Truth in the Highways as a Soldier of the Idea of a Canal." Quoted in McCullough, *The Path Between the Seas*, 277, and Bunau-Varilla, *Panama: The Creation*, 175.

20. "The bugle note had been heard." Bunau-Varilla, *Panama: The Creation*, 175.

20. Bunau-Varilla's tour of the United States has been documented in Ibid., 174-180.

21. "Towards midnight." Ibid., 184.

21. "Every time I was in need of a man he appeared." Ibid., 177.

22. "It is for you now." Ibid., 186-187.

22. "At last, at eight o'clock." Ibid., 187.

23. "Violent assault committed by a foreign adventurer." Quoted in Ibid., 188.

23. The report of the Walker Commission has been documented in McCullough, *The Path Between the Seas*, 266.

24. Information on Bunau-Varilla securing the reversal by the French company can be found in Bunau-Varilla, *Panama: The Creation*, 209.

24. "Go and ask the president." Quoted in Ibid., 213.

25. "Now, look, that damned cowboy." Quoted in Mark Sullivan, *Our Times*, vol. II (New York: Scribner's Sons, 1928), 380.

25. "The bride at every funeral." Nicholas Roosevelt, *Theodore Roosevelt: The Man as I Knew Him* (New York: Dodd, Mead & Co., 1967), 71.

25-27. For background information on Roosevelt, see W. DeGregorio, *The Complete Book of U.S. Presidents*, 4th ed. (New York: Barricade Books, 1993).

26. "Concha warns about 'the President's vehement character'." Letter from Dr. Vicente Concha, September 13, 1903, quoted in *The Story of Panama*, 693.

27. Mahan's influence on Roosevelt has been documented in McCullough, *The Path Between the Seas*, 251-253.

27. "Such powers as no Monarch, or King, or Emperor ever possessed." Quoted in Seitz, *Joseph Pulitzer, His Life and Letters*, 375.

27. "You and I, there are no others." *World* (October 23, 1908).

27-28. Roosevelt's reversal of the Walker Commission's report has been documented in *The Story of Panama*, 120.

28. The reinstatement of Cromwell has been documented in *The Story of Panama*, 122, 244-46.

29. "Gigantic Wall Street syndicate." *World* (April 16, 1903).

29. "Look at the coast of arms." Bunau-Varilla, *Panama: The Creation*, 191.

30. "NEWS PUBLISHED." Ibid., 246, and McCullough, *The Path Between the Seas*, 317.

30-31. All speeches by Senator's Morgan and Hanna are from the *Congressional Records* (57th Congress, 1st Session), quoted in McCullough, *The Path Between the Seas*, 319-20.

30. Hanna's speeches are reported in McCullough, *The Path Between the Seas*, 319.

31. "Mais il est formidable." Quoted in Thomas Beer, *Hanna* (New York, Octagon Books, 1973), 265.

31. "Oh, do make him sit down." Quoted in McCullough, *The Path Between the Seas*, 321.

31. "I do not want to be interrupted." Quoted in Ibid., 322.

32. "I warn that distinguished citizen." Quoted in *The Story of Panama*, 647, 651.

32. "He hoped to see indignation." Bunau-Varilla, *Panama: The Creation*, 240.

32. The *Washington Star* cartoon is described in Ibid., 246.

32. "I hastened to call on all the postage-stamp dealers." Ibid., 247.

33. "You want to be very careful, Theodore." Quoted in Sullivan, *Our Times*, vol II, 319.

3. *Colombia's Gamble*

Detailed information regarding the negotiations with Colombia came from a voluminous brief submitted by the *World* to Rainey's congressional investigation and published in *The Story of Panama*, under exhibit K: *Compilation of Facts* (hereinafter *Compilation of Facts*). It includes copies of all the cables sent and a day-by-day description of the events. To gather this information, Henry Hall of the *World* traveled to Bogotá and obtained Colombia's *Blue Book*, published by President Reyes in 1909, which safeguards the official documents and correspondence of the republic. Cromwell's brief also provides insights as to his role.

PAGE

35. Concha's refusal to negotiate has been documented in *Compilation of Facts*, 639.

35. For background information on Concha, see *Compilation of Facts*, 637, and *The Story of Panama*, 209.

35-36. Cromwell forces Concha to negotiate. See *Compilation of Facts*, 639.

36. For background information on John Hay, see McCullough, *The Path Between the Seas*, 256-258.

36. "Splendid little war." Quoted in DeGregorio, *The Complete Book of U.S. Presidents*, 4th ed., 364.

37. "The echoes of the outer world." Bunau-Varilla, *Panama: The Creation*, 263.

38. "The Governor will forbid its being printed." Ibid., 254.

38. Cromwell cutting a compromise with Colombia has been documented in *Compilation of Facts*, 640-641.

39. Concha advises Marroquín to reject amendment. Ibid., 654.

39. Instruction from Marroquín "in order to render the amendment" is quoted in Ibid., 656.

40. For information on the seven U.S. invasions of Panama, see *The Story of Panama*, 33.

40. For information on the Bidlack-Herrán Treaty of 1846, see Ibid., 4.

41. "This uncle of ours." Quoted in *Compilation of Facts*, 662.

41. Marroquín response to Concha's resignation as "unpatriotic and inadmissible" appears in Ibid., 657.

41. Concha's departure has been documented in *Compilation of Facts*, 664, and *The Story of Panama*, 143.

41-42. Roosevelt warns that no nation "need have any fear" in a message to Congress, December 2, 1902, quoted in *Compilation of Facts*, 664.

42. The instructions from Marroquín to Herrán to sign treaty can be found in Ibid., 665.

42. Hay grants Cromwell authority to negotiate treaty. See Harding, *The Untold Story*, 17-18.

42. Hay's ultimatum to Herrán is quoted in *Compilation of Facts*, 668.

42. "Do not sign canal treaty." Ibid., 668.

43. Cromwell's action to defeat the amendments proposed by Morgan has been documented in Ibid., 672.

43. For information about Bogota's reaction to the treaty, see Ibid., 673, 675.

44. Information about the Colombian demands for an indemnity from the Compagnie Nouvelle and Cromwell's reaction can be found in *The Story of Panama*, 36.

44. "The United States considers this suggestion." Quoted in *Compilation of Facts*, 662.

44. "If Colombia should now reject the treaty." Quoted in Ibid., 674, and Harding, *The Untold Story*, 19-20.

45. "President Roosevelt is determined to have." *World* (June 13, 1903).

45. Statements from Colombian senators are quoted in *Compilation of Facts*, 674, and Bunau-Varilla, *Panama: The Creation*, 270-271.

45-46. For Bunau-Varilla's views on the Colombian Senate debate, see Bunau-Varilla, *Panama: The Creation*, 263-264.

46. The source of the cable from Beaupré to Hay is *Compilation of Facts*, 675.

46. "To whom, in fact, was this wholly inadmissible." Ibid., 662.

47. Congressman Rainey's statement is quoted in *The Story of Panama*, 20.

47. "Unless I had acted as I did." Ibid., 20.

47. "Persons interested in getting the $40,000,000." *New York Herald* (August 29, 1903).

47. "We might make another treaty." *New York Herald* (August 14, 1903).

4. *Panamanian Cohorts*

Information about the revolution in Panama comes from *The Story of Panama*. Henry Hall spent almost three years interviewing Panamanian patriots, analyzing navy department and Panama Railroad Company files to present a day-by-day account of what happened. Other sources are José Agustín Arango's own version of the story, *Datos para la Historia de la Independencia del Istmo* (Panama 1922) (hereinafter *Datos*), other memoirs of patriots and newspaper clippings of the *Panama Star & Herald*.

PAGE

49. Arango's actions to foment a revolution have been documented in *Datos*, 3.

49. Cromwell's plans to find "some other satisfactory way" have been documented in *Compilation of Facts*, 677.

50. "The once proud city had fallen in a state of apathy." Robinson, Tracy, *Fifty Years at Panama, 1861-1911* (New York: Trow Press, 1911), 1.

51. For information about Beers mission, see *The Story of Panama*, 66.

52. Information on the first meeting gathering Panamanians and Americans can be found in *The Story of Panama*, 301.

53. For background information on Amador, see *McCullough, The Path Between the Seas*, 342.

54. "Father, I'm sick, come." Quoted in *The Story of Panama*, 310.

55-57. The secret code among Panamanians has been published in Ibid., 688-689.

59. Cromwell's offer to Duque of the presidency of Panama has been documented in Ibid., 311-312.

59. The source of Hay's meeting with Duque is Ibid., 312.

60-61. Herrán sends his government a wire: "Revolutionary agent of Panama here." Ibid., 312.

60. For information about the meetings between Amador and Cromwell, see Amador, *Memorias*, quoted in *Compilation of Facts*, 694.

61. Amador sends "Disappointed" cable. *The Story of Panama*, 314, 694.

61. Willis Johnson's response to Amador's requests is quoted in *Compilation of Facts*, 700.

61. Cromwell's cable "while there may be no real foundation" is quoted in *The Story of Panama*, 314.

62. Prescott tells the Panamanians they "must be fools." Ibid., 315.

62. Amador's statement "I took leave of him" is quoted in *Compilation of Facts*, 694.

62. The source of Cromwell's brief stating he did "not judge it necessary to enter into the details" is *Compilation of Facts*, 695.

62. Hall's "left the fat" statement can be found in Ibid., 696.

5. *Teddy's Conspiracy*

The source for most of the information in this chapter is Bunau-Varilla's *Panama: The Creation, Destruction and Resurrection*, pages 288-331.

PAGE

65. "Is the rumor true." Bunau-Varilla, *Panama: The Creation*, 289.

66. The source of Amador and Bunau-Varilla's meeting and statements is Ibid., 291-292.

66. Amador sends a one word cable: "Hope." *Compilation of Facts*, 697.

67. Amador's confession to Prescott has been documented in Ibid., 700.

67. "I fear we may have to give a lesson," letter from Roosevelt to Hay, August 19, 1903, quoted in Henry F. Pringle, *Theodore Roosevelt, A Biography* (New York: Harcourt, Brace & Co., 1931), 311.

68. "Oh, Mr. President," quoted in Phillip Jessup, *Elihu Root*, vol. I (New York: Dodd, Mead & Co., 1938), 404-405.

68. "Your excellency knows the vehement character of the President," Herrán letter to Marroquín, September 13, 1903, quoted in *Compilation of Facts*, 693.

68. Bunau-Varilla's conversation with Loomis appears in Bunau-Varilla, *Panama: The Creation*, 310.

69. Bunau-Varilla's conversation with Roosevelt appears in Ibid., 311.

70. "Privately, I would say," letter to Albert Shaw, quoted in Howarth, *Panama: Four Hundred Years*, 233.

70-72. The conversation between Amador and Bunau-Varilla after Bunau-Varilla returns to New York is quoted in Bunau-Varilla, *Panama: The Creation*, 313-316.

72-73. The conversation between Bunau-Varilla and Hay is quoted in Ibid., 318.

73-74. Conversation between Bunau-Varilla and Amador on October 17 is quoted in Ibid., 321.

74. *Mi hijito* letter from Amador to his son Raoul, reprinted in Harding, *The Untold Story*, 73-75, and *The Story of Panama*, 71.

75. Raoul Amador's statement that "the old man has been down" is quoted in Harding, *The Untold Story*, 86-87.

75. Information on the secret meeting of Amador with Roosevelt can be found in *Compilation of Facts*, 700.

76. Cromwell's cable "Your virile and masterful policy" is quoted in Ibid., 702.

76. Bunau-Varilla's conversation with Amador on October 19 is quoted in Bunau-Varilla, *Panama: The Creation*, 324.

77-81. The cable code between Bunau-Varilla and Amador is reprinted in *Compilation of Facts*, 712-713.

82. "On the fifth, it will be too late." Bunau-Varilla, *Panama: The Creation*, 338.

82. "I built the subtle diplomatic structure. Ibid., 333.

6. *Seducing the Patriots*

The events prior to, during, and after the Panama revolution presented in chapters 6,7 and 8, are described in great detail in *The Story of Panama*, beginning on page 329. Much of the military preparations for the revolution are described in Esteban Huertas' *Memorias* (Panama: Publicaciones Continentales, 1959).

PAGE

83-84. Information about Amador's meeting with the patriots is found in *The Story of Panama*, 330.

84. Duque joins the revolution. Ibid., 337.

84. Amador's residence becomes hotbed of the revolution. Ibid., 337.

85. For background information on Huertas, see Huertas, *Memorias*, 19.

86. Arango's conversation with Huertas is quoted in Ibid., 38.

86. The source of de Obaldiá's cable is *The Story of Panama*, 332.

87. Arias's "you are an old man" statement is quoted in Ibid., 330.

88. Amador's cable to Bunau-Varilla is reprinted in Bunau-Varilla, *Panama: The Creation*, 327.

88. Bunau-Varilla's reaction to the cable is found in Ibid., 328.

88-89. Conversation between Loomis and Bunau-Varilla quoted in Ibid., 331.

89. Cable from Bunau-Varilla to Amador quoted in Ibid., 333.

89. Roosevelt claims officers stopped in Panama "as an unpremeditated incident of their return journey" in the State of the Union Address, Jan. 4, 1904, House Document No. 1 (58th Congress, 2nd Session).

89-90. Report of officers printed in *Compilation of Facts*, 704-705.

91. Roosevelt's order to send ships has been documented in *The Story of Panama*, 434, and *Compilation of Facts*, 715-716.

92. The meeting of Arango with Meléndez has been documented in *The Story of Panama*, 334.

92. The conversation between Amador and Huertas is quoted in Huertas, *Memorias*, 39,40.

93. The conversation between Huertas and Diaz is quoted in Ibid., 41.

94-95. For information about the arrival of gunboats in Colón, see *The Story of Panama*, 338.

7. Hamlet Revolution

PAGE

97. Amador's attempt to hide news of arrival of the *Cartagena* has been documented in *The Story of Panama*, 339.

97. For Hubbard's decision to let the Colombian troops disembark and statements, see Ibid., 339.

98. "We have all gone too far to give up now." Quoted in *The Story of Panama*, 339, and Harding, *The Untold Story*, 78.

98-99. Background information on Shaler can be found in the *New York Tribune* (January 2, 1904).

100. Ruiz's confession has been documented in *The Story of Panama*, 340.

100. "I pointed out to him," and other Tovar statements are quoted in Ibid., 340.

101. The navy's orders are printed in Ibid., 334-335.

101. Cromwell's cable from Paris is printed in *The Story of Panama*, 253.

102. Darling's cable "Railway company has declined" is quoted in Ibid., 341.

103. Information about the ride of Aminta Meléndez can be found in Ibid., 341, and McCullough, *The Path Between the Seas*, 367-368.

103. The conversation between Amador and Huertas is quoted in *The Story of Panama*, 342.

103-105. Information on Huertas's activities on the night of November 3 are found in Huertas, *Memorias*, 44-48.

104. Huertas's conversation with Diaz is quoted in Ibid., 47-48.

105. Information about the Colombian general's reception is found in *The Story of Panama*, 342-343.

106. Tovar's statement "There was nothing that did not show" is quoted in Ibid., 342.

Porras's "trust no one" statement is quoted in Ibid., 343.

107. Tovar's conversation with Huertas is quoted in Huertas, *Memorias*, 50.

107. Shaler's refusal to transport the Colombian troops is described in *The Story of Panama*, 390-391.

108. "I am not in proper dress," quoted in Huertas, *Memorias*, 51.

109. De la Guardia's confession has been documented in *The Story of Panama*, 344.

110. Conversation between Huertas and Amador can be found in Ibid, 335, and Huertas, *Memorias*, 54.

110. The cable from Loomis is printed in *The Story of Panama*, 335.

111. Conversation between Tovar and Huertas in the Chiriquí barracks can be found in Huertas, *Memorias*, 58-59.

112. Information about Salazar arresting the Colombian generals can be found in Huertas, *Memorias*, 60, and *The Story of Panama*, 346.

113. Diaz's "You have saved us" statement is quoted in Huertas, *Memorias*, 62.

114. The aftermath of the Colombian generals' arrest has been documented in *The Story of Panama*, 347.

113. Cable of Ehrman to Loomis printed in Ibid., 347.

114. de Obaldiá's arrest has been documented in Ibid., 347.

114. The letter from the Junta to Shaler is printed in Ibid., 348.

115. The meeting of the municipal council and the Panamanian declaration of independence has been documented in Ibid., 349.

117. Cable "A Su Excelencia el Presidente de los Estados Unidos" is quoted in Ibid., 350.

117. Cable from State Department to Ehrman printed in Ibid., 351.

8. *Birthday of Bribery*

PAGE

119. The cable from the junta to Meléndez appears in *The Story of Panama*, 389.

120. The cable from Colombia's foreign ministry to Herrán appears in Ibid., 390.

120. The letter from Hubbard to Torres appears in Ibid., 391.

122. The cable from Darling to Hubbard and the return cable appears in Ibid., 393.

122. "For about half an hour their attitude was most threatening." Quoted in Ibid., 393.

123-124. Amador's search for money on November 4, 1903 has been documented in Ibid., 394, 396.

124. "The soldiers are barefooted." *New York Tribune* (January 4, 1904).

124-125. Amador's and Huertas's speeches to soldiers are quoted in *The Story of Panama*, 396-397.

126. Amaya's testimony can be found in Ibid., 400.

126. Tovar's testimony can be found in Ibid., 400-2.

127. The ceremony honoring Huertas has been documented in Ibid., 404.

127-129. The events in Colón and Meléndez's bribing Torres has been documented in Ibid., 406.

129. "Now, how about paying," quoted in Ibid., 406.

130. The proclamation in Colón can be found in Ibid., 408.

131. Boyd's cable has been printed in *New York Herald* (November 3, 1903).

9. *Treachery*

The events in Washington D.C. after the Panama revolution presented in chapters 9 and 10 are described in detail in Bunau-Varilla's *Panama: The Creation, Destruction and Resurrection.*

PAGE

133. The conversation between Bunau-Varilla and Loomis is quoted in Bunau-Varilla, *Panama: The Creation*, 343.

133-134. Conversation between Lindo and Bunau-Varilla is quoted in Ibid., 345.

134. Information on Lindo sending money to Panama is found in *Compilation of Facts*, 721, and Bunau-Varilla, *Panama: The Creation*, 348.

134. "The silence of Amador." Quoted in Ibid., 348.

135. Warning of Bunau-Varilla "I decline any responsibility" is quoted in Ibid., 348.

135. The cable from Hay to Beaupré and Ehrman appears in *The Story of Panama*, 414, and Bunau-Varilla, *Panama: The Creation*, 350.

135. The cable from Beaupré to Hay appears in *The Story of Panama*, 345.

136. The cable appointing Bunau-Varilla minister appears in Bunau-Varilla, *Panama: The Creation*, 349.

136. The cable from de La Espriella thanking Bunau-Varilla appears in Ibid., 351.

137. Bunau-Varilla's letter to Hay appears in *The Story of Panama*, 415, and Bunau-Varilla, *Panama: The Creation*, 351.

137-138. Conversation between Hay and Bunau-Varilla is quoted in Bunau-Varilla, *Panama: The Creation*, 358.

138. The response cable from de la Espriella to Bunau-Varilla appears in Ibid., 359.

138. The cables from Ehrman to Hay about Bunau-Varilla's authority appear in *The Story of Panama*, 414, and Bunau-Varilla, *Panama: The Creation*, 359.

138. The instructions for Bunau-Varilla that the junta brought with it appears in Bunau-Varilla, *Panama: The Creation*, 360.

140. Information about Cromwell's meeting with Panamanian patriots can be found in *The Story of Panama*, 238.

140-141. The conversation between Curtis, Hanna, and Roosevelt is quoted in Curtis, *Memoirs*, and Charles Averinger, *Review of Books* (1963).

141. "It seemed to me as if I were in the position of a legendary hunter." Bunau-Varilla, *Panama: The Creation*, 353.

141-142. Information about the signature ceremony can be found in Ibid., 365-66.

142. "The Man Behind the Egg." *New York Times* (November 14, 1903).

143. "Not one minute [is] to be lost." Bunau-Varilla, *Panama: The Creation*, 367.

143. The letter to Hay from Bunau-Varilla appears in Ibid., 368.

143. "I [am] thus led to the conclusion." Ibid., 143.

144-145. Information on Farnham detaining Amador is found in *The Story of Panama*, 425, 722.

145. "I had to shield." Bunau-Varilla, *Panama: The Creation*, 372.

145-146. The letter from Bunau-Varilla to Hay has been printed in Bunau-Varilla, *Panama: The Creation*, 373.

146. Article III of the Hay-Bunau-Varilla treaty and Article III of the Hay-Herrán treaty have been printed in Harding, *The Untold Story*, 39.

147. "So long as the delegation has not arrived." Bunau-Varilla, *Panama: The Creation*, 374.

147. Hay's confession to Spooner has been quoted in Alp Dennis, *Adventures in American Diplomacy* (New York: E.P. Dupton Co., 1927), 341, and Howarth, *Panama: Four Hundred Years*, 233.

148-149. For information about the Panama Canal treaty signature ceremony, see Bunau-Varilla, *Panama: The Creation*, 375-77.

10. *The Rape of the Isthmus*

PAGE

151. The conversation between Bunau-Varilla, the Panamanian patriots, and Hay is quoted in Bunau-Varilla, *Panama: The Creation*, 378-379.

152-153. The confrontation between Bunau-Varilla and Cromwell has been documented in Ibid., 393.

153. Information about the Bowling Green Trust loan can be found in *Compilation of Facts*, 722.

153. The transfer of $75,000 from Bunau-Varilla to J.P. Morgan has been documented in *Compilation of Facts*, 721,722.

153. Bunau-Varilla decides to take the matter out of "inexpert hands." Quoted in Bunau-Varilla, *Panama: The Creation*, 380.

153. The cable of November 20 from Bunau-Varilla to de la Espriella has been printed in Ibid., 381.

154. Bunau-Varilla determines to seek revenge. Ibid., 381.

154. The cable of November 25 from Bunau-Varilla to de la Espriella has been printed in Ibid., 384.

155. The cable from the Panamanian junta to Bunau-Varilla can be found in Ibid., 384.

156. Bunau-Varilla's confrontation with Drake is described in Ibid., 402.

156. The cable from Drake to Beers can be found in *Compilation of Facts*, 724, and *The Story of Panama*, 406.

157. "The canal was stolen property." *Times* (December 29, 1903).

157. "The Panama Revolution." *World* (January 17, 1904).

157. Evidence that Cromwell inspired *World* press article is found in Bunau-Varilla, *Panama: The Creation*, 424.

157. "You certainly have, Mr. President." Quoted in Jessup, *Elihu Root*, vol. I, 404-405.

158. Oscar Strauss memo of November 6, 1903 is quoted in McCullough, *The Path Between the Seas*, 380.

158. Roosevelt's message to Congress on January 4, 1904 has been documented in House documents no. 1 (58th Congress, 2nd Session), reprinted in *The Story of Panama*.

159. Statements by senators during the Senate debates are quoted in Bunau-Varilla, *Panama: The Creation*, 427.

159. For information on General Reyes's offer, see Ibid., 399-400.

159. "As if by a derisive trick of fate." Quoted in Ibid., 425.

160. Bunau-Varilla's private thoughts. Ibid., 429.

161. Bunau-Varilla's hands are unexpectedly seized by Cromwell. Ibid., 428.

161. Information about Amador's inauguration can be found in McCullough, *The Path Between the Seas*, 398.

162. Cromwell's ceremony giving the Panamanian flag to Roosevelt has been documented in *Compilation of Facts*, 725.

162. Information about Morales mission can be found in Harding, *The Untold Story*, 81.

162. "After years of absence" and the rest of Cromwell's speech can be found in the *Panama Star & Herald* (December 3, 1904).

163-164. Cromwell getting control of disbursement of funds has been documented in *The Story of Panama*, 247-49, 409, and *Compilation of Facts*, 731.

163. Comparison between the purchase of the Panama route and all prior land purchases by the United States is made in McCullough, *The Path Between the Seas*, 400.

164. Details about the payment to Panama is found in *The Story of Panama*, exhibit E, 471.

164. J.P. Morgan's trip to Paris is documented in McCullough, *The Path Between the Seas*, 400.

165. The handover ceremony from the French company to the United States is described in Ibid., 402

165. The amount of profits earned by shareholders is described in Ibid., 401.

165. *New York Times* (February 4, 1904).

165. The testimony of Hutin and other people can be found in Earl Harding Papers, Special Collections, Lawinger Library, Georgetown University.

165. "Let the dirt fly!" and other Roosevelt comments about Panama are printed in *North American Review* (February 1912), *The Story of Panama*, 29, and Theodore Roosevelt, *An Autobiography* (New York: Charles Scribner's Sons, 1920), 524.

166-167. Morgan's hearings on Cromwell have been documented in Hearings before the Senate Committee on Interoceanic Canals on the Senate Resolution Providing for an Investigation of Matters Relating to the Panama Canal, Senate Document 401 (59th Congress, 2nd Session) (Washington: Government Printing Office, 1907).

167. Cromwell's refusal to answer has been documented in Ibid., 3137-3138, also reprinted in *The Story of Panama*, 522.

167. "What's the use?" *New York Times* (March 22, 1906).

167. "There was a long period." Quoted in Harding, *The Untold Story*, 47.

11. *Who Got the Money?*

The main sources for the resolution of the Pulitzer investigation are Earl Harding's *The Untold Story* and *The Story of Panama*.

PAGE

170. "I have never known," and the results of investigations by lawyers of the French company have been documented in *The Story of Panama*, 280, and Harding, *The Untold Story*, 63.

170. For information on the Pulitzer reporters' findings in Panama, see *Compilation of Facts*, 698.

171. Amador's statement that "if the American government finds out" is quoted in *Compilation of Facts*, 693.

171. "As clean as a hound's tooth," and other testimonies of Panamanians patriots can be found in Harding, *The Untold Story*, 69-71.

172. Information and quotes from the Sullivan & Cromwell brief can be found in *The Story of Panama*, 252, 161.

172-174. Information about the meeting and conversation between Raoul Amador and Harding can be found in Harding, *The Untold Story*, 72-73.

173-174. The original *Mi hijito* letter and other Amador documents have been printed in Ibid., 73-75.

174. "Father told me" and other statements of Raoul Amador before the court have been printed in *The Story of Panama*, 700, and Harding, *The Untold Story*, 86-87.

175. Arias and other patriots revealing information to the court have been documented in Harding, *The Untold Story*, 83.

175. For the source of the "Hope" cable, see Ibid., 85, and *The Story of Panama*, 699.

175. Icaza's and Duque's testimony can be found in *Compilation of Facts*, 732.

175-176. The *Official Gazette* accounts have been published in *Compilation of Facts*, 733.

177. Eduardo Icaza and Donaldo Velazquez's testimonies have been printed in *The Story of Panama*, 412.

177. Information regarding the payment to Salazar, Tascón, and Huertas's trip to Europe can be found in *Compilation of Facts*, 733.

177. Information on the payment to the railroad employees can be found in Ibid., 733.

177. Information on the payment to Amador can be found in *Compilation of Facts*, 733-4, and *The Story of Panama*, 417.

177-178. Donaldo Velázquez statements are quoted in *The Story of Panama*, 416.

178. Hasera's testimony can be found in Ibid., 409.

178-179. Information regarding Drummond's tendering of incriminating documents can be found in Harding, *The Untold Story*, 55-57.

179-180. The original "Memorandum of Agreement" has been printed in Ibid., 58-59.

183. The Windsor Trust book has been printed in Ibid., 59,60.

184-185. The original ledger sheets have been printed in Ibid., 61-63.

186. For testimonies in France, see Hall Hereford (folder 51), testimony of M. Charbonell, Earl Harding Papers, Special Collection, Lawinger Library, Georgetown University; Peirce, *The Roosevelt Panama Libel Cases* (New York: Greenwich Book Publishers, 1959), 44.

188-189. For information regarding the resolution of the libel suit, see *The Story of Panama*, 263-264; Peirce, *The Roosevelt Panama Libel Case*; and World, *The Roosevelt Panama Libel Case Against the New York World* (New York: Press Publishing Co., 1911).

189. "I took the Isthmus" speech was printed in the *San Francisco Examiner* (March 24, 1911); *The Story of Panama*, 578; and in Theodore Roosevelt's *"I took the Isthmus" and Editorial Comment by American Newspapers* (New York: M.B. Brown and Company, 1911). According to Roosevelt, the correct quote is "I took the Canal Zone," not the Isthmus.

190. Roosevelt's statement "I took the canal because Bunau-Varilla brought it to me" is quoted in Philippe Bunau-Varilla, *The Great Adventure of Panama* (New York: Doubleday, Page & Co., 1940), 34, and McCullough, *The Path Between the Seas*, 384.

190. The Rainey resolution has been printed in *The Story of Panama*, 3.

190. Rainey's accusation that Cromwell is "the most dangerous man in America since Aaron Burr" is printed in Ibid., 17.

191. "On the whole." Howarth, *Panama: Four Hundred Years*, 243.

192. Information regarding what happened to the Pulitzer records can be found in Harding, *The Untold Story*, 57-58. The records are now part of the Earl Harding Papers, Special Collections, Lawinger Library, Georgetown University.

192. Evidence is still disappearing. Conversation with historian Jorge Conte Porras in Panama.

193-194 Information about relations between the U.S. and Colombia can be found in *The Story of Panama*, 20.

194. Bunau-Varilla's activities after Panama are documented in McCullough, *The Path Between the Seas*, 616.

194. Information about the Panamanian demand to Cromwell to account for management of the Constitutional Fund can be found in Harding, *The Untold Story*, 95.

196. "If they had not revolted," quoted in *Outlook* (October 7, 1911).

196. "Grass grew over the episode," Seitz, *Joseph Pulitzer, His Life and Letters*, 385.

Epilogue: A Chapter of Dishonor

The main source of the material in the Epilogue is John Major's admirable *Prize Posession: The United States and the Panama Canal, 1903-1979* (Cambridge, New York: Cambridge University Press, 1993).

PAGE

198. "The Panama Canal is our jugular vein." Maurice Ries, *Legion Magazine* (March 1957).

199. "We bought the canal." *New York Times* (March 30, 1974).

199. "We stole it fair and square." Quoted in Major, *Prize Possession*, 58.

199. "Panamanians would eventually resort to violence." Cyrus Vance, *Hard Choices, Four Critical Years in Managing America's Foreign Policy* (New York, 1983), 141, and Major, *Prize Possession*, 345.

199. Torrijos's statement that "two courses are open to me" is quoted in Major, *Prize Possession*, 345, and William J. Jorden, *Panama Odyssey* (Austin: University of Texas Press 1984), 322-3.

199. "Like the poor looking through the lodge gates." Jan Morris, "Panama, an imperial specimen." *Destinations: Essays from Rolling Stone* (Oxford: Oxford University Press, 1980), quoted in Major, *Prize Possession*, 347.

200. "A military nightmare, another Vietnam," Jack Hood Vaughn, *Washington Monthly* (October 1973), 34.

200. The debates by the Senate can be found in Senate Committee on Foreign Relations, *Hearings on Panama Canal Treaty*, and the House Committee on International Relations, Hearing on Proposed Panama Canal Treaties (95th Congress, 1st Session) (Washington: Government Printing Office, 1978).

200. The neutrality clause in the Torrijos-Carter Treaty has been printed in Major, *Prize Possession*, 350.

200. Statement of Understanding, October 14, 1978, in which Panamanians demand that the clause not be "interpreted as a right of intervention," has been printed in Major, *Prize Possession*, 350,353, and Jorden, *Panama Odyssey*, 562-3.

203. Brzezinski statement that "Washington will move in" is quoted in Major, *Prize Posession*, 349.

204. "The past is dead." *New York Times* (January 10, 1979).

Bibliography

PRIMARY SOURCES
1. Manuscript and Archive Collections
Manuscript Division, Library of Congress

Bunau-Varilla, Philippe Jean. Papers, 1880-1940. Edited by admirers of Bunau-Varilla, these papers are interesting but lack objectivity.

Hay, John. Papers, 1900-1905.

Roosevelt, Theodore. Roosevelt's Letters.

William Taft. Papers.

Office of the Naval Intelligence, 1888-1914. Records of the Office of the Chief of Naval Operations. Panama, 1903-1911 (19 volumes). Record Group 38. National Archives. These records offer considerable analysis and character assessments of leading Panamanian politicians.

War department, No. 1, Notes on Panama, Document 217, 1903. This is the "unpremeditated report" from two army officers sent to Panama to plan the revolution.

The Panama Canal, 1897-1914. Records of the second Isthmian Canal Commission, 1905-1914. Record Group 185. National Archives. These documents contain a huge amount of information, much of which was secret and confidential. Political information appears scattered throughout the records.

National Archives

U.S. Congress, Senate, Committee on Foreign Relations. A convention transpired between the United States and the Republic of Panama for the construction of a canal to connect the waters of the Atlantic and Pacific oceans, signed November 18, 1903. This is the Hay-Bunau-Varilla treaty.

Records of the Compagnie Nouvelle du Canal de Panama. Records of the Compagnie Universelle du Canal Interoceanique. These are the records that the United States received from the French company when it purchased its assets in 1904.

Records of the Isthmian Canal Commission. The records of the Walker Commission investigating the Nicaragua and Panama route.

Department of State, 1903-1910. Consular letters from Colón. Instructions to Colón. Consular letters from Panama City. Instructions to Panama City. Dispatches from United States minister in Panama. Instructions to United States minister in Panama. Notes from Panamanian minister in Washington. Notes to Panamanian minister in Washington. Panama Legation Archives, Foreign Office Series. The official government correspondence. Particularly revealing of the actions of government officials during the Panama revolution. Includes private letters, newspaper clippings, pamphlets, and frequently the comments of high government officials appended on the original documents.

2. Official and Semi-Official Publications
United States

Congressional Record. (Washington, D.C.: Government Printing Office).

Hearings before the Senate Committee on Interoceanic Canals on H.R. 3110. Senate Document 253, 57th Congress, 1st Session. (Washington, D.C.: Government Printing Office, 1902).

U.S. Congress, Senate, Committee on Foreign Relations. Correspondence concerning the convention between the United States and Colombia for the construction of an interoceanic canal across the Isthmus of Panama, 1903. (Washington, D.C.: Government Printing Office). Background information for the Hay-Herrán treaty with Colombia.

U.S. Congress, House of Representatives, Committee on Foreign Affairs.

Message from the president of the United States transmitting, in response to resolution of the House of Representatives of November 9, 1903, all correspondence and other official documents relating to the recent revolution on the Isthmus of Panama, 1903. (Washington, D.C.: Government Printing Office). Congressional critics of Roosevelt forced the administration to release this official correspondence. It purported to show the government's complete innocence in the independence of Panama.

State of the Union Address, January 4, 1904. House Documents No. 1. 58th Congress, 2nd Session. (Washington, D.C.: Government Printing Office). Roosevelt's answers to his critics regarding the independence of Panama.

U.S. Congress, Senate, Committee on Foreign Relations. Message of the president of the United States transmitting a statement of action in executing the act entitled "An act to provide for the construction of a canal connecting the waters of the Atlantic and Pacific Oceans," 1904. (Washington, D.C.: Government Printing Office, 1904). Examination of Roosevelt's desires to build an Isthmian canal, although not necessarily in Panama.

U.S. Department of State. Relations between the United States with Colombia and the Republic of Panama, 1904. Concise documentation of Washington's attitude towards Panama and Colombia after Panama's independence.

U.S. War Department, General Staff. Notes on Panama, November, 1903. A compilation of local sources provides a glimpse of Panama in 1903.

Hearings before the Senate Committee on Interoceanic Canals on the Senate Resolution Providing for and Investigation of Matters Relating to the Panama Canal, 1906. Senate Document 401, 59th Congress, 2nd Session. (Washington, D.C.: Government Printing Office, 1907). Senator John Tyler Morgan's investigation of Cromwell's activities in Panama and other matters. Contain many valued testimonies, including several by Panamanians.

The Story of Panama: Hearing on the Rainey Resolution before the Committee on Foreign Affairs of the House of Representatives, January 26 through February 20, 1912. United States Congress, House Committee on Foreign Affairs. (Washington, D.C.: Government Printing Office, 1913). These hearings were precipitated by Roosevelt's "I took the Isthmus" statement. They contain a voluminous record of first-hand testimony, letters, and allegations, all given under oath. They present a "fantastic intertwined, fact-laden testimony."

Hearings before the House Committee on International Relations on Proposed Panama Canal Treaties. 95th Congress, 1st Session. (Washington, D.C.: Government Printing Office, 1978). The House of Representatives' Torrijos-Carter treaty debates.

Hearings before the Senate Committee on Foreign Relations on the Panama Canal Treaty. 95th Congress, 1st Session. (Washington, D.C.: Government Printing Office, 1978). The Senate's Torrijos-Carter treaty debates.

Panama

Panama, Gaceta Oficial. 1903–1910. The official government publication of decrees, pronouncements, etc. The material from November 1903 to June 1904 contains revealing information about the newly independent county's expenses.

Instituto Nacional de Panama, Documentos históricos sobre la independencia del Istmo de Panama. Panama, 1930. A source of original government records dealing with the 1903 period.

Panama, Anales de la convencion: February 26, 1904 a Julio 30, 1904. Serial I-III, No. 1-65. (Panama: Imprenta Nacional, 1904). Interesting record of Panama's first national legislative assembly.

Panama, Biblioteca y archivo nacional. Biblioteca de la Universidad. Selected articles, pamphlets, etc., concerning Panama. Microfilmed by UNESCO, 1959. Reels 91-101, Serial No. 6552, Library of Congress, Washington, D.C. Contains a considerable number of government documents and primary pamphlets published during the early years of independence.

Panama, Comision originadora con motivo de los 100 años del nacimiento del procer de la República: Carlos Antonio Mendoza o la lealtad. (Panama: Imprenta La Academia, 1956). A laudatory examination of the author of Panama's declaration of independence's activities during the revolution.

Panama, Mensaje de la Junta de Gobierno Provisional a la Convención Nacional Constituyente. Panama, *Imprenta Star & Herald*, 1904. Junta justifies its acceptance of the Hay-Bunau-Varilla treaty.

Arosemena, Carlos C., and Nicanor A. de Obarrio. Datos historicos acerca de los movimientos iniciales de la independencia, relatados por los proceres. Panama: Impresta La Academia, 1937. First hand reminiscences of two early supporters of the independence movement.

Museo del Canal. Panama, Republic of Panama. An illuminating tour of the canal history in pictures and photographs.

3. PRIVATE COLLECTION

Earl Harding Papers. Special Collections, Lawinger Library, Georgetown University.

SECONDARY SOURCES
1. Books and Pamphlets

Arango, José Agustín. *Datos para la Historia de la Independencia del Istmo*. Panama: 1922.

Arrocha Graell, Catalino. *Historia de la Independencia de Panama, 1821-1903*. Panama: The Star & Herald Company, 1933.

Bacon, Alexander S. *The Wooly Horse*. New York: 1909.

Beal, Howard K. *Theodore Roosevelt and the Rise of America to World Power*. Baltimore, Maryland: Johns Hopkins Press, 1956.

Beatty, Charles. *De Lesseps of Suez: The Man and His Times*. New York: Harper and Bros., 1956.

Beer, Thomas. *Hanna*. New York: Octagon Books, 1973.

Biesanz, John and Mavis. *The People of Panama*. New York: Columbia University Press, 1955.

Bishop, Farnham. *Panama, Past and Present*. New York: Appleton Century Co., 1913.

Bishop, Joseph Bucklin. *The Panama Gateway*. New York: Charles Scribner's Sons, 1915.

———.*Theodore Roosevelt and His Time*. 2 volumes. New York: Charles Scribner's Sons, 1920.

Boyd, Federico. *Exposicion historica acerca de los motivos que causaron la separacion de Panama de la Republica de Colombia*. Panama: Star & Herald, 1911.

Boyd, Jorge E. *Doctor Jorge E. Boyd's Open Letter to President Porras Refuting Bunau-Varilla's Book with Regards to the Independence of Panama*. Panama: Star & Herald, 1913.

Bunau-Varilla, Philippe. *Panama or Nicaragua* (pamphlet). New York: 1901.

———. *Panama: The Creation, Destruction, and Resurrection*. New York: Robert M. McBride, 1920.

———. *The Great Adventure of Panama*. New York: Doubleday, Page and Co., 1920.

———. *From Panama to Verdun: My Fight for France*. Philadelphia: Dorrance and Co., 1940.

Cameron, Ian. *The Impossible Dream: The Construction of the Panama Canal*. New York: Morrow, 1972.

Carles, Rubén Darío. *The Centenial City of Colón*. Panama, 1952.

———. *Horror y Paz en el Istmo, 1899-1902*. Panama: Editora Panama America, 1950.

Castillero Reyes, Ernesto. *La causa inmediata de la emancipación de Panamá*. Panama: Imprenta Nacional, 1933.

Cornish, Vaughan. *The Panama Canal and Its Makers*. Boston: Little Brown & Co., 1909.

Davis, Richard Harding. *Captain Macklin*. New York: Charles Scribner's Sons, 1906.

De Mallet, Matilde Obarrio. "Bosquejo de la vida colonial de Panama." *Boletín de la Academia Panameña de la Historia*. Enero Abril de 1934.

Dean, Arthur H. *William Nelson Cromwell, 1854-1948*. New York: Ad Press, 1957.

DeGregorio, W. *The Complete Book of U.S. Presidents*, 4th edition. New York: Barricade Books, 1993.

Dennis, Alp. *Adventures in American Diplomacy*. New York: E. P. Dupton Co., 1927.

Dreyfus, Alfred and Pierre. *The Dreyfus Case*. New Haven, Connecticut: Yale University Press, 1956.

DuVal, Captain Miles P., Jr. *And the Mountains Will Move*. Stanford, California: Stanford University Press, 1947.

———. *Cádiz to Cathay: The Story of the Long Struggle for a Waterway Across the American Isthmus*. Stanford, California: Stanford University Press, 1940.

Hardeveld, Rose van. *Make the Dirt Fly*. Hollywood, California: Pan Press, 1956.

Harding, Earl. *The Untold Story of Panama*. New York: Athene Press, 1959.

Howarth, David Armine. *Panama: Four Hundred Years of Dreams and Cruelty*. New York: McGraw Hill, 1966.

Huertas Ponce, Esteban. *Memorias y bosquejo biográfico del general Esteban Huertas: Prócer de la gesta del 3 de noviembre del 1903*. Panamá: Publicaciones Continentales, 1959.

Huntington, C. P. *The Nicaragua Canal*. (pamphlet) 1900.

Jessup, Philip C. *Elihu Root*. New York: Dodd, Mead and Company, 1938.

Johnson, Willis Fletcher. *Four Centuries of the Panama Canal*. New York: Henry Hold & Co., 1907.

Jorden, William J. *Panama Odyssey*. Austin, Texas: University of Texas Press, 1984.

Keller, Morton, ed. *Theodore Roosevelt*. New York: Hill and Wang, 1967.

LaFaber, Walter. *The Panama Canal: The Crisis in Historical Perspective*. New York: Oxford University Press, 1979.

Legters, Lynman H. ed. *Area Handbook for Panama*. Washington, D.C.: Government Printing Office, 1962.

Mack, Gerstle. *The Land Divided: A History of the Panama Canal and Other Isthmian Canal Projects*. New York: Alfred A. Knopf, 1944.

Mahan, Captain A.T. *The Influence of Sea Power Upon History*. Boston: Little, Brown & Co., 1890.

Major, John. *Prize Possession: The United States and the Panama Canal, 1903-1979*. New York: Cambridge University Press, 1993.

McCullough, David. *The Path Between the Seas*. New York: Simon & Schuster, 1977.

Miner, Dwight Carroll. *The Fight for the Panama Route*. New York: Columbia University Press, 1940.

Miró, Rodrigo, ed. *Documentos fundamentales para la historia de la nacion Panameña*. Panama: Imprenta Nacional, 1953.

Morison, George S. *The Isthmian Canal* (a lecture delivered before the Contemporary Club, Bridgeport, Connecticut), 1902.

Morris, Jan. "Panama, an Imperial Specimen." *Destinations: Essays from Rolling Stone*. Oxford: Oxford University Press, 1968.

Neimeier, Jean Galbraith. *Panama Story*. Portland, Oregon: Metropolitan Press, 1968.

New York World. *The Roosevelt Panama Libel Case Against the New York World*. New York: Press Publishing Co., 1911.

Ortega, B. Ismael. *La independencia de Panama en 1903*. Panama: Imprenta Nacional, 1930.

——. *La jornada del día 3 de noviembre de 1903 y sus antecedentes*. Panama: Imprenta Nacional, 1931.

Parks, E. Taylor. *Colombia and the United States, 1765-1934*. Durham, North Carolina: Duke University Press, 1945.

Peirce, Clyde. *The Roosevelt Panama Libel Cases*. New York: Greenwich Book Publishers, 1959.

Pringle, Henry F. *The Life and Times of William Howard Taft: A Biography*. New York: Farrar and Rinehart.

——. *Theodore Roosevelt: A Biography*. New York: Harcourt, Brace & Co., 1931.

Rainey, Congressman Henry T. *The Story of a Trip to Panama* (pamphlet). Washington, D.C.: 1907.

Robinson, Tracy. *Fifty Years at Panama, 1861-1911*. New York: Trow Press, 1911.

Roosevelt, Nicholas. *Theodore Roosevelt: The Man as I Knew Him*. New York: Dodd, Mead & Co., 1967.

Roosevelt, Theodore. *An Autobiography*. New York: Charles Scribner's Sons, 1920.

——. *"I took the Isthmus," and editorial comment by American newspapers*. New York: M. B. Brown and Company, 1911.

Sands, William Franklin. *Our Jungle Diplomacy*. Chapel Hill, North Carolina: The University of North Carolina Press, 1944.

Seitz, Don Carlos. *Joseph Pulitzer, His Life and Letters*. New York: AMS Press, 1970.

Simon, Maron J. *The Panama Affair*. New York: Charles Scribner's Sons, 1971.

Shaw, Albert. *A Cartoon History of Roosevelt's Career*. New York: Review of Reviews, 1910.

Sullivan, Mark. *Our Times*, vol. II. New York: Scribner's Sons, 1928.

Susto, Juan Antonio. *Homenaje al doctor Manuel Amador Guerrero en el centenario de su nacimiento*. Panama: Imprenta nacional, 1933.

Swanberg, W. A. *Pulitzer*. New York: Charles Scribner's Sons, 1967.

Taylor, Bayard. *Eldorado, or Adventures in the Path of Empire.* New York: G. P. Putnam, 1850.

Thayer, William Roscoe. *The Life and Letters of John Hay.* Boston: Houghton Mifflin Co., 1915.

The National Cyclopaedia of American Biography. New York: James T. White and Company, 1893-1965.

Valdés, Ramón M. *La independencia del Istmo de Panamá: sus antecedentes, sus causas y su justificación.* Panama: Imprenta Star & Herald, 1903.

Vance, Cyrus. *Hard Choices: Four Critical Years in Managing America's Foreign Policy.* New York: 1983.

Westerman, George W. *Carlos Antonio Mendoza: Padre del acta de independencia de Panama.* Panama: Ministerio de educación, 1957.

Whitehead, Richard H. *Our Faith Moved Mountains.* Newcomen Society, 1944.

2. Newspapers, Magazines, and Journals

American Heritage Magazine
American Historical Review
Atlantic Monthly
Le Matin (Paris)
Le Temps
Legion Magazine
New York Evening Post
New York Herald
New York Journal
New York Times
New York Tribune
North American Review
Outlook
Panama Star & Herald
Review of Books
Review of Reviews
Times (London)
Washington Monthly
Washington Post
Washington Star
World

Index